THE MARTIAL ARTS CINEMA
OF THE CHINESE DIASPORA

THE MARTIAL ARTS CINEMA OF
THE CHINESE DIASPORA
ANG LEE, JOHN WOO, AND
JACKIE CHAN IN HOLLYWOOD

KIN-YAN SZETO

Southern Illinois University Press
Carbondale and Edwardsville

14 13 12 11   4 3 2 1

Library of Congress Cataloging-in-Publication Data
Szeto, Kin-Yan, [date].
The martial arts cinema of the Chinese diaspora : Ang Lee, John Woo,
    and Jackie Chan in Hollywood / Kin-Yan Szeto.
        p. cm.
Includes bibliographical references and index.
    ISBN-13: 978-0-8093-3021-8 (pbk. : alk. paper)
    ISBN-10: 0-8093-3021-0 (pbk. : alk. paper)
    ISBN-13: 978-0-8093-8620-8 (ebook)
    ISBN-10: 0-8093-8620-8 (ebook)
1. Martial arts films—United States—History and criticism. 2. Lee,
    Ang, 1954– —Criticism and interpretation. 3. Woo, John, 1948– —
    Criticism and interpretation. 4. Cheng, Long, 1954– —Criticism and
    interpretation. I. Title.
PN1995.9.H3S94 2011
791.43′657—dc22   2010038673

CONTENTS

ACKNOWLEDGMENTS

This book has benefited from the contributions of many people. I extend my deepest gratitude to Margaret Drewal, Chuck Kleinhans, and Dwight Conquergood for their insight, guidance, and inspiration that shaped this project. Their advice and encouragement have driven me to expand my own horizon and abilities. I am grateful to the Hong Kong Film Directors' Guild, the Hong Kong Film Archive, Centro Digital Pictures, and the China Film Archive for providing resources. I wish to thank the Lilla Heston Fellowship, the China Times Cultural Foundation Young Scholar Award, and the Appalachian Foundation Fellowship for their financial support in making this research project possible. I would also like to thank the editorial board and production staff at Southern Illinois University Press for their help and professionalism at every stage in the process of production. I am very appreciative of the generous comments and suggestions from the anonymous reviewers. *Modern Chinese Literature and Culture* has kindly granted me permission to include in my book the revised version of the previously published essay "Jackie Chan's Cosmopolitical Consciousness and Comic Displacement" (*Modern Chinese Literature and Culture* 20.2 [2008]: 229–60).

THE MARTIAL ARTS CINEMA
OF THE CHINESE DIASPORA

INTRODUCTION: COSMOPOLITICAL CONSCIOUSNESS, FILM, AND TRANSNATIONALISM

"Action is a world language, thus Hong Kong's action films were accepted by Cantonese speakers and Mandarin speakers, by Southeast Asian countries which didn't understand Chinese, and gradually, by Europe and America" (Zhang Che 20). Zhang Che, a major Hong Kong martial arts film director between the 1960s and 1970s, comments on the successful crossover of Hong Kong action films based on the fact that action is a world language. Similarly, Ang Lee gives his insights on the success of Hong Kong/Chinese martial arts (or martial arts–inspired) films in Hollywood: "[W]hen it comes to martial arts, we are an inspiring force in filmmaking. Those are films we excel at, and there is something special about them. I cannot think of another genre that we do better than America" (qtd. in M. Berry 359). In the 1990s, Hollywood witnessed an influx of Hong Kong film stars, among them Jackie Chan, Chow Yun-Fat, and Michelle Yeoh; filmmakers, such as John Woo, Tsui Hark, Stanley Tong, Ronny Yu, and Kirk Wong; and martial arts choreographers, including Yuen Woo-ping and Corey Yuen. Ang Lee, a director originally from Taiwan, now makes films mainly in the United States. His *Crouching Tiger, Hidden Dragon* (2000) is both an homage to and a recuperation of the Hong Kong martial arts movie, a genre generally composed of stylized violence and dazzling fight choreography.

The martial arts cinema, or martial arts–inspired cinema, including *Crouching Tiger, Hidden Dragon, Face/Off* (1997), *Rumble in the Bronx* (1994), and others are all highly visible and successful films featuring cosmopolitical directors and stars, including Ang Lee, John Woo, and Jackie Chan. In the shared and intermingling world of transnational filmmaking, Lee from Taiwan and others from Hong Kong are transnational film artists who embody cosmopolitical perspectives and knowledge. The strategies they deploy are not essentialist; rather, they include a wide variety of encounters, negotiations, and affiliations as they face off with larger infrastructures like those of Hollywood. That is to say, their positionalities are not fixed but are multiple and flexible. Subjects achieve cosmopolitical perspectives as they engage complex experiences of displacement and accommodation among national and transnational forces.

The impact of the martial arts film in mainstream Hollywood is ubiquitous. From *The Matrix* trilogy (1999–2003) to *Rush Hour III* (2007), Hong Kong fight choreography has been incorporated into Hollywood films. The migration of foreign stars, directors, and technicians to Hollywood is not a new phenomenon. Charlie Chaplin and Alfred Hitchcock are among the "imported" stars and directors who made a great impact in Hollywood. While the various new waves in Europe during the 1960s once influenced American directors, today's East Asian cinema—particularly the Hong Kong/Chinese martial arts cinema, together with its filmmakers, stars, and other film artists—has become the major source of inspiration and participation in today's Hollywood.

Historically, the role of modern Chinese economic and cultural participants has engaged in the transnational linkages and flows of capital, images, and people (G. Wang; Ong, "Flexible"). Although citizenship is conventionally thought of as membership based on the political rights and participation within a sovereign state, globalization has made economic calculation a major element of the diasporic subject's choice—a choice not so much of citizenship but of the imagining of subjecthood based on the recognition of multiple modernities. The disjunctures created by the histories of colonialism, imperialism, or other political and sociocultural circumstances result in subjects' multiple displacements. Thus, the multiple displacements in the translocal terrains form subjects and agents whose endeavors are in dialogue with national, transnational, postnational, and political discourses.

This book examines commercially successful films that depict or were inspired by Chinese martial arts and that were made by major film artists of the Chinese diaspora—Jackie Chan, John Woo, and Ang Lee—in Hollywood. I have chosen these film artists in particular over others such as Tsui Hark, Stanley Tong, Yuen Woo-ping, Zhang Yimou, Quentin Tarantino, and the Wachowski brothers. Though Tsui Hark and Stanley Tong are directors who crossed over between Hollywood and Hong Kong in the 1990s, they now mostly make films in Hong Kong and Mainland China instead of shuttling between the film industries. Yuen Woo-ping, the martial arts choreographer for *The Matrix* trilogy, has been the action advisor/choreographer for many other Hollywood projects, including Tarantino's *Kill Bill* films (2003–04). However, as a choreographer, he has limited control during the creative process, compared to a director. Tarantino's *Kill Bill* films assimilate Asian popular cinema, including the spectacle of Hong Kong martial arts choreography, without questioning the correlation between revenge and violence. For example, the *Kill Bill* films perpetuate the theme of individualistic revenge and do not question the association of ideal femininity with violence/revenge, as embodied by Uma Thurman's bride/killer character (Szeto par. 11). Zhang Yimou's *Hero* (2002) is another example of a transnationally successful martial arts film that has earned international recognition but does not problematize the myths of gender and sexuality in patriarchal culture. The film conforms the rebellious martial arts heroes/heroines to the authoritarian government and examines the status of the individual's freedom versus the state's indoctrination and control (E. Chan 272–74). In light of this, the Wachowski brothers' *Matrix* trilogy also sustains the hegemonic status of white masculinity and shows Hollywood's assimilation of Hong Kong action cinema, a topic that I will discuss below.

I also chose Ang Lee, John Woo, and Jackie Chan over powerful stars like Chow Yun-Fat, Jet Li, Gong Li, Zhang Ziyi, and Michelle Yeoh because Lee, Woo, and Chan are subjects who reflect cosmopolitical consciousness. In this book, I discuss these three directors over stars and other film talents because they exemplify several important qualities: they actively participate in the directing, production, and planning of their films; they have been commercially successful in both the Chinese-language film markets and Hollywood; and they demonstrate various forms of geopolitical knowledge and consciousness in their transnational filmmaking. These film artists from the Chinese diaspora of Hong Kong and Taiwan embody the histories of colonialism; the geopolitics of race, masculinity, and power; and the experiences of transnational filmmaking.

This book examines how the transnational filmmakers and/or film artists such as Lee, Woo, and Chan embody and deploy cosmopolitical perspectives in their martial arts or martial arts–inspired films. For example, since the 1980s, Chan has consistently and dramatically grown in popularity in international media markets—beginning in Asia, then spreading to the United States, Europe, and the rest of the world—thus indicating his broad appeal across national and cultural lines. Indeed, he is the most commercially successful Asian film personality since Bruce Lee. Largely due to this success, Chan also has asserted a high degree of creative, technical, and administrative control over his film projects, not only as a star but also as a director, producer, choreographer, and/or writer. Similarly, Woo and Lee have been both directors and producers in many of their Hollywood-funded projects. Such administrative control over their projects has enabled these film artists to choose or participate in their films in ways that include engaging with and undermining dominant ideologies involving such categories of identity as Asianness, masculinity, and femininity. Related to these qualities, Lee, Woo, and Chan also demonstrate various forms of knowledge and action that, in another context, have been termed "cosmopolitical," a topic I explore in this book. Together, these qualities demonstrate that these film artists embody complex geopolitical identities that are significant commercial and ideological forces in today's global media landscape.

The critical literature on cosmopolitanism constitutes two major perspectives. The first proposes the possibilities of global democracy and world citizenship. The other allows a framework for investigating a new definition of political belonging in a world in which transnational linkages socially, culturally, and politically result in new strategies of identification beyond the nation-state. Cosmopolitanism occupies a complex place in the analysis of global citizenship. Some recent analyses of cosmopolitan democracy by David Held (106–9), Daniele Archibugi ("From the United Nations"), and Archibugi and Held (12–15) refer to such notions of cosmopolitanism, citing Immanuel Kant (Archibugi, "From the United Nations" 134). Ulf Hannerz ("Cosmopolitans" 239; *Transnational* 103–9) and John Urry (*Consuming* 167; *Sociology* 156–57, 183–84), on the other hand, analyze the global dimensions of cosmopolitanism, consumption, and travel.

Historically, the concept of cosmopolitanism, as Pheng Cheah notes, arose as "a central concept of the eighteenth-century French philosophes, [and] *cosmopolitanism* is derived from *kosmo-polites*, a composite of the Greek words for 'world' and 'citizen,' by way of the *esprit cosmopolite* of Renaissance humanism. It primarily designates an intellectual ethic, a universal humanism that transcends regional particularism" (22). Cheah reiterates Kant's notion of perpetual peace and cosmopolitanism in a new light as he suggests, "What Kant calls 'a universal *cosmopolitan existence*' refers to nothing less than the regulative idea of 'a perfect civil union of mankind'" (23). Though cosmopolitanism in its ideal invokes a universal history and, in Kant's case, the universal history that positions the West as the center, Cheah argues for the moral necessity to think in terms of the "cosmopolitical" and acknowledges the fact that Kant's notion of cosmopolitanism has become the source of contemporary normative theories. Cheah points out:

> Kant's cosmopolitanism signifies a turning point where moral politics or political morality needs to be formulated beyond the polis or state form, the point at which "the political" becomes, by moral necessity, "cosmopolitical." His vision remains the single most important philosophical source for contemporary normative theories of international relations, including accounts of global civil society and the international public sphere. (23)

Cheah contends, however, that historically, Kant's sense of the cosmopolitan is more a philosophical republicanism and federalism designed to reform the absolutist dynastic state and precedents of the modern theory of nationality (23–24). The context in which scholars use and refer to Kant's cosmopolitanism cannot be separated from the Enlightenment tradition from which it emerged.

Sheldon Pollock and his colleagues also rework the notion of cosmopolitanism in their introduction to the *Public Culture* special edition on "cosmopolitanisms" and suggest "a new *cosmopolitan politics* [my emphasis] is expressed in the idiom of 'arbitrage,' that is, doing better in the domain of social power, identities, and communities what multinational corporations already do well in the domain of business" (588). The new "cosmopolitan politics" as assessed by Pollock and his colleagues involves the various dimensions of social power, identities, and communities at the disjunctures, displacements, and ruptures in local and global fields. It is summarized by Ackbar Abbas's notion of "arbitrage" in his article about the cities of Hong Kong and Shanghai ("Cosmopolitan" 783). Abbas suggests that arbitrage refers to everyday strategies for negotiating the disequilibria and dislocations that globalism has created. Arbitrage in this sense does not allude to the exploitation of small temporal differences but refers to the larger historical lessons that can be drawn from our experiences of the city (786). But such strategies do not occur only out of our "cosmopolitan" experiences of locality, such as the city, as Abbas has argued.

In "Cosmopolitical Democracy," Archibugi uses the notion of cosmopolitical to refine her earlier notion of "cosmopolitan democracy" and proposes the model of "cosmopolitical democracy." Archibugi prefers the word "cosmopolitical" to "cosmopolitanism," as the latter suggests a general image of liberal global unity. When the nation-state loses many of its traditional powers, Archibugi argues, democracy requires a cosmopolitan political authority above it. She writes: "What distinguishes cosmopolitical democracy from other such projects is its attempt to create institutions which enable the voice of individuals to be heard in global affairs, irrespective of their resonance at home. Democracy as a form of global governance thus needs to be realized on three different, interconnected levels, within states, between states and at a world level" (8). The cosmopolitical in this sense is related particularly to the recognition of sovereign equality that proposes supranational bodies or constitutions that form the basis of democracy.

In this book, I further rework the notion of the cosmopolitical differently from Kant's "moral politics" in the global civil society and Archibugi's idea of a hierarchy in which the nation-state comes together to cooperate in an international project. Rather, I want to posit the notion of the cosmopolitical as a transnational, interactive, and complex emergent identity and consciousness that human agents assume and deploy strategically in their navigations of multiple dislocations. There is nothing automatically political about cosmopolitanism in the sense of crossing borders or living in diaspora. An individual's cosmopolitics arises from the experiences of multiple shifts in consciousness that occur in the process of acquiring the tactical knowledge needed to operate from a number of geopolitical locations. Subjects embody cosmopolitical consciousness as they experience multiple dislocations through globalism, colonialism, and histories of diaspora and learn to navigate their temporal, spatial, and historical contradictions, surviving in the world and achieving their goals.

Displacement and the travel of people, capital, and images produce a variety of different, emergent experiences that reveal the inadequacy of the nation as a category. The cosmopolitical does not disregard the politics of the nation at play. It resists the assumption that human sociopolitical belonging in the world today is naturally and inevitably articulated at the nation-state level. Although nationalism is still persistent in today's politics, the emergence of other forms of alliances cannot be disregarded. Cosmopolitics in this sense involves engaging in various knowledge systems and forms and diverse sociopolitical contexts and discourses. The cosmopolitical suggests an engagement in multiple systems and cultural forms that require people's resilient and inventive strategies for survival in today's global media landscape.

Writing on the "appropriating, cutting, and mixing" that people living or working in cross-cultural environments often perform, versus simply conforming to "homogenizing, normalizing disciplines," James Clifford uses the term "cosmopolitical perspective" to describe a process of identity formation that creatively engages with multiple and often conflicting sociopolitical sensibilities (367, 369). This perspective emerges from Clifford's observation that "identity is never only about location, about shoring up a safe 'home,' crucial as that task may be in certain circumstances. Identity is also, inescapably, about displacement and relocation, the experience of sustaining and mediating complex affiliations, multiple attachments" (369).

Following Clifford's formulation, I examine how Ang Lee, John Woo, and Jackie Chan act as cosmopolitical agents. These film artists' cosmopolitical perspectives emerge from experiences of displacement from their native homeland of either Taiwan or Hong Kong and continue to develop and act in an increasingly transnational environment of media production, distribution, and consumption. Colonialism, Chinese nationalism, and Western Orientalism and imperialism—along with their associated patriarchal discourses—shaped these film artists' complex identities. The film artists have not been passive observers or victims of these forces but instead have deployed cosmopolitical consciousnesses tactically in navigating through them, with an inventive resilience that has enabled them not only to survive but also to succeed commercially. All these film artists' perspectives inevitably collide and collude with hegemonic forces such as patriarchy and masculinist ideology.

I have chosen to critically investigate the above-mentioned directors over female stars such as Michelle Yeoh, Gong Li, and Zhang Ziyi. Actresses such as Michelle Yeoh, Gong Li, and Zhang Ziyi are highly visible Chinese movie stars that attract significant amounts of attention to Hong Kong/Chinese-, Taiwanese-, or Hollywood-produced films. Michelle Yeoh plays a Chinese Bond girl/action heroine in *Tomorrow Never Dies* (1997), and her persona is based on the tough martial arts/action heroine she has established in Hong Kong cinema. Zhang Ziyi also succeeds in being highly visible and successful as an internationally well-known actress on the global stage. Zhang began to catch global audiences' attention after starring in Ang Lee's *Crouching Tiger, Hidden Dragon*. Zhang, Yeoh, and Gong Li play geishas in *Memoirs of a Geisha* (2005), which reinforces the stereotypical images of Asian women as gentle and submissive. As stars, they do not have as much creative control over the roles and narratives as do the directors. Film directors such as Lee, Woo, and Chan, and their works are not self-consciously "political" in the usual sense of the term. Rather, the history of displacement, including colonialism, nationalism, imperialism, and Western Orientalism, results in geopolitical perspectives that are political in the sense that the subjects' embodied histories and experiences result in cosmopolitical interventions. Lee, Woo, and Chan and their cosmopolitical consciousnesses are not absolute or static but are always subject to the complex transnational context where political agency must act with tactical expediency—sometimes confronting, sometimes cooperating with hegemonic forces to achieve strategic goals.

Cosmopolitical consciousness is different from the notion of "double consciousness" as used by W. E. B. Du Bois in *The Souls of Black Folk*. Du Bois recognized that the contradictions in African American life informed more than one perspective, which at once accounts for the experience of the marginalization of African Americans and for the perspectives of white-dominated public discourses (16). Paul Gilroy later elaborates on Du Bois's model, adding a third, diasporic component, because double consciousness merely reifies a black/white binary that simplifies the complexities of the postcolonial black Atlantic as a form of "transcultural, international formation" (4). Moving beyond doubleness and "thirdness," I propose the notion of "cosmopolitical consciousness" that engages transnationally in potentially contradictory discourses and complicated histories of gender, ethnicity, and class. A cosmopolitical consciousness traverses contentious and changing power fields. The subject embodies multiple planes of power struggles as he or she navigates different historical, cultural, economic, and sociopolitical differences and makes use of such histories and experiences of displacements and disjunctures as sites of empowerment and agency. It is neither the same as double consciousness nor binary but a cosmopolitical knowledge of the differentiated local and translocal forces in a global context.

In the globalized framework of encounter and exchange, sexual, racial, and gender politics are similar to other kinds of transnational identities in that they are imbued with power relations. These power relations are connected to inequalities that result from histories of colonialism, nationalism, patriarchal domination, imperialism, and globalization. The objective of this book is to examine how these directors' cosmopolitical identities get at the complex terrain of sexual, racial, and gender politics that are at once national, regional, local, and cross-cultural. In the study of sexual, racial, and gender politics in a transnational frame, we need a mapping of different conceptions of the body, femininity, masculinity, homosocial bonds, and political economies of the family.

A cosmopolitical approach that addresses inequalities as well as new formations explores the nature of sexuality, ethnicity, and gender at the juncture of globalization. This critical perspective addresses the inequities as well as those aspects of global capitalism that are mobile and subject to territorialization and reterritorialization of power. The hegemonic forces such as nationalism and patriarchy operate in such a way that sexual and gender politics reproduce heteronormative narratives. A cosmopolitical perspective comes to fore and engages with the contexts of gender, race, and sexuality in both East and West contexts. It is my objective to rethink how hegemonic forces act on popular cinema as a primary locus of difference and inequality and to explore how martial arts films demonstrate the martial masculinities and femininities that collide and collude with the geopolitics of the body, including Western stereotypes of the Orient in the global context.

In this book, I examine how Ang Lee's successful film *Crouching Tiger, Hidden Dragon* is an example of such cosmopolitical knowledge. The once art-house filmmaker showed that he could invade the mainstream market with his 2000 martial arts film. The ability to make profitable and critically acclaimed films in various genres involves geopolitical awareness and knowledge in commercial and art-house filmmaking. *Crouching Tiger, Hidden Dragon* is proof of Lee's success in both arts and commercial cinema, and the film shows Lee's critical reflection toward Chineseness, Asianness, and femininity as repressed domains and markers on a transnational scale.

As one of the most famous and respected directors from Hong Kong, John Woo is now also an important filmmaker in Hollywood. Known for his choreographed action sequences featuring balletic shoot-outs, Woo's films often engage with themes of loyalty and honor and the place of the loner hero in a world full of corruption and violence. In 1997, Woo released *Face/Off*, his third Hollywood film. In it is Woo's trademark shoot-out with slow-motion bullets and choreography. This film that earned Woo's official and successful entry into Hollywood cinema contains not only American influences but also Hong Kong/Chinese martial arts cinema influences. After *Face/Off*, Woo continued to make several other Hollywood films, including *Mission: Impossible II* (2000), *Windtalkers* (2002), and *Paycheck* (2003). Woo has proved he can make films transnationally without sacrificing the themes and styles that have won him acclaim in his latest Chinese-language films, such as *Red Cliff* and its sequel (2008–09). The limiting category of Chinese, Asian, or American cannot fully encompass the transnational film trajectory of John Woo. As a director, he traverses various borders and becomes an active social subject with multiple geopolitical consciousnesses.

Jackie Chan is another cosmopolitical film director-actor-producer-choreographer who became popular in his native Hong Kong in the late 1970s, and his popularity slowly spread across the globe, from Asia, Africa, and Europe to the United States. His introduction to U.S. audiences came in several 1980s Hollywood projects, including *The Big Brawl* (1980), the *Cannonball Run* series (1981, 1984), and *The Protector* (1985), and he later emerged as a bankable star and notable artist finally in the United States with the 1996 release of *Rumble in the Bronx*. Since then, Chan has made several highly successful films with American studios, such as the *Rush Hour* films (1998–2007), and many more with Hong Kong studios (*The Accidental Spy* [2001], *The Medallion* [2003], *New Police Story* [2004], *The Myth* [2005], *Rob-B-Hood* [2006], and *Shinjuku Incident* [2009]). While Hollywood appropriates the folk customs and traditions of Hong Kong/Chinese martial arts, the Hong Kong/Chinese film industry reappropriates Jackie Chan's Hollywood success and marketability into its media to enhance a new phase in Hong Kong cinema's transnational trajectory. Chan's cross-national paradigm shift reveals the workings of the asexual martial artist stereotype as a deliberate history of the exploitation and racialization of Asians and Asian Americans in Hollywood film history. Chan's example shows that his transnational film practices and the global marketability of his star image provide tools for mapping and remapping the terrain of the Hong Kong film industry and its relationship with global Hollywood. His works inevitably and controversially collide and collude with power politics, such as hegemonic masculinity, global capitalism, and nationalism. Chan not only engages in various discourses and contexts of power struggles but also (and more important, as a star, filmmaker, choreographer, and producer) embodies the consciousness of marginalization, otherness, and inequality and the awareness of the ways that enable him to work as a major filmmaker in today's global Hollywood.

Martial arts cinema's transnational success has encouraged Asian film industries, such as those in Hong Kong and Mainland China, to target their martial arts film products for the world and particularly Hollywood markets. Commercial success does not mean that transnational filmmaking is necessarily politically compelling or challenging, however, especially in terms of critical dialogues with the discursive formations related to martial arts cinema transnationally. Hong Kong film director/choreographer Yuen Woo-ping's martial arts choreography has transformed forever the ways action films are made both in Hollywood and the world. Yuen works transnationally between Hong Kong and Hollywood and, as mentioned above, choreographed for the Wachowski brothers in *The Matrix* trilogy. Yet, being transnational does not necessarily mean being cosmopolitical. The Wachowski brothers' *Matrix* trilogy seeks to sustain the hegemony of the "false consciousness [that] consists of thinking locally and not globally" by the assimilation of Hong Kong action cinema into Hollywood (Feng 17). While the dominant global film industry, like Hollywood, shows increasing awareness of Hong Kong martial arts cinema in its creative consciousness, the martial arts or martial arts–inspired action genre also becomes a transnational interstitial site for the phenomenal Chinese entry into Hollywood, exemplified by Lee's *Crouching Tiger, Hidden Dragon* and Chan's and Woo's works. Martial arts films are inseparable from the power of the performative body that is implicated in the body politics in a geopolitical context. Martial arts films, with the spectacular display of stunning choreography, wirework, athletic skill, and Chinese tradition, flourish by negotiating the complex and conflicting experience of colonial modernity and postcoloniality in a global context. In their various ways, these film artists have either made martial arts films or produced works highly influenced by the martial arts film traditions. By embracing contemporary new media technology (as inspired by *The Matrix*), the film artists combine styles, forms, narratives, traditions, genres, and ideologies of martial arts cinema and engage with the issues of action/martial arts film genre's encounter with new media and technology.

It is my objective to interrogate the cultural, political, historical, and social circumstances that gave rise to the transnationalization of martial arts cinema. My purpose is also to explore the Hong Kong/Chinese martial arts film genre as an instance of an emerging phenomenon of the transborder flows of images, people, and capital in Hollywood and the Chinese diaspora. The increasing permeability of boundaries in filmmaking problematizes the conceptual and analytical framework that is portrayed as either Asian or American. It is in this critical context that the issues of postcolonialism, nationalism, gender, and ethnicity in comparative and transnational frameworks become important, urgent, and significant subjects. To examine martial arts cinema of the Chinese diaspora in Hollywood critically is to explore this new sphere.

To examine critically the cosmopolitical practices of the artists who transgress boundaries of East and West in their filmmaking also demands a rethinking of political agency in the changing geopolitics of transnationalism. In this sense, subjects encompass the consciousness of the multiple linkages and displacements that result in the transition from national to transnational associations and disjunctures as the terrain of enunciating agency and imagining identities. Such a critical framework initiates a paradigmatic shift in thought and political action. To think and act cosmopolitically means that political and cultural actors no longer move, situate themselves, and act in a space of nation-states exclusively but in a coexisting world society. This is a different way to conceptualize, imagine, and identify oneself.

In this book, I examine how certain film talents have not only worked in mainstream Asian and American cinema but also introduced different aspects of Hong Kong/Chinese martial arts film traditions that forever transformed the ways action films can be perceived and understood in world cinema today. The crossover trend between Hollywood and the Chinese diaspora results in the transformation of film styles, themes, genres, and traditions and also in the contestation of such issues as identity politics and the geopolitics of gender and ethnicity in the transnational terrain. In this book, I examine the diverse dimensions of history, tradition, cultural politics, representations, gender and ethnicity, and new media associated with the popularity of martial arts cinema in Hollywood and the Chinese diaspora. The transnationalization of martial arts cinema can be seen as an instance in which cultures and cinemas originate from Asia and then cross over to America, whereas martial arts cinema itself (including kung fu and *wuxia*, or knight-errant/swordplay, films) was already a hybrid form of performance, encompassing various martial arts traditions, influences from *wuxia* novels, theater, acrobatics, dance, special effects, Japanese samurai films, and Hollywood musicals.

In chapter 1, I outline the history of martial arts as it relates to the incorporation into literature, theater, and films. It proceeds with a historical construction of the complex regional networks and diasporic associations among the Hong Kong film industry and Southeast Asian markets, including Taiwan and Hollywood. In chapter 2, I analyze how the discourse of ethnicity is articulated through the politics of gender cross-culturally in Ang Lee's Chinese language *wuxia* film *Crouching Tiger, Hidden Dragon*, and then I turn to the Hollywood-produced *Matrix* trilogy for comparison. In chapter 3, I examine how the culture of Chinese legendary *xia* has also long fascinated director John Woo in the themes of homosocial bondings and righteous heroism. I then critically explore the ways that Woo contests the concepts of loyalty and honor in a global context. In chapter 4, I trace the film trajectory of Jackie Chan transnationally from colonial and (neo)colonial Hong Kong to the context of global Hollywood. In conclusion, I link these films and film artists together and highlight their similarities and differences demonstrated in their cosmopolitical consciousnesses.

MARTIAL ARTS CINEMA, THE CHINESE DIASPORA, AND HOLLYWOOD

The martial arts cinema originated in the Shanghai film industry in Mainland China, with the 1928 release of the film *Burning of the Red Lotus Monastery*, based on the martial arts novel *Legend of the Strange Hero*. The regional networks, diasporic connections, and border-crossing movement of goods, capital, and people drew Hong Kong and Shanghai together in an intracity nexus that sustained the survival and flourishing of popular cinema. Between 1935 and 1950—a time of incessant violence, occupation, civil war, imperialism, and colonial expansion in China— millions of people were displaced, and extreme poverty spread across the Mainland. As Stephen Teo notes, "Historians have usually pointed to the outbreak of war on the Mainland as a turning point in Hong Kong's film industry. It led to the growth of the local film industry as Hong Kong absorbed migrants fleeing Shanghai" (*Hong Kong* 7).

In the 1930s, the Chinese film industry's center gradually shifted to Hong Kong. Prior to the Japanese bombing of Shanghai in 1932 and the occupation of the city in 1937, Hong Kong operated under the shadow of the Shanghai film industry. Shanghai was the most cosmopolitan treaty port, and its film industry served as the meeting point of foreign ideas, technology, and culture as they made their way throughout China. By 1934, the Tianyi studio (the precursor to Shaw Brothers) began to move its operation to Hong Kong. Poshek Fu writes: "The [Hong Kong film] industry quickly expanded. By 1935–37, Hong Kong was producing about thirty talkies a year, a remarkable increase from the annual output of four or five silent films in the 1920s. Two studios—Tianyi and Daguan—were the shaping force in this expansion. And they also revealed the cosmo- politan, border crossing nature of early Hong Kong cinema" (*Between* 56).

The Shanghai studio Tianyi, remade in Hong Kong as Shaw Brothers, together with Daguan helped to establish Hong Kong as the regional center of Cantonese film culture by the mid-1930s. The cosmopolitan nature of the Hong Kong film industry was seen in its early days of talkies, as the city had been a key nodal point in the transnational pan-Chinese cultural network from Shanghai and Singapore to San Francisco and Los Angeles (Fu, *Between* 57). During the Japanese invasion of Hong Kong in the 1940s, Hong Kong filmmakers fled and totally shut down the film industry.

Hong Kong cinema took advantage of the import of capital and Shanghai filmmakers and revived swiftly after the Japanese invasion. While the film industries in Mainland China and Taiwan went through nationalization and decolonization, the Hong Kong film industry became the only prospering place in the world that had the resources, talent, and freedom to make Chinese entertainment films. Shaw Brothers continued to pioneer the new school of Mandarin-language swordplay (*wuxia*) films in the 1960s. The company dominated the film entertainment business in the transnational pan-Chinese world between the 1950s and 1980s, and it retains control over the largest television network in Asia today. Shaw Brothers' influences include its expansion in Singapore during the 1930s and 1940s and then its significance in Hong Kong from the 1930s onward (Fu et al., "Zou"; M. Chan; Cheuk).[1]

In the 1960s studio era, dialogue in Hong Kong cinema was in Mandarin, and the target audience was the ethnic Chinese community outside Hong Kong. Hong Kong cinema did not have the political power and economic influence of Hollywood, but its system was no less commercial and competitive. As a British colony, Hong Kong adopted a cultural and capitalistic laissez-faire policy that provided economic and political freedom to the entrepreneurs. Ding-Tzann Lii refers to the notion of "yielding" and its relation to marginal experiences, particularly in the case of the Hong Kong film industry that is an instance of "marginal imperialism" (125). Expanding Michael Taussig's notion of "mimesis" that has a rejuvenating yielding relation to nature, Lii describes instead the model of transformation of the Other by the imperial self. Thus, the yielding self envisions a different model of self and Other relationships that is organized around the more flexible and playful exchange of differences that characterizes "mimesis." Lii distinguishes between incorporation, where the "Other" is transformed by imperialism, and yielding as a "synthesis which transcends both the self and the Other" (134). The Hong Kong film industry therefore encompassed a different model from Hollywood "core" cinema. Hong Kong films were mainly produced for overseas markets, and it was common to have Chinese and English subtitles and, more important, different versions and editions for various film markets (132). The films the Hong Kong industry produced targeted this flexibility and reciprocity that transposed, displaced, and disrupted multiple terrains of space and time, making this particular instance of transnational filmmaking cosmopolitical.

Many scholarly works have been written about both the industrial and cultural aspects of Hong Kong cinema's transnational linkages and histories. Frank Bren and Law Kar's *Hong Kong Cinema: A Cross-Cultural View* examines Hong Kong's contribution to world cinema and looks at Eastern and Western influences upon the medium through its historical development from the late 1890s to the 1970s. The account of Hong Kong cinema after the 1970s occupies only fourteen pages of the entire volume. A more updated approach in tackling the transnational trajectory of Hong Kong martial arts cinema after the 1970s therefore becomes necessary.

Leon Hunt's *Kung Fu Cult Masters: From Bruce Lee to "Crouching Tiger"* chronologically examines stars, directors, and choreographers who have contributed to the local and international success of Hong Kong/Chinese martial arts cinema. The book represents a broader base of literature that approaches the martial arts film practice primarily as a fanzine phenomenon and emphasizes the notion of "authenticity" derived from martial arts performance, choreography, and kinetic aspects of the human body that propel these kung fu masters into stardom beyond the Chinese-speaking world (17, 21–47). In light of a cosmopolitical perspective, the film artists I discuss in this book problematize Hunt's general historical overview of "authentic" physical performance genre. In particular, this book examines the transnational identities that the film artists embody and how their works contest the dichotomy of Asian/white, body/mind, and martial arts/technology.

While Hunt sees the martial arts performance as the authentic Other in his analysis, Kwai-Cheung Lo's *Chinese Face/Off: The Transnational Popular Culture of Hong Kong* devotes four chapters to examining the transnational phenomenon of Hong Kong martial arts cinema within the global forces that continuously contest what Chineseness means as a form of ethnic and cultural politics. Lo revolves around issues of Hong Kong culture and identity within a transnational frame rather than around the film artists' cosmopolitics within a global context. The existence of Chinese filmmakers making non-Chinese-language films calls into question the old paradigm of "Chineseness" and "ethnic cinema." The cosmopolitical filmmakers' unique transnational experiences extend beyond the national and ethnic identity model as their works challenge the critical assumption of Chineseness as an encompassing analytical model for filmmakers with Chinese cultural heritage in an increasingly globalized context. In fact, film artists such as John Woo, Jackie Chan, and Ang Lee converse with multiple facets of identities (in which Chineseness is only one of them) as their works intersect with the politics of the Chinese diaspora in Hollywood. The crossover of directors, stars, and choreographers from Asia to America inevitably intersects with the history of Asian or Asian American politics in mainstream Hollywood cinema.

Darrell Y. Hamamoto and Sandra Liu's edited volume *Countervisions: Asian American Film Criticism*, for example, engages Asian American film criticism from its beginnings in the 1960s and 1970s. Essays in the collection represent various possibilities for reexamining the Orientalist cinematic representations and performances of Asian American actors from earlier in the century.[2] The book concentrates on examples of contemporary Asian American and Asian film and video and investigates the possible political interventions Asian American filmmakers can make to contest the impact of racial inequality on minority communities. The final essay in the book, "Cultural Identity and Diaspora in Contemporary Hong Kong's Cinema," is Julian Stringer's analysis of three Hong Kong films, including Jackie Chan's *Rumble in the Bronx*, which launched Chan's second-wave entry to Hollywood. Stringer notes that it was unusual to include a discussion of Hong Kong films in an anthology of Asian American film criticism and observes the artificial divisions between Asian American and Asian film practices in analyzing emerging phenomenon. These explicit categorical divisions exclude other possible historical, political, and cultural imaginings of the phenomenon.

Roger Garcia's edited volume *Out of the Shadows: Asians in American Cinema* pays homage to the directors, actors, choreographers, and technicians of Asian origins who have also worked in Hollywood. The book consists of essays that outline the history of Asian representations, Asian/Asian American filmmaking, and the reception of Asian films in America. It includes interviews and provides a series of insightful and contrasting perspectives from these talents. *Out of the Shadows* offers a mixture of personal and critical perspectives that point at the competing accounts of Asianness and Americanness in the contemporary interstitial spheres of transnational filmmaking that need further examination.

David Bordwell's *Planet Hong Kong: Popular Cinema and the Art of Entertainment* compares and contrasts Hong Kong cinema with Hollywood in the context of film style and notes the technical and narrative differences between the tighter Hollywood dramaturgy and Hong Kong cinema's more episodic plot structures. Bordwell insists that the broad transcultural appeal of Hong Kong action films is based on the universal stylistic "pause/burst/pause scheme" that accentuates the fantasy of "the human body's efforts to burst its earthly bonds" (220, 224). He also prefers a stylistic approach rather than a cultural studies approach in his analysis. The Hong Kong/Hollywood interaction occurs not only on the technical or stylistic level but also, and more important, sociopolitically and culturally in the films and with their filmmakers. In fact, the pleasures of martial arts come not only from its dynamism and energy but also from the foregrounding of the hero/heroine's body with the ability to wield power of liberation and overcome social and political oppression. The filmmakers are manifestations of their complicity and intervention with established modes of local and Hollywood filmmaking.

As Jenny Lau indicates in the edited volume *Multiple Modernities: Cinema and Popular Media in Transcultural East Asia*, the legacy of Western modernity operates on a mass level most notably in Asian media cultures such as cinema (1–10). The cross-hybridization of cinematic culture, particularly in the examples of martial arts cinema, reflects the translation of chivalric codes, genre, technique, and spectacle between and within Chinese and American contexts. Thus, the task of examining the transnational martial arts cinema is to consider directors who have traveled from outside of Europe and the United States to work in Hollywood, most notably in recent years from East Asia, and to critically inspect a different model to rethink the politics of agency, identities, and belonging in today's world.

In fact, the film talents from Asia, from Ang Lee to Jackie Chan, not only participate in mainstream Hollywood but also inflect their transnational filmmaking with cosmopolitical awarenesses. Martial arts cinema is a diasporic film practice that questions the historical and national ideologies that define hero and heroine in Hong Kong and Hollywood films. The genre's influence belongs to the Chinese diaspora in that it was not completely embedded in Mainland Chinese, local Taiwanese, or Hong Kong culture. Historically, Hong Kong cinema enacted its transnational engagement by first embracing the regional and global Chinese diasporic communities to extend beyond its local market. In this way, the Hong Kong film industry became Southeast Asia's regional cinematic powerhouse. The Chinese martial arts cinema, especially *wuxia* films, originating from the Mainland and flourishing in Hong Kong, also became a Chinese diasporic film genre that allowed those of Chinese origins in other parts of the world (including the United States) to imagine their cultural heritage and relation to China. Taiwanese filmmaker Ang Lee made *Crouching Tiger, Hidden Dragon* based on his imagination of China. Martial arts cinema with its popularity extended beyond the local market, and the Hong Kong action cinema positioned itself as a key player in the world film market.

June Yip's account of New Taiwanese cinemas focuses on the Taiwanese nativist tradition in the wake of self-reflection and awareness of nationalist sentiments and makes a distinction between that nativist tradition and the nostalgia tradition of the Mainland refugee writers. The emergence of New Taiwanese cinema addresses the interests in indigenous traditions as a site for self-reflection on the "national crisis." Ang Lee, a second-generation mainlander whose parents moved to Taiwan from Mainland China following the Nationalist government's defeat during the Chinese civil war in 1949, makes Chinese- and English-language films in Asia and America. This complicates the cultural and sociopolitical locality of Taiwan, defying the prescriptions of the local and the global.

In another article, "Tai Wan Dian Ying Yu Di San Shi Jie Dian Ying Lun Shu" ("Taiwanese Cinema and Third World Film Criticism"), Qiu Zhi-Yong uses Teshome H. Gabriel's concept of "third world cinema" and applies this analytical construct to discuss contemporary Taiwanese cinema. Qiu notes the international success of Ang Lee's *Crouching Tiger, Hidden Dragon* in his concluding statement while also acknowledging the awkward fact that the film was considered a national film in Taiwan, a Hollywood film in Mainland China, and a foreign language film in the West (52). Although Qiu notes that the rigid classification of third world cinema is inadequate, he reiterates the insufficiency of the third world cinema's alternative analytical paradigm that sees itself solely from a marginal and oppositional position in relation to Hollywood's dominant mode of production.

In fact, the critical paradigm of the cosmopolitical considers in detail transnationally mobile directors who work with popular martial arts or marital arts–inspired genres, like Ang Lee or John Woo. It is therefore necessary to contest the notion of "third world" not only in relation to the two industrializing economies, Hong Kong and Taiwan, but also in the ways in which we understand the transnational trajectory of filmmakers who come from the Orient. The ability to make commercial and critically acclaimed films in various geopolitical contexts involves cosmopolitical awareness. Lee makes not only martial arts films but films of various genres, ranging from the art-house comedy *The Wedding Banquet* (1993) and the wartime drama *Ride with the Devil* (1999) to the comedy *Taking Woodstock* (2009). *Crouching Tiger, Hidden Dragon* draws heavily on Hong Kong talent. Chow Yun-Fat starred, while Yuen Woo-ping was action choreographer. Both Peter Pau, the cinematographer, and Tim Yip, the costume designer and art director, were Oscar nominees. Lee has also talked about how Han-Hsiang Li's *Liang Shan Ba Yu Zhu Ying Tai* (aka *The Love Eterne*, 1963) greatly influenced him (Lyman E1). The film was among the numerous Shaw Brothers' historical costume dramas and martial arts films popular in Taiwan in the 1950s and 1960s when Lee grew up.

Filmmaker King Hu also had great impact on Lee's *Crouching Tiger, Hidden Dragon*. Hu made films both in Taiwan and Hong Kong. His internationally acclaimed film *A Touch of Zen* (1971) was a swordplay film that gained its most widespread visibility because of the regionally global powerhouse of the Hong Kong film industry. King Hu's film was considered a Taiwanese *wuxia* film and was included in books on Hong Kong cinema (F. Lu 138; Teo, *Hong Kong* 92–93; Urban Council, *Hong Kong Swordplay* 279). As Stephen Teo mentions in *King Hu's A Touch of Zen,* the film *A Touch of Zen* is "a model of a pan-Chinese production of its time, being directed by a native of Beijing based in Hong Kong, who expanded his career into Taiwan where he made the bulk of the film with Taiwanese and Hong Kong actors and crew members (the final sections of the film being filmed in Hong Kong). Such a pan-Chinese production strategy allows one to claim that the film is a Hong Kong production as well as a Taiwan production, and its strategy of a double heritage linking the Hong Kong and Taiwan film industries is one of the significances of *A Touch of Zen*" (1–2). In comparison to King Hu's double linkage with Hong Kong and Taiwan film industries, Ang Lee's dream of China is cosmopolitical in its engagement with the martial arts film genre as a translocal zone of transnational interaction, global consumption, and critical consideration of ethnic identities, such as Chineseness. This phenomenon brings to light the transnational linkages among the filmmakers, writers, and businesspeople in between the Chinese film industries in Hong Kong, Shanghai, and Taiwan and in other world film industries such as Hollywood.

Cosmopolitical subjects embody histories of exile and displacement and succeed in making films transnationally by strategically colliding and colluding with power. To collide and collude with power does not mean the subject is apolitical. It is only a different strategy in encountering, interrogating, and revealing the working power in today's interconnected world of globalism. To examine and critically engage in a discussion of martial arts cinema is therefore to move beyond the national and the geopolitical polity in considering the interconnections of filmmaking practices across different national, cultural, and historical boundaries that also lead to new understandings of notions of self and Other, Orientalism and Occidentalism in a globalized context. The transnational trajectory of the Chinese diaspora in Hollywood addresses and navigates multiple fields of power, struggles, and inequality from the historical processes of colonialism, Orientalism, Chinese nationalism, imperialism, displacement, migration, and exile.

The Popular *Wuxia* Film Genre

Wuxia films depict chivalry and swordplay and originated as a northern Mainland tradition that was evocative of ancient Chinese culture and history. By contrast, the kung fu films of Hong Kong developed by incorporating martial arts techniques that were usually thought of as a southern style of more recent historical period. The difference between *wuxia* and kung fu is that the former is based on sword fighting and the latter on fist fighting. Kung fu films emphasize body and training. The phrase "kung fu" in Cantonese means accomplishment or skill cultivated through long and hard work. *Wuxia* films are usually set in Chinese dynasties and other mythical fantasy periods that are the conventions of the genre. As Stephen Teo notes, "[T]he effortless facility of sword-fighting heroes and heroines to leap, somersault and generally levitate in defiance of gravity generated a fairytale effect" (*Hong Kong* 98). *Wuxia* novels inspired the earliest *wuxia* films in China. In 1922, Zhang Shichuan founded the Mingxing Film Company, Shanghai's most important studio. Between 1928 and 1930, he produced and directed eighteen episodes of *Burning of the Red Lotus Monastery*, which was based on the *wuxia* novel *Legend of the Strange Hero*. As Lin Nien-Tung notes: "In their evolution, martial arts films have moved away from a heavy reliance on magical feats, and within this process of secularization, arrived at a realistic portrayal of martial skills and an adhesion to martial ideals. This significant transition can be traced in the different remakes of *Burning of the Red Lotus Monastery*" (12).

Burning of the Red Lotus Monastery uses flying daggers, tornado palm power, traps, and weightless leaps achieved with suspension wirework, and the serial featured 300–400 martial artists. These stylistic and formalistic features influenced most prominently the *wuxia* films in Hong

Kong after World War II (Lin 13). The different branches of Chinese martial arts cinema found their origin in *wuxia* films. *Wuxia* films build on the fantasy elements and traditions, including the use of special effects. Originating in Shanghai in the 1920s, *wuxia* films began in the silent era and incorporated special effects, adaptations from comic books and serialized novels, and the folkloric tradition of Chinese opera and acrobatics. During the years of the civil wars, filmmakers relocated to Hong Kong and Taiwan, where martial arts and *wuxia* films continued to be made.

Historically, the *wuxia* film genre derived from modern *wuxia* fiction. *Wuxia* novels are a unique form in Chinese literature, and the term has a rough literal translation as "martial knight/adventurer/knight-errant" (*wu* are things pertaining to warfare, and *xia* is a type of chivalric person). Hence, *wuxia* fiction might translate as tales of martial adventure or chivalry. *Xia*, sometimes called "knight-errant" or "swordsman," now generally refers to the martial arts hero who appears in martial arts swordplay films with origins in ancient Chinese history.

The first time Chinese philosophers linked *wu* and *xia* together in the same context was in the School of the Legalists, or Fa, and its representative figure Han Feizi (280–233 B.C.). The School of Fa held that human beings are basically egotistical and require strong sanctions and a rigorous application of the law to prevent them from being self-serving and disrupting society. Han Feizi condemned the Confucians and the *xia* for placing the moral code above the law. He included both the Confucian scholars and the *xia* in "The Five Vermin" and asserted, "The Confucians with their learning bring confusion to the law; the knights [*xia*] with their military prowess violate the prohibitions. Yet the ruler treats both groups with respect, and so we have disorder" (Han Fei Tzu 105). *Xia* were criticized as being extremist and counter-hegemonic, as they did not regulate their behavior but rather used violence and martial skills to challenge the doctrine of the central administration of the state. As film critic Ng Ho notes, "The more chaotic the era, the greater the demand of the legendary *xia*" (84). Such an understanding of the icon of the swordsman, related to social and political uncertainty, contextualizes the remarkable adaptation of the *xia* hero in film. The world of the *xia* is different from that of society. This imaginary world operates in an order that is outside the mainstream society and the rule of law, called *jianghu* ("rivers and lakes").

The most comprehensive and definitive account of *xia* comes from *Records of the Grand Historian of China* (also known as *Shiji*) completed by Sima Qian (145–86 B.C.).[3] He defines the phrase *you xia* (wandering knight) as one who embodies the qualities of *ren* (forgiveness for all), *xin* (trust), and *yi* (uprightness and selflessness) (2:453). Sima Qian gives accounts of several *xia* in his records. His biographies became the major literary account of *xia* that influenced *wuxia* fiction, and later on such a concept of *xia* also influenced the portrayal of heroes and heroines in martial arts films.

The *wuxia* film heroes and heroines have roots in their literary counter-parts in *chuanqi* (literally meaning "strange legends") of the Tang Dynasty (A.D. 618–907), that is, fables or native tales often written in the vernacular, and the *huaben* tales of the Song Dynasty storytellers (A.D. 960–1279) (Ye 21). *Huaben* included detective stories and tales of martial heroism. The growth of colloquial fiction began in the Ming Dynasty (A.D. 1368–1644) (Ye 22). One of the representative novels of this period was an epic of classical Chinese literature called *San Guo Yan Yi* (*Romance of the Three Kingdoms*), a Chinese historical novel based upon events near the end of the Han Dynasty (206 B.C.–A.D. 220) and the Three Kingdoms era of China. John Woo's *Red Cliff* films are inspired by this novel.

Huaben fictions influenced the style and content of *wuxia* novels in the Republican period (1912–49) (Ye 26). The *wuxia* novel on which Ang Lee based his film is Wang Dulu's *Crouching Tiger, Hidden Dragon*. The novel is a work of the "Old School" of the Republican period in China. The years after the establishment of the People's Republic of China from the 1950s on mark the next phase, the Guangdong (and Hong Kong) School of *wuxia* fiction, represented by the works of Gu Long, Wo Longsheng, Liang Yusheng, and Jin Yong (Ye 62). Many of the martial arts novels have been adapted into films, including Tsui Hark's *Zu: Warriors from the Magic Mountain* (1983) and Wong Kar-Wai's *Ashes of Time* (1994).

Cantonese and Mandarin, two dialects of the Chinese language, had significant roles in the formulation of martial arts cinema. Cantonese is the local dialect in Hong Kong, whereas Mandarin is the official language of the Mainland. Mandarin played an important part in Hong Kong cinema's early days, especially during the Sino-Japanese War from 1937 onward, and the civil wars between the Communists and Nationalists brought about a further migratory wave of Chinese filmmakers from Shanghai to Hong Kong between 1946 and 1949 (Teo, *Hong Kong* 11). Hong Kong's Cantonese-dominated cinema had shared its place with Mandarin films, particularly with the *wuxia* films made in Mandarin during the 1960s.

The two major filmmakers King Hu and Zhang Che helped to launch the Mandarin-speaking *wuxia* film trend in the 1960s that dominated the local film market. King Hu's *Come Drink with Me* (1966) and Zhang Che's

The Magnificent Trio (1966) represented the new wave. The following year, Zhang's *The One-Armed Swordsman* (1967) and Hu's *Dragon Inn* (1967) broke Southeast Asian box office records. King Hu and Zhang Che represented two different approaches. Zhang focused on the male characters and demonstrated the exhibition of the male body, action, and violence. As a major Mandarin filmmaker, Zhang represented the transition from *wuxia* film to kung fu film, as he made films in both categories. His representative works include *The One-Armed Swordsman, The Assassin* (1967), *The Golden Swallow* (1968), and *The Boxer from Shantung* (1972). Zhang helped to start the trend of martial arts films that favored male protagonists and that had themes of male individualism and fellowship under the phrase Zhang called *yang gang* (masculine attributes).

Zhang Che had his own repertoire of actors and directing assistants, and many important filmmakers and actors had worked with him, notably John Woo, who had been his assistant director. Zhang's *yang gang* films center on individualistic male *xia* and the brotherhood code of *yi*. Themes of bloodshed and visceral violence are common sights in his films. With Zhang, a new brand of *wuxia* film emerged, one increasingly influenced by Japanese samurai action films. Japanese cinema's popular samurai films like *The Tale of Zatoichi* (1962) and Akira Kurosawa's works such as *Seven Samurai* (1954) had also influenced *wuxia* films. Fight scenes in *yang gang* films depend on depicting heroes as having developed fighting skills and physical proficiency through years of training. The martial arts hero in *The One-Armed Swordsman*, for example, is an ascetic hero whose personal ambition is revenge. Martial arts heroism is no longer geared toward the traditional humanistic ideals to which a hero usually aspires. This trend of violent sword fighting (influenced by samurai films) or combat action influenced John Woo, who transformed the traditional *xia* into an urban setting in his contemporary action thrillers.

In comparison, King Hu's *Dragon Inn* clearly introduces cultural forms and effects from the Mainland, including Beijing opera. These influences can be seen in Hu's transplantation of staging, acting, and music—including the use of minimal percussive and musical instrumentation, such as the *ban* (wooden board)—from the opera to his films. As an important Mandarin film director of the 1960s and 1970, King Hu committed himself to making one particular film genre, the *wuxia* film. Hu's *Come Drink with Me* and *Dragon Inn* accomplished new martial artistry with the use of inventive cinematic techniques, action choreography, and wirework.

A Touch of Zen is an adaptation from Pu Song-Ling's seventeenth-century collection of tales *Liao Zhai Zhi Yi* (*Strange Stories from a Chinese Studio*). In this film, King Hu focuses on the patriotic and political ideals of his *xia* characters. When shown at the 1975 Cannes Film Festival, *A Touch of Zen* was awarded the Special Prize for Technical Achievement, making it the first Chinese-language movie to win a major prize at a Western festival. Hu's fight scenes made acrobatic moves more dynamic by using editing at the instant something or someone touches the frame or screen edge—what David Bordwell terms the "glimpse" ("Richness"). The film pushed the *wuxia* film genre to a new standard, particularly with its vision of the world of martial arts and its technical excellence in camera work, choreography, and editing. Hu's films set the tone for future cinematic innovations in *wuxia* and kung fu films, from those of Tsui Hark to Ang Lee. Lee in particular has skillfully revitalized Mandarin *wuxia* film traditions, including *xia* heroism, for international consumption.

The next milestone in the *wuxia* genre occurred in the early 1980s as a new generation of filmmakers schooled in Japanese and Hollywood filmmaking became the standard-bearers for Hong Kong's New Wave. Ackbar Abbas's *Hong Kong: Culture and the Politics of Disappearance* argues that Hong Kong's colonial experience, which lasted for more than 150 years, and its return to Chinese sovereignty in 1997, thanks to the Sino-British Joint Declaration of 1984, resulted in a change from "reverse hallucination" to a "culture of disappearance whose appearance is posited on the imminence of its disappearance" (7). Post-1984 also initiated a period in which Hong Kong consciously underwent change as its seemingly stable colonial status began to confront the imminent return to its Chinese homeland. Abbas points to the emergence of the New Wave in 1979 and the signing of the Sino-British Joint Declaration in 1984 as two events enabling the city to see itself with new eyes; "the new Hong Kong cinema . . . has found Hong Kong itself as a subject" (*Hong Kong* 23). Directors of Hong Kong New Wave in the late 1970s, like Tsui Hark, Ann Hui, Allen Fong, and Yim Ho, were trained in film schools in the United States and Britain. Zhang Che's protégé John Woo also emerged during the 1970s and later created the singularly impressive modernization of the *wuxia* genre by making Chow Yun-Fat his prototype of the contemporary *xia* hero in *A Better Tomorrow* (1986); he fought for justice and trust with guns instead of swords in Woo's gangster films. The 1980s and 1990s saw the rise of international visibility of the Hong Kong martial arts cinema and contemporary action thrillers as these films caught the attention of the West. In fact, Hong Kong underwent sociopolitical and cultural changes in the 1990s that intersected with the transnationalization of stars, filmmakers, and choreographers in Hollywood. Hong Kong's return to Chinese sovereignty began a whole process of struggle fought out at multiple social, cultural, and political levels. The stories of martial arts heroes and heroines also influenced the contemporary popular print culture, such as *manga*. The highly successful *The Storm Riders* (aka *Feng Wen*, 1998) was adapted from the Hong Kong martial arts *manga* series. The film incorporates computer-generated effects in its action composition. The combination of action and new technology dated back to Tsui Hark's *Zu: Warriors from the Magic Mountain*, for which he hired Hollywood special effects experts and in which he introduced the innovative style of visual effects and animation to Hong Kong martial arts films (C. Li). At the same time, kung fu, *wuxia*, and contemporary action thrillers extended the influences beyond the boundary of Hong Kong to the West. Directors such as Luc Besson, Oliver Stone, and Quentin Tarantino have expressed enthusiasm for the Hong Kong martial arts and action film genres (Shek Kei, "Brief" par. 29). In 1999, the fusion of Yuen Woo-ping's choreography with computer-generated imagery (CGI) in the American sci-fi film *The Matrix* extended the fascination with Hong Kong action films. American director Tarantino also introduced some classics of the martial arts genre to Western viewers in *Kill Bill* and its sequel. Following the success of *The Storm Riders*, Hollywood's interest in Hong Kong action in *The Matrix*, and the *Crouching Tiger, Hidden Dragon* phenomenon, today's filmmakers aim at exploring the huge Hollywood market and other means and forms of film production and distribution that appeal to world audiences.

The Transnationalization of Kung Fu Films

In the 1970s, the *wuxia* films gradually lost their attraction among audiences and gave way to kung fu films. By the early 1970s, *The Chinese Boxer* (1970) was often seen as the first major kung fu film that formed the basis and popularity of the kung fu film genre, but it wasn't until Bruce Lee's appearance in kung fu films that the genre was brought to its international acclaim and recognition. In his study of the reception of kung fu cinema in the United States, David Desser considers the kung fu craze of the 1970s a "a deceptively complex moment in American cultural history, when a foreign cinema grabs hold of the box-office as never before and eventually gives rise to a new and significant genre in American cinema"

(39). Desser sees the kung fu enthusiasm that burst into American consciousness in the 1970s as possibly related to the rebelliousness of black and youth audiences as well as to the American trauma of the Vietnam War. Kung fu entered the mainstream American imaginary as the subject of the television show *Kung Fu* (1972). The concept came into popular use along with the international success of Bruce Lee's films and refers to combat films in which the protagonists fight mostly with their fists. The genre is particularly unrivaled in Hong Kong cinema.

The incorporation of Chinese martial arts gained prominence when the film industry in Hong Kong produced the first Wong Fei-hung film in 1949. Wong Fei-hung (1847–1924) was a famous martial artist, teacher, and medical doctor in Guangdong during the late Qing Dynasty (1644–1912) and early Republican period in China. Throughout the 1950s and 1960s, Kwan Tak-hing played the title role in nearly eighty Wong Fei-hung films (Teo, *Hong Kong* 51). Kwan's Wong embodied Confucian virtue and patriarchal authority. The success of the Wong Fei-hung films helped to maintain the legend of the Cantonese folk hero and also consolidated the tradition that required that actors must be skilled enough in martial arts to perform physically in films. Both Jackie Chan and Jet Li have revisited the role of Wong Fei-hung in their later works. While the Wong Fei-hung films consolidate Confucian themes of patriarchy, patriotism, and hierarchy, the historical and fantastic worlds in *wuxia* films tend toward Buddhist and Taoist thought and attitudes. The Wong Fei-hung films set the prototype for the later prosperity of kung fu films in the 1970s and in its revitalization in the *Once Upon a Time in China* series (1991–97).

The golden age of kung fu films in the 1970s can be connected to the competition between Shaw Brothers, Golden Harvest, and Ng See-Yuen's Seasonal Films studios. (Ng's film company helped with the success of Jackie Chan in his collaborative works with Yuen Woo-ping, such as *Snake in the Eagle's Shadow* in 1978). Shaw Brothers, the largest studio in Hong Kong prior to the emergence in the 1970s of Golden Harvest, made films mainly in Mandarin, which accounted for the largest export market in Southeast Asia. Some of the most innovative directors of the martial arts film genre working for Shaw Brothers prior to the 1980s included King Hu and Zhang Che. Golden Harvest, a new film production and distribution company at the time, was the major film company in Hong Kong that helped to launch the international success of Bruce Lee. Another international star that Golden Harvest succeeded in promoting was Jackie Chan (Fore, "Golden Harvest"). The company became the largest film production and distribution company in Hong Kong. Martial arts films expanded Hong Kong cinema's market, which grew from twenty to eighty countries between 1950 and 1995 (Leung and Chan 145).

Hong Kong kung fu films broke loose from their ethnic Chinese diasporic population in Chinatown to downtown theaters all over the world. By the time Warner Brothers produced the *Kung Fu* television drama series in 1972 and such Hong Kong kung fu films as *Five Fingers of Death* (1972) and *Fist of Fury* (1972) were distributed in 1973, kung fu had become an inextricable part of American—and global—popular culture. Bruce Lee's Hong Kong– and Hollywood-produced films elevated the traditional Hong Kong martial arts film to a new level of popularity and acclaim and sparked a major surge of interest in Chinese martial arts in the West.

Bruce Lee was the major figure in Hong Kong cinema that brought martial arts films and Hong Kong cinema to international recognition, reaching more than ninety countries and transcending race and language. *The Big Boss* (1971) and *Fist of Fury* (aka *The Chinese Connection* in the United States) were Lee's first two major films and helped to initiate the kung fu craze in Hong Kong, America, and the rest of the world. According to the 1977 documentary *Bruce Lee, the Legend*, although Lee was born in San Francisco as an American citizen, he had problems becoming a Hollywood star. Lee played numerous roles in Hong Kong films at an early age, then returned to the United States and played a few minor roles in films and television, but he could not break down the barriers that denied Asian actors leading roles. As the documentary mentions, Lee was disappointed after losing the role of Kwai-chang/Caine in the American *Kung Fu* television series and returned to Hong Kong to make *The Big Boss*.

Only after Bruce Lee became the greatest star in Asia and his films grew to be the largest-grossing Asian films up to that time was Hollywood willing to feature him in the movie *Enter the Dragon* (1973). Hsiung-ping Chiao contextualizes Lee's films within modern Chinese history, highlighting the Hong Kong colonial background, and considers Lee's anticolonial sentiments as an explanation for his popularity among audiences in Southeast Asia and the American inner city. Chiao suggests that overseas Chinese can identify with the kung fu films, as they can connect their experiences of colonialism, imperialism, racism, or other forms of inequality and reconfigure their cultural identities in contexts outside of Mainland China. Chiao notes, "The blatant and exultant advocation of national identity was congenial not only to Chinese, but literally to all people who felt that they had been degraded by Western Imperialism" (37).

In "Kung Fu Film as Ghetto Myth," Stuart Kaminsky argues that Lee's films express underclass needs and values. He observes that kung fu films appeal to audiences who can identify with the minority protagonist, and the genre becomes a form that deals with the problem of social injustice. Kaminsky sees that the reception of Lee's films in the United States held political and racial significance. In fact, Lee also remasculinized Asian males, playing a significant part as an expression of Asian American politics and culture in years to come. Asian or Asian American characters on-screen are usually depersonalized and dehumanized representations.[4] Lee became an iconic figure particularly to the Chinese, as he portrayed Chinese national pride and Chinese nationalism in his movies.

The flexibility of the reception and interpretation of kung fu as a cross-cultural imaginary (as an extension of what Ding-Tzann Lii notes as a "yielding" relationship to different film markets and viewers) also reflects the transnational appeal of minorities' and other communities' consciousness of Lee's films in their encounters with social and political injustices. Bruce Lee's antiracist and anticolonial sentiments found resonance not only among Chinese but with broader audiences, including Asians, Asian Americans, African Americans and other minorities in the United States, and Africans, such as Tanzanians (Joseph).

Bruce Lee became an important figure who crossed multiple levels of discourses, national borders, and cultures. The multiple possibilities in the readings of Lee's films point to the history of reception and transnational filmmaking associated with the martial arts genre. Lee's films have created the transnational linkages and readings for Hong Kong/ Chinese martial arts films. Kung fu films provide an alternative model of masculinity that creates a noncultural specific imaginary not only for Hong Kong subjects and ethnic Chinese but also for other minorities. It was not until Bruce Lee's rise that Asian actors began to assume leading roles. Other Asian stars like Jackie Chan and Jet Li would follow.

While Bruce Lee was an important film artist who brought martial arts cinema to international recognition, Jackie Chan was the next leading action hero to come out of the Hong Kong film industry. The different trends of kung fu comedies, such as the northern-style kung fu from Yuen Woo-ping and Jackie Chan, first gained popularity in the 1970s. As Shek Kei comments:

> Contemporary kung-fu cinema has split into two interesting sub-genres both of them calculatedly entertaining and oriented towards acrobatics: the Northern style martial arts film, and the *kung-fu* comedy. . . . [M]artial artists/directors, including Yuen Woo-Ping,

Sammo Hung and Jackie Chan, have worked to integrate Northern styles with slapstick comedy, and their films have given *kung-fu* cinema its biggest successes since the death of Bruce Lee. ("Development" 35)

The precision, kinetic power, and death-defying stunts in later works by Jackie Chan and Sammo Hung derived from the skills acquired through Chinese opera training and then years of work as stuntmen. Chinese martial arts have a historical association with Beijing opera. *Da* is martial arts with acrobatic action.[5] Combat routines in Chinese opera, such as the Beijing opera, combine martial arts and the dramatic arts, and actors and actresses must undergo strict physical training from childhood before they acquire the skills and techniques to perform their roles.[6] There are also extra characters, now more commonly known as *dayingxiong* (martial/fight heroes), who play minor or supporting roles in martial arts fight scenes on stage (Jiang 163; Xu 193–94). The *longhu* (dragon and tiger) masters in Cantonese opera derive from the tradition of *dayingxiong* in Beijing opera. Zhang Che notes:

> The components of dance or martial arts in Cantonese opera were not profound but they later imbibed influences from Peking [Beijing] opera making them akin to the serialised libretto play of the Shanghai school. Most *Longhu* masters learned from Shanghai artists, such as Yuen Siu-tin (father of Yuen Woo-ping) and Yu Zhanyuan (teacher of Jackie Chan and Sammo Hung, and father of Yu So-chau) . . . who originally hailed from Shanghai. (20)

Hong Kong martial arts films have originated from these traditions of martial arts, theater, literature, history, and philosophy. Martial arts have close relationships with theater practices, and this also paved the way for the later incorporation of martial arts performance into film. The majority of Hong Kong martial arts filmmakers or actors, such as Jackie Chan and Sammo Hung, were trained in opera. Both Chan and Hung, for instance, were *longhu* masters in films for a long time before they gained major parts as actors or filmmakers. They studied at Yu Zhanyuan's Chinese Drama Academy as they learned and trained in martial arts for acrobatic stage performance. Chinese theater not only influenced martial arts choreography but also, together with Chinese *wuxia* literature, established the tradition of martial arts heroes in film.

Action star/director/choreographer Robin Shou's documentary *Red Trousers: The Life of the Hong Kong Stuntmen* (2004) traces the origins of the profession of the red trousers—a term originating from the Beijing

Opera School that referred to the color of the pants worn by the stunt-men. These are the people who brought their martial arts training from the stages of the operas to the sets of the action movies. In the documentary, Shou notes that there are major differences between martial arts practice and martial arts training under the Beijing Opera School. The latter requires more flexible adaptation of acrobatics and physical movements for performances on stage than does the martial arts practice. The generations of "red trousers," like Jackie Chan, Sammo Hung, and others, have set the high standards for Hong Kong stuntmen, performers, and fight choreographers.

Greg Dancer suggests that what he calls "real" and "fantastic" traditions in martial arts films coexist, one founded on the artifice and mastery of technology, the other on virtuosity and the performativity of kung fu (45). For example, King Hu's films depend on precise choreography and visual tricks, like unusual camera angles, selective framing, and editing (45). Jackie Chan has been compared to Gene Kelly for his athleticism and fondness for incorporating inanimate objects into his choreography (47). But martial arts seen in films are no longer the martial arts practice. That is why the performance in film is generally considered to be more flexible and acrobatic in comparison to the martial arts practice. The martial arts films engage with the performativity of the martial arts by asserting their status of spectacle and performance. The performative aspects of martial arts have achieved enormous influence on literature, theater, and film, and the world of Chinese opera has been the source of several generations of film stuntmen, stars, and choreographers, a tradition that peaked with Jackie Chan, Sammo Hung, Yuen Woo-ping, and others. These have been the most gifted physical performers of the genre.

In the 1990s, in the wake of Jackie Chan's top-billed appearance in the martial arts–incorporated action film *Rush Hour* (1998), the new international cinematic vocabulary absorbed and transposed stylistic, thematic, and sociopolitical concerns. The discussions of these phenomena have had to consider films beyond the fixed geographical boundaries of Hong Kong and have had to evaluate the diverse discourses that the demands and challenges of transnational capital have stimulated in the global marketplace. The urge to provoke new critical vocabularies to examine these emerging phenomena is reflected in the discussion of Jackie Chan's transnational film trajectory. In his analysis of Hong Kong identity in relation to Jackie Chan's global rise, Kwai-Cheung Lo points out the inherent contradictions that Chan's films pose to the social and political imaginary of Chineseness as a stable marker of ethnic identity.

Lo considers Hong Kong's construction of cultural identity to be based on a "certain negation of Chineseness"—thus "Hong Kong's transnational crossing to Hollywood initiates another negation that negates the very symbolic realm common to Chineseness" ("Double Negation" 467).

While Lo examines Chan's transnational film trajectory within the paradigm of Hong Kong's cultural identity and Chineseness, Gina Marchetti notes that Chan has transformed himself into a Hollywood star without severing his ties to Hong Kong, Japan, and non-Asian fans by creating a "ghetto myth" of transnational multiculturalism ("Jackie Chan" 157). The popular reception of Chan's films has had an impact on his film productions in the United States, and his films have proved very popular with transnational audiences. Chan's political intervention in mainstream Hollywood, however, does not offer an overtly multiculturalist politics. Instead of examining Chan's transnational film trajectory as "double negation" of "the very symbolic realm common to Chineseness" or as the "ghetto myth" of transnational multiculturalism, this book proposes a paradigmatic shift in Jackie Chan's transnational film trajectory to a cosmopolitical consciousness and agency (Lo, "Double Negation"; Marchetti, "Jackie Chan").

In analyzing the works of Chan, Ang Lee, and John Woo from a cosmopolitical viewpoint, I am participating in a scholarly effort to critique and offer productive alternatives to multicultural, polycultural, and transnational theories regarding local, ethnic, and national identity in mainstream cinema. Vijay Prashad, for example, problematizes multiculturalism, asserting that the world's cultures are interrelated rather than mutually divisive. Taking Bruce Lee's kung fu films as symbols of anti-imperialist solidarity, Prashad illustrates the polycultural affiliations among oppressed third world communities and America's ethnic populations during the late 1960s and 1970s. Prashad's polycultural critique rightly rejects essentialist, multiculturalist notions of ethnic identity but also retains the fallacious binary structure of the "unmarked" white/first world and "hybrid" ethnic/third world cultures and considers political resistance to be possible only from the stance of peripheral opposition. In examining Hong Kong's transnational influences and contribution to world cinema, Meaghan Morris explores a "cosmopolitan model of how to understand global cinema from local contexts that are neither 'centered' by Hollywood nor excluded or disavow its influence" ("Introduction" 13–14). Although Morris's cosmopolitan model investigates the transnational linkages that are attributable to film in general, a cosmopolitical perspective arises from the process of border-crossing and dislocation and tackles the strategic knowledge and tactical resistance for displaced transnational subjects to act across hegemonic power structures, both locally and translocally.

In extending and refining the arguments of Prashad and Morris, I argue that these cosmopolitical filmmakers offer more nuanced models for human identity that show how agents navigate multiple temporal, spatial, historical, and geopolitical positions, particularly within the global capitalist system, and the paradoxes or contradictions these may engender in colliding and colluding with mainstream ideologies and institutions. With attention to these filmmakers' transnational film trajectories and their successes in transnationalizing martial arts cinema from its Chinese origins, I address the filmmakers' efforts to achieve and maintain commercial success and to disrupt power inequities locally and internationally.

Transnational filmmakers such as Ang Lee, John Woo, and Jackie Chan embody cosmopolitical perspectives and knowledge. The strategies they deploy are not essentialist; rather, they utilize a wide variety of encounters, negotiations, and affiliations as they face off with larger infrastructures like those of Hollywood. That is to say, their positionalities are not fixed but multiple and flexible. Subjects achieve cosmopolitical perspectives as they engage complex experiences of displacement and accommodation among national and transnational forces. The interventions that filmmakers mount on Hollywood's hegemony are pushed further by their various political positions. Each of these interventions into Hollywood and Hong Kong/Chinese films is indeed cosmopolitical. That is, these filmmakers, who make films transnationally and embody multiple geopolitical consciousnesses, resist the hegemony of Hollywood's gender and racial politics and its confidence in its inviolability of its privileges in relation. The political positionalities in the transnational arena often involve gaps and discrepancies among different social, political, and cultural contexts of the translocal. The film artists take multiple positionalities and crack gender and racial codes that go unquestioned in Hollywood and Hong Kong/Chinese products. To examine highly successful martial arts cinema is to examine cosmopolitical consciousness as a new way of theorizing identity.

ANG LEE'S *CROUCHING TIGER, HIDDEN DRAGON*: GENDER, ETHNICITY, AND TRANSNATIONALISM

Cosmopolitical director Ang Lee made the Chinese-language film *Crouching Tiger, Hidden Dragon* in 2000, winning international acclaim and commercial success. The film's budget of $15 million was the highest ever for a Chinese-language film at the time and became the most commercially successful foreign film ever to be distributed worldwide, grossing more than $200 million in global box office receipts (Rose 4). Ang Lee was born in Taiwan, studied theater acting and directing at the Taiwan Academy of Arts in Taipei, received a bachelor's degree in theater at the University of Illinois at Urbana-Champaign, and continued his MFA in film at New York University. By the time he made *Crouching Tiger, Hidden Dragon*, Lee had already completed three Chinese-language films and three Hollywood projects. In 1995, British screenwriter and actress Emma Thompson invited Lee to adapt Jane Austen's classic *Sense and Sensibility* on the silver screen. Then Lee took on the American suburbs of the 1970s in *The Ice Storm* (1997) and the war-torn American South in *Ride with the Devil*.

Crouching Tiger, Hidden Dragon includes such transnational artistic talents as Chow Yun-Fat (Hong Kong), Michelle Yeoh (born in Malaysia but began her film career in Hong Kong), Zhang Ziyi (Mainland China), Chang Chen (Taiwan), and Cheng Pei-pei (Hong Kong). Cinematographer Peter Pau and fight choreographer Yuen Woo-ping are both from Hong Kong. Composer Tan Dun (born in Mainland China) prepared the musical score and drew upon the Chinese American cellist Yo-Yo Ma and pop singer Coco Lee, born in Hong Kong but raised in San Francisco. Lee's longtime collaborator, American screenwriter James Schamus, cowrote the screenplay with Taiwanese writers Wang Hui-Ling and Tsai Kuo-Jung.

The production team and crew members are from all over China, Asia, and the United States. The assistant directors gave instructions in Cantonese, Mandarin, and English (Cheshire 79). The film's production and investment was truly transnational. Lee's cosmopolitical perspective emerges from the fact that "[b]etween all of the different writers, [Lee] was the guy who was in the middle, who was in between the two worlds [the Chinese- and English-language worlds]" (Lee et al. 130).

In Jingbei Zhang's biography of Lee, *Shi Nian Yi Jiao Dian Ying Meng* (*Ten Years and a Dream of Film*), Lee noted that many people thought *Crouching Tiger, Hidden Dragon* was a purely Hollywood-produced Chinese-language film. Sony Pictures Classics and Columbia Pictures Film Production (Asia) purchased only the distribution rights but not its copyright. Good Machine International, led by Lee and his partners, owns the film's copyright (381–82).

Though the film was commercially successful in the West as well as in Taiwan, it was received with mixed feelings in Hong Kong and the Mainland. When Lee brought his *Crouching Tiger* Oscar for Best Foreign Film to Taiwan, he was considered a "faithful son returning triumphant from his overseas success" and was claimed as "(Taiwan) Chinese" through his description of "his filial piety—filial piety signifying as paradigmatically 'Chinese' cultural values" (Martin 151). However, Lee noted that many Mainland critics criticized the film as being not authentically Chinese, while in Hong Kong and the rest of Asia, the martial arts genre was in decline (in M. Berry 344, 346). Kenneth Chan identifies two main critiques of *Crouching Tiger, Hidden Dragon*. Cultural essentialists want a "true" and "authentic" representation of Chinese culture and its filmic history, while anti-Orientalists argue against exoticizing one's own culture and capitalizing on the popularity of an Orientalist gaze. In this chapter, I investigate how *Crouching Tiger, Hidden Dragon* cannot be considered solely within the framework of the national cultures of either China or America because of the cosmopolitical consciousness that the film encompasses.

The discourses of national and ethnic identity very often intertwine so that national and transnational frameworks negotiate questions of identity through the discourse of gender. In particular, I examine Ang Lee's use of *xia* characters in the *wuxia* film genre to transgress the hegemonic, binary split between public and private, masculine and feminine. He invokes strong female fighters and effeminate male warriors and questions the gender construction within the larger framework of Taoism and transnational feminism. In this light, I critically analyze how the female and male *xia* characters in the film defy traditional gender representations, such as *wen* and *wu* masculinities, in which public and private, masculine and feminine get played out through emotion, technology, and choreography in the contexts of Hong Kong/Chinese and Hollywood cinemas.[1]

The subordination or suppression of individuals to patriarchy and community is a pervasive theme in Lee's films. James Schamus, a collaborator of Lee's in his first three Chinese-language films, *Pushing Hands* (1991), *Eat Drink Man Woman* (1994), and *The Wedding Banquet*, commented:

> If the [three films] . . . could be said to have a common theme, it is the question of the father, of the role of the patriarch in a world where the patriarchy is under justifiable fire. In one way, *The Wedding Banquet* is very much about making the institution of fatherhood safe for the contemporary world, while *Eat Drink Man Woman* is about contemporary fatherhood's comically disruptive attempts at reconfiguring itself. (xi–xii)

After dealing with the crisis of the patriarchal figure, Lee, in his first English-language film, *Sense and Sensibility*, chronicles the life, romance, and experiences of two sisters whose father has just passed away. The film is an adaptation of Jane Austen's novel that contrasts the lives of Elinor, who withholds all her emotions and feelings, and Marianne, who openly expresses her likes and dislikes. While Lee's first three Chinese-language films are now known as the "father trilogy," dealing with the challenges that face the patriarchal figure, his *Sense and Sensibility* centers on the role of the woman and on the absence and death of a significant patriarchal figure.

His next English-language film, *The Ice Storm*, was based on Rick Moody's 1994 semi-autobiographical novel of the same title, and Lee chose to focus on the failing patriarchy in the American society of 1973, when the Nixon-Watergate scandal was at its peak. The film portrays insecure fatherhood, shown through two contrasting fathers, Ben and Jim. In his next project, *Ride with the Devil*, Lee focused on a small group of southerners after the American Civil War, based on Daniel Woodrell's 1987 novel, *Woe to Live On*. Rather than making a grand Civil War spectacle, Lee chose marginal figures—the "dutchy" Jacob Roedel, the "nigger" Daniel Holt, and the woman Sue Lee—to portray a personal journey that changes the lives of these people. *The Ice Storm* and *Ride with the Devil* in each case provide astute perspectives on familiar, classic, and/or historical accounts of American society.

Lee's next Hollywood film, *The Hulk* (2003), presents an alternative viewpoint to the American comic by offering a Freudian father-and-son theme. *Brokeback Mountain* (2005), for which Lee won an Academy Award for his direction, depicts the disastrous emotional and moral consequences faced by two homosexual cowboys whose surrounding (and to some extent internalized) environment of social intolerance causes and then exacerbates their erotic self-repression. In fact, self-repression is a theme that appears in several of Lee's movies, including *Sense and Sensibility*, *The Ice Storm*, and *The Hulk*. *Lust, Caution* (2007) deals with the subordination of public questions of war, revolution, and national survival to the private emotion of loyalty, vanity, and betrayal. Given Ang Lee's different points of view in relation to mainstream cinema and narrative, *Crouching Tiger, Hidden Dragon* shows his success in both arts and commercial cinema, and he turns his critical reflection toward Chineseness, Asianness, and femininity as repressed domains and markers on a transnational scale. Most prominently, the Chinese male and female warriors that Lee creates are caught between the discourse of Orientalism and the cultural authenticity of the *wuxia* or swordplay genre in Hollywood that also demonstrates how "the less powerful (cultures) negotiate the imposition of the agenda of the powerful" (Chow, *Primitive* 201).

Crouching Tiger, Hidden Dragon broke ground for the commercial success of martial arts films like Zhang Yimou's *Hero* and *House of Flying Daggers* (2004). *Hero* manifests Sinocentrism and Orientalist Eurocentrism as civilization, in the film, is at the hands of a centralized government that represents "all under heaven" (Chiu par. 46). The historically subversive martial arts heroes/heroines have to submit their individualism to "heaven's will." The film demonstrates collective trust and "fascist" glorification of "superpowerdom" at the expense of individual freedom and even the suppression of "division, differences, and heterogeneity" in the global capitalist system (E. Chan 272–74). In Zhang Yimou's next martial arts film, *House of Flying Daggers*, Zhang Ziyi's character, Mei, is a *xia* heroine and government rebel as well as an idealized object of sexual desire for the two major male characters, played by Takeshi Kaneshiro and Andy Lau (Szeto par. 11). The two films do not problematize the myths of gender and sexuality in patriarchal culture. *Hero*, for example, subordinates the status of the individual's freedom to the state's indoctrination and control. These two films were successful commercially, but they do not demonstrate the kind of cosmopolitical consciousness that shows in *Crouching Tiger, Hidden Dragon* as Lee strategizes the cultural and sociopolitical awareness of emotional repression and the polity of feminine agency as the site of contestation, both locally and translocally.

Qing (Emotion and Passion) and *Xia*

Crouching Tiger, Hidden Dragon has it roots in Chinese *wuxia* fiction, Hong Kong *wuxia* films, and classical Taoist culture that enhanced the childhood imaginations of many Asian filmmakers, including Ang Lee. Lee adapted Wang Dulu's (1909–77) *wuxia* novel of the same title, one of the representative works of the so-called Old School of the Republican period in China; it belongs to the literary tradition of *xia-qing*, or "knight-errant in love." Historically, the *wuxia* film genre derived from *wuxia* fiction. The original novel, set in the imaginary world of China during the Qing Dynasty, describes in detail how Yu helps Lo discover his own history and take revenge for his father's death. But Lee cuts this part about Lo and concentrates instead on Jen, another major female character in the novel.

The young Jen Yu (Zhang Ziyi), the daughter of Governor Yu, is at the center of the film's narrative, an affluent but unhappy young woman who desires to flee her arranged marriage for a life of adventure. She befriends Yu Shu-Lien (Michelle Yeoh), a woman warrior whose remarkable skills are exceeded only by the fruitless longing she feels for Li Mu-Bai (Chow Yun-Fat), a noble hero who possesses the four-hundred-year-old Green Destiny sword. The story begins as Mu-Bai tries to give away the sword to a prominent and respectable official in Beijing. Jen steals the sword in order to experience an adventure in *jianghu*, literally "rivers and lakes," or the public sphere of adventure. Rounding out the major characters are the film's ambivalent female antagonist, Jade Fox (played by Cheng Pei-pei, a veteran Hong Kong action heroine of the 1960s), and Lo (Chang Chen), Jen's love interest in the desert interlude.

One main feature of the *wuxia* film narrative is the heroic deed. The major characters demonstrate respectable qualities such as *yi* (uprightness and selflessness) and *xin* (trust) in *jianghu*, or the public sphere. Lin Nien-Tung suggests:

> The martial hero in the cinema is a commoner who "keeps his promise, advocates integrity far and wide, and sacrifices his life despite the world." . . . He [the martial hero] may be the protagonist in Zhang Che's films, who annihilates a single opponent, a household, a village, or a county for the sake of settling private hostilities. Or he may be the patriot in King Hu's films, a Mohist disciple who uses force with a broader vision for humanity. (16)

Thus, Lee also modifies some of the ideas and concepts of *xia*, who generally embody heroism and justice, instead portraying strong female *xia* who are also ambiguous in relation to the traditional definition of *xia* as embodiments of *yi* and *xin*. Lee's adaptation of Wang's novel takes on a new form of anti-heroism accomplished through the incorporation of romance and emotion into the *wuxia* genre's portrayal of the *xia* heroes' moral integrity. Men with *wu* masculinity are supposed to avoid women entirely and often violently eliminate the feminizing threat of desire for women (Louie 30). In the world of swordplay film and literature, the ideal martial heroes are usually the ones who exert control over any desire they might feel for women and demonstrate martial masculinity that honors brotherhood instead of romantic or sexual relationships with women. In Lee's projection of many emotions in the drama and action of the *wuxia* film genre, he is particularly interested when *qing* (emotion) conflicts with *yi* (uprightness and selflessness), an important attribute of *xia* (J. Zhang 269). Lee contests the basis of *wu* masculinity and feminizes his male warriors by depicting either their suppressed desire for or emotional reliance on women. In choosing to adapt Wang's novel with its melodrama, romance, and emotion, Lee rejuvenated the *wuxia* film genre.

The strong female *xia*, Jen Yu in Wang's novel, who attempts to act independently and overcomes obstacles with her skills in martial arts, appealed to Lee, who was attracted to her defiance of social constraints and her literal image as a "monsteress" and also to the dynamics and "*yin/yang*[2] hybrid gray area" between the two female characters Jen and Yu Shu-Lien (qtd. in J. Zhang 274, 275). Lee chose the feminine as the site of intervention to contest themes of loyalty and submission to authority generally embodied by the major historical and literary accounts of *xia* and thus tries to rework the concept of *xia* in his *wuxia* film. Lee, most prominently, empowers the female characters in the public sphere and feminizes the male in the private sphere. As Kaja Silverman notes, "[W]hat passes for 'femininity' is actually an inevitable part of all subjectivity. . . . [W]hat is needed . . . is not so much a 'masculinization' of the female subject as 'feminization' of the male subject" (149). However, the empowerment of the female subject and feminization of the male subject have more complicated meanings when the discourses of gender collide and collude with those of emotion.

In foregrounding atypical emotional struggles for this genre, Lee feminizes his male characters. If women and femininity are often relegated to the depoliticized realm of the private sphere and emotional attachments, the feminization of the male characters in the film is significant. It reworks the binary of public and private, masculinity and femininity. In mainstream cinematic representation, and action cinema in particular, the male heroes are glorified by the attributes of *wu* masculinity and are masculinized in the public sphere. Very often, such films also exclude men from the private sphere and feminize them in their expressions of emotion and love.

The greatest change Lee made to the novel was his addition of the death of hero Li Mu-Bai as the climax of the story. Lee portrays a *xia* in crisis. The major male *xia*, Li Mu-Bai, sickened by the corruption and violence he has witnessed in *jianghu*, the public sphere of adventure, wants to retreat by giving up his sword. But he is also a man unable to resist temptation and desire, and he cannot fully give up his passion for the sword and the power he exercises in the public sphere. He is in constant battle with himself and hesitates in his love relationship with Yu Shu-Lien. In crisis, Mu-Bai reveals his struggles with emotion, love, temptation, and desire. He avenges his master's death by killing Jade Fox. However, the code of honor that Mu-Bai defends is also questionable, as his master slept with Jade Fox but refused to teach her martial arts.

Lo, another male character in the film, hardly fulfills the ideal of being a *xia*, either. Lo's character is feminized in the sense that he assumes the stereotypical feminine characteristics of emotion and vulnerability in the intimate, domestic, and nurturing private sphere normally absent in the representation of males. The film shows Lo as a bandit whose general position in the public sphere of political and economic leadership is depoliticized, as the audience sees him openly declaim his emotion and weep while interrupting Jen's marriage procession. Lo's feminized image is enhanced by his lack of determination in the love relationship and in contrast to Jen's yearning for risk and adventure.

In the tradition of *wuxia* film, the female characters (with the general exception of the female *xia*) are mostly shown as dependent on men and as projections of the male characters' love interests. In *Crouching Tiger, Hidden Dragon*, Lo is depicted as emotionally dependent on Jen, and Jen is shown to be an active female agent who pursues her love, affection, and desire; thus, the characters invert traditional gender roles. In the love scene between Jen and Lo, she always strives metaphorically to be "on top." Jen also refuses to leave with Lo before the night of her wedding. She wants to gain control of her public life in *jianghu*; she also learns to become a desiring subject rather than remain the peripheral, inactive desired object that patriarchy arranges.

In most cases, powerful female characters are visible in *wuxia* films because they become upholders of the patriarchal code of *xin* and *yi*. The agenda is to show patriarchy co-opting strong female figures. The female *xia* characters are derived from Chinese martial arts and Beijing opera traditions that have roots in folk legends of women warriors. Martial arts films have captured the heroic feats of women, from the King Hu epic *Come Drink With Me,* starring Cheng Pei-pei, to *Crouching Tiger, Hidden Dragon* with its heroines. The action heroines have been popular since early *wuxia* films. Yet, such portrayal of strong female characters is also based on the given social discrimination in traditional China that "[w]omen fighters . . . are specified as the *xianu* [women warriors]," and for them to venture into martial accomplishments, they must "do so in a manner which will further prove the exclusivity of male rights implicit in this construct" (Louie 12). In the martial arts novels, women warriors avenge wrongs, and their achievements are acknowledged only if "they reinforce the 'superiority' and 'normality' of masculine ideals" (12). Thus, for the woman warrior to fight against evil or to fight for the communal values of *yi* and *xin* means that she is willing to risk her own safety in the service of the common good without expectation of reward.

Crouching Tiger, Hidden Dragon both sums up the *wuxia* tradition and questions the motivations of the female *xia* in traditional *wuxia* films. No female character is immune to the suffering that patriarchy inflicts, not even Yu Shu-Lien, the woman who appears to attain peace at heart. But her inner peace is only a suppression of the rules and laws that prohibit her and the man she loves, Li Mu-Bai, from fully expressing their affection for each other. Shu-Lien takes the lead in transporting the treasured sword Green Destiny to Beijing and demonstrates that she is an independent female *xia* character. Yet, she adheres strictly to a Confucian scale of obligation by respecting the dead husband of her short-lived marriage and retaining a painfully platonic relationship with her husband's friend, Mu-Bai. As strong as Shu-Lien is in her forceful martial arts techniques, she cannot, metaphorically, manipulate the same determination to fight against the constraints of feudalism and patriarchy. Shu-Lien reveals her true emotion only when she expresses her love for Mu-Bai before his death.

In the film, Jen Yu disguises herself as a man and tries to penetrate the male-dominated circle of warriors in *jianghu* in order to transcend her role that society restricts her to as a woman. She does not enact images of the canonical or stereotypical female warrior who upholds the code of honor in terms of *yi* and *xin*, but she is an individual who ventures into *jianghu* beyond the status as valuable sexual property and socially defined merchandise between men. The outcome is, of course, that Jen finds herself all alone and the cause of disaster. She is not able to reconcile herself to the form of femininity her society desires and expects. Her way of life poses too great a threat to the accepted separation of spheres, in which the only value a woman has is in her body. Through the skills of combat and martial arts, Jen gains entrance into the very guarded public sphere of male domination. Martial arts are still a male preserve. The sword that Mu-Bai tries to give up is an apparent phallic symbol of power that manifests itself in masculine superiority. In accessing the masculine role in the public sphere, Jen's attempt to steal the sword becomes symbolic of the moment a woman tries to wield masculine power concretely in the public sphere. The film shows the shifting boundaries that conceptually, politically, and physically elude the dichotomy of public and private, masculine and feminine.

Female *xia* can choose either the traditional life (like Yu Shu-Lien) or live without acceptance into the patriarchal society. Jade Fox and Jen Yu are the antitheses of Shu-Lien. Both have chosen to forsake the submissive female life and to chase after their desires and wishes. Jade Fox is a villain, but her life of crime is mainly due to the lack of respect she has received from male counterparts. Her bitterness has stemmed from the fact that Mu-Bai's master slept with her but refused to be her martial arts master because she is a woman. Jade Fox thus killed him and learned martial arts on her own. With Jade Fox's brief appearance on-screen, Ang Lee underlines the extreme injustice in which patriarchy locks out the potential for women to learn martial arts, the supposed male domain of the public sphere. The disavowal of the inequality of woman and man in the public and private spheres is an undertone in the movie. As Julia Kristeva points out, the abject is a sign of the divided subject, as the zone of the "in-between, the ambiguous, the composite" (4). The powerful feminine figure Jade Fox, whom the formal code of *jianghu* repelled and made abject, is generally considered to be the major villain in the movie. She is the inscription of sexual and social Otherness that the general code of *jianghu* wants to expel. The greatest evil in the film, however, is not Jade Fox but the patriarchal world that helps to create her.

Unlike traditional *wuxia* films, where honor is granted to the hero, *Crouching Tiger, Hidden Dragon* consistently delays this honor, and the hero, Li Mu-Bai, dies at the end of the movie. As David Bordwell writes: "The revenge motive took on moral resonance through the Confucian scale of obligations: The child owes a duty to the father, the pupil to the teacher. The *wuxia* plot often presents a struggle between social loyalty and personal desires" ("Hong Kong" 15–16). Mu-Bai adheres to this Confucian scale, because it was his duty and obligation to take revenge on his master's murderer, Jade Fox. As a male *xia*, Mu-Bai tries to attain Tao, the path of liberation, but fails, as he is still confined within Confucianism and patriarchy. The exception among the female fighters is Jen Yu, the only character to completely break away from the traditional representations of her gender by resisting Confucian principles and submissiveness to men. Although she is a woman in love, Jen refuses to return to Xinjiang with her lover Lo, and as a daughter/bride, she escapes from an arranged marriage monitored by her parents. Jen decides to completely embrace her talents and break the bonds of her aristocratic life. After experiencing the way of the warrior in *jianghu*, Jen chooses to transcend all responsibilities that the patriarchal world demands of her—be it love or a traditional role as a wife, bound to a husband. Rather than submit to the Confucian codes of social loyalty, she throws herself off a mountain and floats gracefully down into a world where she is free from all constraints. She refuses to adhere to the Confucian scale that binds Yu Shu-Lien to her duty, leads Jade Fox to her bitterness and revenge, and forbids Li Mu-Bai from obtaining Tao. By breaking with social obligations, she thus questions both the traditional female *xia* and the conventional male *xia* who are blind to their personal desires, bound to the hegemonic codes of patriarchy and Confucianism. The female warriors resist the normative roles as wife and mother confined in the household space, the major function assigned the female by the patriarchy.

In fact, *Crouching Tiger, Hidden Dragon* pays tribute to the different types of woman warrior figures, interestingly juxtaposing and reworking the representations of women on-screen. The film includes martial arts actresses of different generations: Cheng Pei-pei of the 1960s, Michelle Yeoh of the 1980s and 1990s, and newcomer Chinese actress Zhang Ziyi. Michelle Yeoh and Zhang Ziyi owe their representations of women warriors to Cheng Pei-pei, called the "queen of *wuxia* film" as the genre's first major female warrior. Cheng Pei-pei's audiences remember her from the 1960s in one of her most memorable roles, the Golden Swallow character in King Hu's *Come Drink with Me*, a film that Lee also pays tribute to.

King Hu was the major director to portray strong female *xia* characters during the 1960s and 1970s. The role of Golden Swallow inaugurated a new characterization of the fighting woman skilled at martial arts practice. If *Crouching Tiger, Hidden Dragon* is a tribute to the Hong Kong martial arts genre, Cheng Pei-pei as Jade Fox reminds us of the tradition she developed in her roles. Historically, in the *wuxia* film genre, very few females have been central characters. But in King Hu's *Come Drink with Me*, Cheng plays the role of a female *xia* who demonstrates the heroism generally embodied by males. Golden Swallow departs from the general attributes of vulnerability and dependency associated with female characters yet still colludes with the stereotypes perpetuated in obedience to Confucian principles. In the film, Golden Swallow engages in combat to save the son of a magistrate (also her brother) whom a gang of outlaws kidnapped. Despite her exceptional fighting skills, a man, Drunken Cat, defeats a group of corrupt abbots and rescues Golden Swallow.

In action cinema, Michelle Yeoh has incontestably been the major actress from the 1980s until now, starring memorably in *The Heroic Trio* (1992), a Hong Kong action film featuring strong female warriors, including actresses Maggie Cheung and Anita Mui. Her work ranges from an impressive number of Hong Kong films, including *Yes! Madam* (1985), *Magnificent Warriors* (1987), *Police Story III: Supercop* (1992), and *Tai Chi Master* (1993) to the Hollywood blockbuster James Bond picture *Tomorrow Never Dies* (1997), in which Yeoh's part as a beautiful but dangerous Chinese spy introduced her to mainstream American audiences. In this film, Yeoh's character is not the Oriental Lotus Blossom but a fiery Chinese spy that resembles a Dragon Lady prototype. Yeoh plays the woman *xia* or action heroine who fights against evil for the communal values of justice in order to uphold social stability. Her visibility as an international actress was an asset to the box office receipts.

Zhang Ziyi, who appeared in Chinese director Zhang Yimou's film *The Road Home* (2000), was a relatively new face to the transnational film audience. As Ang Lee notes, Zhang Ziyi as a new actress enables various possibilities, discoveries, and explorations (in J. Zhang 320). Zhang's "unknownness" at the time enabled the possibility of transporting an alternative interpretation of mythical "Chineseness," one that is unfixed and allows the emergence of new possibilities (in J. Zhang 320). This is an advantage compared to Yeoh's overexposure as a Bond girl or as an excellent fighter alongside Jackie Chan in *Police Story III: Supercop*. Lee also carefully considers the international appeal and marketability of his stars, such as Michelle Yeoh or Chow Yun-Fat, as the latter is one of the biggest stars from Hong Kong and Asia and has completed several Hollywood projects since *The Replacement Killers* (1998). Chang Chen, who plays Lo in *Crouching Tiger, Hidden Dragon*, has starred with Tong Leung Chiu-Wai in Wong Kar-Wai's *Happy Together* (1997).

Hong Kong martial arts films have long explored women as warriors in many works. Some of the *wuxia* films of the 1990s, such as director

Ronny Yu's *The Bride with White Hair* (1993), paint a seemingly more progressive feminist fable. Yu's film is based on the PRC Communist opera and film classic *The White-Haired Girl* (1950), about a woman whose hair turns white as she escapes from an evil landowner's oppression; eventually the Communists save her. In *The Bride with White Hair*, when the female protagonist finds that the world has no more room for her, she simply denounces it. She transforms into a monstrous figure who becomes the world's enemy and not its victim. The strong female warrior in the film emerges as a symbol of indestructible female power and anger. While Ronny Yu's strong female *xia* fiercely denounces the world in an oppositional manner, Ang Lee develops a heteroglossia to explore the intricacies of various female subject positions.

Crouching Tiger, Hidden Dragon portrays strong heroines who take charge of their actions and challenge the heroes' patriarchal order. Heteroglossia may mean multiple, but not necessarily unilaterally opposed. Mikhail Bakhtin notes, "[T]he centripetal forces of the life of language, embodied in a 'unitary language,' operate in the midst of heteroglossia" (271). Thus, the forces that lead to unity must struggle against the ever-present forces of heteroglossia that work to make language opaque. The *wuxia* novel is an unorthodox but popular form of literature. Heteroglossia intervenes in constructions of gender, creates multiplicity, and destabilizes and contests official discourse intent on constancy.

The movie shows the effeminate males and the different subject positions available to women. Only Yu Shu-Lien, who cautiously follows the rules of patriarchal authority, survives. The other remaining male figures are the old official Te and Jen Yu's "weepy" lover Lo. After all, the family (society) of the patriarchy is destabilized, and it evokes the endless process of adjusting many dissenting interests into changing coalitions and reciprocal concessions. The film challenges the centrality of the masculinist master narratives in *wuxia* by locating its perspective in the figure of the young female protagonist, Jen. By refracting a genre through a gender consciousness, Lee shifts the historiographic perspective to *qing* and the private sphere of the protagonists; such a perspective is not usually regarded as central to the traditional narrative in *wuxia* film. Ang Lee has used a diversity of male and female representations in *wuxia* film to examine the emergence of different subject positions. In so doing, he contests the hegemonic foundation of patriarchy and Confucian ideology that determines the dichotomy of public and private, masculine and feminine, empowered and disempowered in traditional *wuxia* films.

The Feminine as the Site of Cosmopolitical Intervention

The feminine position becomes the interstitial space in which issues of gender and ethnicity are carefully crafted within the realm of a utopian and fantastic fiction of imaginary China. The woman warrior is also an interstitial site for Lee to interrogate the meanings of identity in the transnational world. Maxine Hong Kingston's imagination in *The Woman Warrior* leads her to reconstruct this apparently Chinese myth as she investigates both her Chinese heritage and American self. In comparison, Lee reworks and adapts the traditions of the female and male *xia* to a new situation, the new audience and the new media of transnational filmmaking. The Chinese landscape with *xia* heroes and heroines is used not so much to reconfirm the ethnic or gender identity but rather to question the basis of such constructions.

Ang Lee notes that his parents are part of the Chinese émigré population of 1949 to Taiwan:

> To me I'm a mixture of many things and a confusion of many things. I'm not native Taiwanese, so we're alien in a way in Taiwan today, with the native Taiwanese pushing for independence. But when we go back to China, we're Taiwanese. Then, I live in the States; I'm a sort of foreigner everywhere. It's hard to find a real identity. Of course, I identify with Chinese culture because that was my upbringing, but that becomes very abstract; it's the idea of China. (qtd. in C. Berry 54)

Lee has repeatedly mentioned that *Crouching Tiger, Hidden Dragon* was for him "a dream of China" (Lee et al. 7) and notes in his biography that he was drawn to making a *wuxia* film because of his longing for "classical China," an abstract *wuxia* world that does not exist in reality (qtd. in J. Zhang 268). The film reiterates established geopolitics of China's exotic Otherness in its landscape, imagery, and martial arts choreography that are acceptable and widely circulated among audiences in the Chinese diaspora and international film market. As Stephen Teo notes: "The *wuxia* genre thus became associated with the northern style which audiences believed was more ancient and historical than the southern style. Novels and movies set their swordplay narratives in medieval dynasties and other mythical fantasies which, in turn, became stylistic conventions in the genre" (*Hong Kong* 98).

Ang Lee pays tribute not only stylistically and thematically to King Hu's *wuxia* film *A Touch of Zen* but also sociopolitically to Hu's diasporic background. As a Mandarin émigré in Hong Kong, King Hu found affiliation with the Beijing opera tradition and the historical and fantastic imagination of ancient China in the Mandarin-language *wuxia* film. Hu's bond with Mainland Mandarin cultures in the diasporic contexts of Hong Kong suggests the complex relationships between homeland and exile in the 1960 and 1970s. The tension between diaspora and its cultural roots resonates in Ang Lee's dream of China thirty years later in *Crouching Tiger, Hidden Dragon*. Raised in Taiwan in a mainlander generation from China, Lee associated romance and fantasy with the martial arts world, and this resulted in his tribute to a Mandarin *wuxia* film instead of a Cantonese Hong Kong *wuxia* film in 2000.

As an Asian filmmaker working in Hollywood, Lee also strives for his creative and artistic integrity. The *wuxia* film allows Lee not only to construct his dream of China but also to defy a China-centered discourse of nationalism. The martial arts genre captures *xia*'s marginality, often as an outsider to the mainstream society. As a diasporic subject from Taiwan, Lee turns to look at Chinese culture anew. The *wuxia* genre cultivates the imaginary China from a diasporic and global perspective. Femininity and feminine agency serve as allegories for the marginal. The valorization of the marginal is an ideological subversion of Sinocentrism that continues with the Mainland Chinese sense of cultural superiority. Thus, the China imagery is suffused with gender politics of marginality and resistance.

In fact, strong women have a long history as warriors in Chinese folklore. The portrayals of strong women images in *Crouching Tiger, Hidden Dragon* can also be traced back to Chinese literature, where women warriors are prominent figures alongside males. Both men and women are likely to be wandering nomads in *wuxia* novels. One example is the tale of the woman warrior Fa Mu Lan who fights in the place of her father. This is an important Confucian tale, as it reminds both men and women to be loyal to the father (patriarchy). Kingston, in her memoir *The Woman Warrior*, uses the story of Fa Mu Lan to imagine a mythical China and reinterprets the tale of Fa Mu Lan to construct her Asian American identity. Kingston allows herself to explore her Asian heritage by setting the myth of Fa Mu Lan in an imaginary Chinese landscape with Chinese figures. She negotiates and constructs her bicultural (Chinese and American) identity with this tension between her American self and her Chinese ancestry. The silence that Kingston's woman warrior confronts is a product both of Orientalism and of the patriarchy in Chinese society.

In *Crouching Tiger, Hidden Dragon*, Lee constructs an imaginary China and chooses this particular myth of the woman warrior to demonstrate a process of identity construction symbolically and metaphorically.

Such a cosmopolitical approach moves beyond the geopolitical position of the United States and is different from Kingston's construction of Asian American identity. It is also different from the Disney animated feature *Mulan* (1998) that further popularizes the image of the Chinese woman warrior and guarantees comprehension across viewer groups by containing a "kernel of American-style individualism in the context of ethnic and gender assertion" that makes the "major shift from the Chinese cultural trait of filial piety to the pursuit of a sense of selfhood" (Wang and Yeh 181). Georgette Wang and Emilie Yueh-yu Yeh note, in comparison to *Mulan*, that in *Crouching Tiger, Hidden Dragon*, "[w]hat causes the difference in the type of hybridity that comes out of the process of transformation is the kind of reculturalization strategy that the filmmaker seeks to adopt and the objectives that the film is expected to achieve" (188). Yet, such a model of reculturalization in a specific cultural context does not demonstrate how Ang Lee works across hegemonic power structures that pervade the histories of the Chinese diaspora.

In the Disney version, *Mulan* creates a strong, active woman warrior who in the end does not break with traditional narrative as she eventually returns home and gets married. In comparison, Jen, the woman warrior in *Crouching Tiger, Hidden Dragon*, defies marriage, love, and filial piety. Lee's strategy of mixing, synthesizing, and hybridizing East and West is cosmopolitical as he targets femininity and feminine agency as the sites of contestation and collusion with mainstream ideology in both Chinese and Hollywood cinemas. *Crouching Tiger, Hidden Dragon* is a portrayal uniquely Asian and Western. Lee uses the myth to deal with his cosmopolitical existence that combines Chinese, Taiwanese, and Asian American experiences. Through the discourse of the feminine subjectivity, Lee navigates and contests hegemonic ideology, including Confucianism and patriarchy, in both Chinese and Hollywood cinematic contexts.

In the film, the "crouching tiger" and the "hidden dragon" mean the hidden emotion and uncertain desire embedded within oneself. Lee says, "The [Chinese] culture is very repressed, but there are a lot of hidden dragons in people—and crouching tigers—that from time to time explode" (qtd. in Cheshire 78). In the novel and the film, Jen Yu's Chinese name, Jiao Long, means "Beautiful Dragon." If tiger and dragon refer to hiding one's strength from others, and thus to the unexplored and unidentified possibility hidden within oneself, then the inscription of the Asian man and woman represents not only the hidden desire and social stereotype that the dominant ideology projects and forces onto the ethnic Other but also the unexplored subjectivities that have yet to emerge.

In the film, Li Mu-Bai tries to indoctrinate her because he was afraid that if she were not properly disciplined, she would become a "poisoned dragon." In Chinese, "poisoned dragon" is an idiom for rebelliousness and antidiscipline. The potential nature of such "poison" is elusive and also highly perceptual, due to the moral codes of Confucianism and patriarchy in the film. Jen's Chinese name, Jiao Long, also literally suggests that she is the Dragon Lady.

Crouching Tiger, Hidden Dragon crosses the domains of Asia and America and engages the politics of race, ethnicity, and gender transnationally across Chinese and American frameworks. Asian and Asian American women are very often feminized and oversexualized in representations like the Lotus Blossom and the Dragon Lady.[3] In *Crouching Tiger, Hidden Dragon,* Jen Yu has a flexible identity: one could call it her "daytime personality" as a Lotus Blossom/soft-spoken aristocratic daughter when she is involved in the elite society, and her "nighttime personality" as a Dragon Lady/woman warrior when she is involved in the secret world of martial arts warriors. Jen's image refuses the framework of the binary opposition and thus essentially breaks with conventions of conformity, obedience, and the power structure both in the East and the West. Lee's cosmopolitical perspective ushers a different voice into the traditional Chinese patriarchal world of martial arts film that glorifies *yi* and *xin* in *jianghu* and the concepts of woman, femininity, and sexuality in a Western context. The film portrays strong female warriors that challenge the Lotus Blossom image. Jen's headstrong and temperamental female warrior image can be interpreted as a Dragon Lady with a violent disposition. The stereotypical sign of the Dragon Lady engages and confronts broader discourses of gender and ethnicity across the Chinese diaspora in Hollywood.

Touching upon the characterization of strong female characters as Jade Fox and Jen, the film does not fit into the mold of the preconceived Western perception of the East as secondary and submissive. Sonia Shah notes in "Slaying the Dragon Lady" that an "Asian American feminist movement" signifies the intervention in which a "different sort of Dragon Lady is emerging—not a cold blooded reptile, but a creature who breathes fire" (xx). Jen Yu is a Dragon Lady as well as a Lotus Blossom: a temperamental woman warrior who also performs her role as a submissive aristocratic daughter occasionally. Yet, her image cannot be thoroughly understood solely as Asian American or Chinese. She follows the path of her freedom and of her temperamental and natural disposition. She shatters the notion of subservient gender relations to the hierarchical order, not only in the Chinese tradition but also in East/West contexts.

In such Hollywood mainstream action cinema featuring strong female characters as *Terminator 2: Judgment Day* (1991) and *Alien 3* (1992), women can succeed only by becoming more masculine or androgynous. For example, the female warrior figure Sarah in *Terminator 2* is seen as a strong character because she accesses male attributes of muscularity and fighting skills. Similar to Yu Shu-Lien, the female characters in *Terminator 2* and *Alien 3* are strong but are submissive to men, whether those men are in the government or in the patriarchal order. Through the use of martial arts, Jade Fox, Shu-Lien, and Jen Yu are all strong female heroines, like the woman warrior prototype Fa Mu Lan. In comparing *Crouching Tiger, Hidden Dragon* with *Thelma and Louise* (1991), another example of a female-led Hollywood film, the latter film affirms the sisterhood between women who succeed when they bond with each other; they endure suffering but also express great triumph and joy at the end. Rather than offering only two feminist positionalities working out their differences, *Crouching Tiger, Hidden Dragon* provides at least three different portrayals of women's dilemmas in contesting their subjectivities and the culturally normalizing stereotypes.

As Fran Martin notes from an American perspective, *Crouching Tiger, Hidden Dragon* is "a contributor to the pop-cultural trend toward 'the action heroine who is both feminist and feminine,'" as seen in TV drama series such as *Buffy the Vampire Slayer* and *Dark Angel* and in films such as *Charlie's Angels* (2000) (156). In general, women are not considered to be powerful unless they have sex appeal. Women with sex appeal have a power over men. For instance, the sexually appealing female protagonists in *Charlie's Angels*, *Dark Angel*, and *Buffy the Vampire Slayer* make their power socially acceptable. *Crouching Tiger, Hidden Dragon*, however, shows that a powerful woman does not have to rely on her body or sexuality to get what she wants. Asian women literally occupy the site of the feminine, performing their ethnicity (as embodied in martial arts performance) in a transnational mainstream film production to legitimatize their visuality.

Images of fierce, fighting Asian women in different ethnic dynamics enable the feminist subject to defy the male in the heteronormative narrative, particularly the hegemonic model of white masculinity. For instance, the female *xia* representation allows a Western feminist interpretation to imagine a possible positionality to defy white male masculinity. Strong Asian women characters do not threaten white males, as they are doubly feminized as a sexualized Other and as a feminized ethnicity; they can be interpreted as deceptively threatening only to their own feminized Asian males. The hegemony of white masculinity displaces forms of threatening female figures, such as Dragon Ladies and women warriors on a transnational level. The male subject or *xia* can be easily equated with Chineseness as a communal and ethnic marker, while woman is considered as an Other and cannot bear the fundamental proposition of ethnicity without succumbing to the bodily and sexual imaginary of her as female. Performing as a feminized ethnicity across different geopolitical domains in the film complicates the territory of the conventional Hollywood narrative. In going transnational, notions of Chineseness have increasingly become diasporic through global capital. The film takes a step further by using the Asian female warriors and their site of alterity from the hegemonic model that white women presume and challenges not only the misogynistic nature of Chinese society but also the American context.

Ang Lee targets the legacy of oppressive orthodoxy in ancient China, with its restricted sexuality due to Confucian ideals and indifference to female subjectivity. Thus, the martial arts practice and philosophy of Taoism embedded in the fantasy film offers a refreshing change from the more traditional views of female warriors in martial arts cinema. Very often, the discourses of gender and ethnicity overlap each other in a film like *Crouching Tiger, Hidden Dragon*, which is "an attempt to keep a kind of narrative focus that I thought would work well both in Asia and in the West" (qtd. in Teo, "'We Kicked'" par. 29). *Crouching Tiger, Hidden Dragon* is also situated in a history of Asian men and women representations within literature, theater, and mainstream cinema, particularly its major distributor, the Hollywood film market and industry. It is there that the axes of nationality, ethnicity, and gender intersect and at the same time constitute each other. Ang Lee makes films transnationally, and, as in this case, his *Crouching Tiger, Hidden Dragon* reveals the multiple geopolitical consciousnesses that collide and collude with the hegemony of Hollywood's gender and racial politics.

The effeminate male character Lo in *Crouching Tiger, Hidden Dragon* coincides with the representations of Asian men in Hollywood (in comparison with other male action heroes in mainstream Hollywood cinema, such as Sylvester Stallone, Bruce Willis, and Steven Seagal). Within a popular history of Asian men depicted as asexual, ethnicity is read as an Other, a feminized space within the history of Hollywood representations. The representations in *The Last Emperor* (1987), *Farewell My Concubine* (1993), *M. Butterfly* (1993), and *The Wedding Banquet* depict homosexual or bisexual Asian characters as the leads. The history of representation of Asian Americans within the framework of America could be read against two tendencies in Hollywood cinema—its Orientalist fascination with Asian martial arts and the long tradition of images of male asexuality generated by Hollywood's practice of stereotyping Asians. Caucasian actors played characters from the Far East, such as Fu Manchu and Charlie Chan, emphasizing the unattractiveness of Chinese men. These representations can be explained in part by the threats to the hegemony of white masculinity nonwhite males have presented.

In a way, the feminizing effect of emotion collides and colludes with hegemonic discourses, as Asian is seen as an effeminate ethnicity in most cinematic representations. Cinematic representations across transnational perspectives are interwoven with the hegemonic model of American politics of gender and ethnicity. Asian as an ethnicity collapses as a feminized race, displaced and represented on behalf of the racialized and sexualized bodies in the performance of martial arts. Yet, Lo's effeminate character can be read in a larger context of the history of Mandarin and Cantonese *wuxia* films.

The film's critical vision of Chinese culture beyond the notion of the nation is more complicated than King Hu's films, as the latter are generally dubbed in standardized Mandarin to avoid the differences in accents. *Crouching Tiger, Hidden Dragon*'s actors do not come just from different regions in Mainland China but from all across Chinese-language-speaking communities: Chow Yun-Fat, Hong Kong; Michelle Yeoh, Malaysia; Zhang Ziyi, Mainland China; Chang Chen, Taiwan. Unlike the Mandarin films of King Hu, *Crouching Tiger, Hidden Dragon* is a Chinese-language film composed of various Mandarin accents.[4] Native Mandarin speakers readily identify Chow Yun-Fat and Michelle Yeoh's accents, but this level of awareness is impossible for the non-Chinese-speaking audience. Unlike Li Mu-Bai, Yu Shu-Lien, and Jen Yu, who inhabit central China, Chang's character Lo is a Xinjiang bandit, an outsider and exile from this "central" Chinese community. His character speaks not only Xinjiang dialect but also Mandarin with a distinct (Taiwanese) accent that reflects his alterity. The seemingly exhibitionist portrayal of epic China in the transnational film market conceals its heteroglossic discourse around the performance of language and its accents.

In this case, the film shows that standardized Mandarin, the official language of China, is a strand in the film that connects to other diasporic-accented versions of the language. Michelle Yeoh's Mandarin is with a Malaysian accent. Chow Yun-Fat underwent special diction lessons for his Mandarin; his first language was Cantonese. The attempt to speak standardized Mandarin can be noted in his enunciation. While Chow and Yeoh had to articulate standardized Mandarin, Chang Chen maintains his Taiwanese accent. Zhang Ziyi speaks standardized Mandarin, which affirms her diegetic role as the aristocratic daughter residing in Beijing. The film narrative further reflects the geopolitical divergences in accents. Both Chow and Yeoh struggled to acquire the official accent of Mandarin, as their characters in the film live in central China. While Mandarin as such does not directly convey a colonizing or imperial charge, its embeddedness within various pedagogical and disciplinary regimes of subjugation (whether these relate to colonization, imperialism, or migration) and its attachment to an official perception of Chineseness generally make it function as a worldwide lingua franca of the Chinese language. More particularly, the film reflects the differences Mandarin has undergone as it is acquired within the official or an immigrant context and then displaced by other prior dialects.

The standardization of the language, so much so as a monolithic representation of Chineseness in the global landscape, is invoked as a homogenizing force in its Orientalist portrayal of the premodern world of Chinese martial arts, yet it generates political meanings only when analyzed in the geopolitical forces in which Mandarin as a language is embedded. The ways in which Ang Lee records the different modalities of Mandarin addresses both the meanings of Chineseness and his reflection on language in a diasporic context. Accented Mandarin displaces the official language, as the enunciative differences reveal the latter as the regime of discipline. The complex variety of linguistic affects and the exiled subject who engages this multiple response and reflection on Chineseness make up a rebelliousness against the ideological impulse of induction into official Chineseness. More precisely, in Lee's film, fluency in standardized Mandarin exposes the disciplinary regime the other actors underwent.

The character Lo is a diasporic subject, and his Chinese name in the film and the novel means "Little Tiger." Lo is cut adrift from the naturalized bonds of the nation-state, since he is a bandit in the wilderness. He is the protagonist in the film who retains his local Mandarin accent. As a male warrior who publicly shows his emotion when his lover deserts him, not only is Lo an effeminate subject, but both his character and his Taiwanese-inflected Mandarin represent the outsider's point of intervention to reflect upon Chineseness as an ethnic and historical continuity.[5] Lo's exile from the traditional concept of *xia* heroism and his Mandarin accent also illustrate a rupture with the general perception of a homogeneous "Cultural China" transmitted through the Orientalist and Sinocentric perception of a heroic Chinese *wuxia* film set in ancient landscape of premodern China. In this case, ethnicity enmeshed with Chineseness and Confucian *xia* heroism can just as well be considered a hegemonic discourse. The different versions of Mandarin also pose a disruption to the seemingly seamless, uniform flow of the ancient China imaginary, which challenges the "systematic *codification and management of ethnicity* that is typical of modernity, in this case through language implementation" (Chow, "Introduction" 8). The film places the performativity of language and heteroglossial differences in conversation with each other. Lee employs multiple Mandarin accents to contest the homogeneity of an imaginary China that travels in the transnational flows of images. These images and sounds trespass borders not simply as preconceived exotic alterities but, rather, as political entities that have multiple resonances and therefore forcefully intervene across a variety of geopolitical terrains.

Viewing the film as a negotiation of multiple forces such as Sinocentrism and Orientalism enables us to understand how filmmakers like Ang Lee provide a counterpoint to hegemonic discourses, such as an ethnic ideology in mainstream cinema. These ethnic ideologies, whether Asianness or Chineseness, standardized Mandarin or its inflected variants, are shown to be complicit in the desire to subjugate Others as ethnic or racial sameness. In this case, the film engages the transnational contexts that overlap different grounds, not only the *wuxia* traditions and the representation of male and female warriors in Chinese cultures and issues of Chineseness in the national (China)/diasporic dynamics, but also crossover into Asian American politics and ethnic representations.

The Spectacle of Fight Choreography

Crouching Tiger, Hidden Dragon is a "martial arts and love epic set against the breathtaking landscapes of ancient China" (Lee et al. 27). There is a long tradition of epic in Hollywood in which filmmakers reinvent and redeploy the cultural stereotypes of the past. *Crouching Tiger, Hidden Dragon* marks a calculated reworking of those old-fashioned Hollywood romantic epics that usually find Europeans venturing into Asia, as in, for instance, *Anna and the King of Siam* (1946), *The King and I* (1956), and *Lawrence of Arabia* (1962); in war epics like *Apocalypse Now* (1979) and the American TV mini-series *Shogun* (1980); and in the Hollywood exposition of China's last imperial dynasty, *The Last Emperor.* Contrary to Hollywood's exploration of China's Otherness, Ang Lee reworks the exhibitionism of the mythical Chinese landscape to enhance global visibility on screen. In this case, the director made use of available technology and appropriated Oriental exhibitionism in an attempt to make it visible as pure spectacle, appealing to the desire for power and knowledge of the ethnic Other.

Spectacle is a major element of the epic, exhibited through sets, costumes, characters, landscapes, and narrative. The locale is also a main ingredient of the epic; a grand geographic milieu can become a central and magnificent backdrop for the *xia*'s actions. For example, in *Crouching Tiger, Hidden Dragon*, while traveling to Beijing to deliver the antique sword Green Destiny for Li Mu-Bai, Yu Shu-Lien rides into the city, which provides an opportunity for Ang Lee to spectacularize the ethnographic display with a sweeping vista of the crowded marketplace. One of the earlier scenes includes the spectacle of two young girls (not unlike the female martial arts warriors displaying their techniques on-screen) performing stunts to entertain passersby and earn a living. The martial arts cinema becomes an exotic Other projected as the strange and intractable cultural Other. At the same time, it also signifies the internal difference latent in the ambivalence of global film markets in which Hollywood is a dominant force.

Homi Bhabha associates desire with the visual and inflects codes of subversion in the ambivalence of stereotypes. He looks to Sigmund Freud in developing the idea of pleasure and in designating the pleasure of watching screen images and also to Jacques Lacan's concept of the mirror phase. A stereotype is like the fetish that simplifies a representation in an "arrested, fixated form" (Bhahba, *Location* 75). There is the combined recognition of difference and its disavowal, an experience of mastery and pleasure as well as self-defensive anxiety. The colonial and thus hegemonic stereotypification, as a form of the manipulation of power and knowledge and a form of technology of the colonizers, can therefore be seen as the uneasy, anxious result of the recognition of difference, the generation of fear and attraction, and its negotiation through denial. Premodern China's exotic landscape and martial arts are stereotypical images of Chineseness that travel in shared cultural and visual domains transnationally. The location of *Crouching Tiger, Hidden Dragon* is in the distant land of an imaginary China. The cinematography portrays an exotic landscape that is more abstract than precise. The Gobi desert can be taken as the scenery of American Westerns in which Lee rejuvenates his knowledge of different filming styles and techniques in both the East and the West. The horse-chasing scenes in *Ride with the Devil* are now transported to *Crouching Tiger, Hidden Dragon*'s desert interval with martial arts and romance.

Crouching Tiger, Hidden Dragon is an ambitious work in its martial arts choreography. Lee pays tribute to *wuxia* film choreography and composition of different eras. What he undertakes is to modify the classic style of *wuxia* film choreography of the fight scene, usually based simply on the spectacle of action. Jen Yu single-handedly fights off a group of rivals at the inn, which is reminiscent of the setting in King Hu's *Come Drink with Me* and *Dragon Inn*. In *Come Drink with Me*, for instance, Cheng Pei-pei plays a solitary woman warrior who fights a band of opponents in one of King Hu's most favored combat settings, the inn. In the famous fight scene in the film, Golden Swallow displays her legendary skills to a group of bandits and defeats them. A similar scene occurs in *Crouching Tiger, Hidden Dragon* in which Jen "is a young girl facing all those mediocre fighters" (Scarlet Chen 158). Golden Swallow fights for honor and the safety of her family, while Jen fights for her own desire to experience the life of a female *xia* in the public sphere of adventure. More, in *Crouching Tiger, Hidden Dragon*, the long shots punctuate the fight scenes. Jen is shown soaring through the space in the inn through the extravagant use of wireworks to suggest flight instead of through the more common use of montage.

Wuxia heroes or heroines in novels are supposed to have the ability to float or hover in the air. The phrases commonly used to describe their movements are "flying across the roofs," "running up the walls," and "walking on the water." The flight sequences in *wuxia* films are rarely revealed in their completeness in order to show visually that these characters actually have special martial arts skills and spiritual powers to make themselves as light as wind. Many martial arts films use fast cutting to magnify the kinetic power of the shots, new modes of digital image processing, and nonlinear editing in the practice of composition and choreography. In martial arts films of the 1990s, like Tsui Hark's works or the legendary transformation of the genre in Wong Kar-Wai's *Ashes of Time*, speed is the common denominator. As Ackbar Abbas writes about Hong Kong—with its cinematic style embodying a postmodern, transnational experience of disjuncture and velocity—film demonstrates "a visual aporia, as if every shot had to be closely attended to because things are always surreptitiously passing you by. This is the *déjà disparu*, a reality that is always outpacing our awareness of it, a reality that the film breathlessly tries to catch up with" (*Hong Kong* 35). The fast juxtaposition of scenes and editing techniques helps to justify Hong Kong's peculiar postcolonial condition, hybrid nature, and unstable social relationships as represented in a cinematic culture that consists of diversity and the rapid accumulation of capital. The films show Hong Kong's unique experience of postcolonialism and an accelerated version of late capitalism in terms of globalization, capital intensive production, and technological transformation.

While film director Tsui Hark examines the interface between movement and computer in his martial arts film *The Legend of Zu* (2001), Ang Lee rethinks the future of martial arts films from a different perspective. His approach to choreography and flying effects is different from other techno-*wuxia* films, like *The Storm Riders*, in which computer-generated special effects enhance the choreography. Lee's aim is to use the new technology and fight choreography, with great ambition, to take into consideration a different set of criteria: the cause and effect of transcultural gazes in the global circulation of martial arts film.

Rapid editing and montage aim to enhance the speed and illusion of movement rather than the authenticity of the flight itself as a cinematic spectacle. This is due in part to technical constraints, as Hong Kong filmmakers traditionally have had to use fast editing to hide the wires for the stunt work. Since filmmakers do not want the thick wires showing in their filming, they also must choreograph the flying sequences carefully. Thus, they typically prefer not to film the whole action in one long take, because they cannot hide the wires from the camera. In describing the wireworks, Kenneth Turan suggests that at times, each actor requires from five to twenty people to manipulate a fight scene. A lot more calculation and coordination is involved in the action choreography. Shooting action scenes are very time-consuming in the ways the shots have to be set up. Turan notes, "Traditionally, the Hong Kong-based genre is short on characterization and emotional nuance. Lee soon found out why 'it's almost against nature' to do the kind of film he envisioned" (52).

Unlike previous wireworks used for the sake of spectacle, Lee employs the long shot to expose the supernatural power of the flight so as to enhance and express the emotion of the characters. Both technology and capital allowed Lee to break physical laws in imagining the flying sequence. He took a literal approach to making these fantastic legends into live-action visual images with the help of modern technology, transforming the dreamy imagery of soaring warriors from *wuxia* novels onto the screen, as viewers see in the chase scene of Yu Shu-Lien and Jen Yu where the two characters fly across the rooftops and run up the walls.

Lee shows the failed relationship between the women Shu-Lien and Jen in a match. Pauline Chen comments, "[T]he fight between Jen and Shu-Lien seems hardly justified by the nature of their quarrel or the substance of their friendship based on sworn sisterhood according to the precept of 'yi'" (72). The ferocity of the fight between Jen and Shu-Lien in fact illustrates the contested dialogism between different subject positions. They start out as friends but become rivals as the film progresses. The match allows the females to expose their temper, emotion, and anger. The fight choreography reveals Jen's natural temperamental deviation and how Shu-Lien is agitated by Jen's ungratefulness. Shu-Lien poses as the example of freedom in comparison to married women, but in fact she is still bound by traditional rules of society that demand female passivity. Many *wuxia* films are full of melodrama. Lee's *Crouching Tiger, Hidden Dragon* redefines this long tradition of the heroic principle from the manifestation of Shu-Lien's chivalric justice to Jen's emotional inclination and sentiment. Lee chooses the feminizing effect of emotion and desire as the logic behind the choreography.

To audiences accustomed to the fast rhythm editing and energy in many Hong Kong martial arts film of the 1990s, the long takes in the flying scenes in *Crouching Tiger, Hidden Dragon* are unfamiliar. In "Love and Swords: The Dialectics of Martial Arts Romance—A Review of *Crouching Tiger, Hidden Dragon*," Stephen Teo comments on the ways Ang Lee's film pays tribute to director King Hu's *A Touch of Zen*: "[Lee] has essentially failed to grasp the substance of the master—Hu's substance always alluding to the heroic principle as the tragic manifestation of chivalric violence" ("Love" par. 13). One of the most memorable fight scenes in *A Touch of Zen* is the combat in a quiet bamboo forest. The action occurs in midair, as the fighters hurl themselves from branches high above the ground in a mixture of fast cuts and editing. In *Crouching Tiger, Hidden Dragon*, Li Mu-Bai and Jen Yu hover over water and fight on top of bamboo trees. In this scene, Mu-Bai intends to introduce Jen to the Wudang school, but Jen resists. The fight between Mu-Bai and Jen has more than pedagogical implications, also implying patriarchal anxiety over female sexuality that might at times challenge patriarchy's hegemonic authority.

When Mu-Bai accused Jade Fox of corrupting Jen and expressed interest in being Jen's master, his action not only has an obvious sexual undertone but also suggests the anxiety of the patriarch in the face of strong and uninhibited female characters. Jen's power is immediately compromised when she matches against Mu-Bai and Shu-Lien. Jen's inability to constrain her temperament and impulsive emotion becomes her biggest downfall during the contest. Jen refuses admission to the Wudang school, another patriarchal system that she fears would poison her, just as her parents, her arranged marriage, and her life as a woman had done. Jen fights for her own desire to experience the life of a female *xia* without the constraints of indoctrination and patriarchy.

In comparing *Crouching Tiger, Hidden Dragon*'s bamboo forest scene with the flight scene in Ronny Yu's renewal of the *wuxia* film genre in *The Bride with White Hair*, for instance, Leslie Cheung's character, Yi-Fan, picks up the fallen Lian, played by Brigitte Lin, and soars up in the air and out of the frame. The camera, however, does not follow Yi-Fan to complete the flying motion. *Crouching Tiger, Hidden Dragon* is also different from such films as *Once Upon a Time in China* (1991). The latter is more properly classified as a kung fu film, because it emphasizes elements of martial arts combat techniques more than swordplay. These two films contrast in interesting ways. When Jet Li's character, Wong Fei-hung, defies gravity in his martial arts performance, the editing does not show entirely his flying sequence, either; the flying effects are presented in fragments with close-ups and rapid editing. The flying choreography shown in its incompleteness is similar to the way the title character in Hollywood's *Spider-Man* (2002) slides up and down buildings through special effects. *Crouching Tiger, Hidden Dragon*'s use of long shot to record bodily movements purposely tries to differentiate itself from the fragmented flight sequences of Hong Kong martial arts films and the special effects that enhanced *Spider-Man*. Lee's reworking of the *wuxia* and martial arts choreography and filming techniques thus becomes significant in a film production targeted at transnational film markets.

Andre Bazin notes, "That depth of focus brings the spectator into a relation with the image closer to that which he enjoys with reality," and as a result, "its structure is more realistic" ("Evolution" 50). Deep focus in this sense ushers in the spectator to the visual richness of a profoundly focused world. Bazin aligns this thinking with those who put faith in reality. Bazin believes that cinematic realism could be achieved only when filmmakers refrained from "trying to deceive us," as evident in the accelerated montage films of Sergei Eisenstein and Vsevolod Pudovkin, and instead focused on "condensing time" rather than attempting to interrelate random images through pure montage (50). In effect, Bazin argues that such filmmakers "rediscovered a possible use related to temporal realism in a film without montage" (50). The use of specific filmic devices and technologies, including depth of focus, allows "reality" to speak for itself.

Crouching Tiger, Hidden Dragon, however, calls attention to the fact that the filmic reality is perceptual and culturally specific. The *wuxia* film becomes a cross-cultural commodity. The mysticism of Chineseness is in essence the fetishized corporeal body in the transnational world. Lee complicates the unilateral picture of the eradication of the body into "simulacrum" that "bears no relation to any reality whatever" (Baudrillard 170). He contemplates the biopolitics of the body and technology, in which the wirework-enhanced martial arts choreography is already a form of special effects. Lee makes use of cinema to open up a new space for recording moving images, both for the East and the West. Cinema, as a Western technology with its inherent obsession with realism, documents *Crouching Tiger, Hidden Dragon*'s manipulation of the body's potential movement.[6] Thus, what the filmmaker demonstrates is not only his cosmopolitical knowledge of the technology of the body (martial arts performance) but also his knowledge of the technology of cinema in the global film market.

In "Flying, East and West," Stanley Kauffmann describes *Crouching Tiger, Hidden Dragon* as a cinematic ballad that indulges in visual and aural spectacle. According to this logic, *Crouching Tiger, Hidden Dragon* consciously poses itself as an "authentic" Other and seemingly reaffirms the Orientalist framework the West has constituted. In turn, the film also enables a strategic posing that plays with the stereotype of the martial artist. Thus, *Crouching Tiger, Hidden Dragon* fulfills the desire that is inherent in the conceptions of filmic reality, and Ang Lee purposely uses the images of the Orient to interrogate this desire. At the same time, the film offers a context for understanding the clean look of new technology-enhanced choreographic filming, and the long shot reminds us of the aura of the performing body that gets lost in technical perfection. Walter Benjamin says, "[F]or the first time—and this is the effect of the film—man has to operate with his whole living person, yet forgoing its aura. For aura is tied to presence; there can be no replica of it" (229). The manipulation of the cinematic techniques and angles in long shots and within one frame provide evidence of the real body in performance, whereas the wiped-out wire lines result from a process of sterilization in order to veil information about the technological involvement. The authenticity as an ethnic Other is accomplished by performing mythical martial arts vividly and convincingly through the technology of cinema.

The ability to remove the wires digitally in the postproduction process allowed the director and his choreographer, Yuen Woo-ping, to use thicker wires to compose the fight scene in the bamboo forest. The deployment of the long shot to record the choreography of flying or gliding on tops of bamboo trees, roofs, or walls allows exotic contemplation of ethnicity as an embodied entity that is subject to the visual power of gaze. Lee makes use of ethnic Others' performing bodies as the marker of the Oriental imagination both within the United States (towards Asians and Asian Americans) and beyond the nation (China and the United States). Thus, by engaging with technology, the film allows a new spectacle and performance of *wuxia* fantasy under transnational fetishistic looks and uses the cycle of voyeuristic desire to upset the linearity of the gaze. The film targets the Cartesian binarism of body and mind. The technology of martial arts and new media are incorporated into the making of *Crouching Tiger, Hidden Dragon* and challenge the semiotic articulation of reality that reaffirms the desire for differential Otherness in transnational cinematic and image consumption. Thereby, the technological effects of the Orient produced in transnational filmmaking displace the authenticity of the cinematic object of Otherness.

Speed becomes a significant factor in the aesthetics of transnational production. Lee's long shot exhibits delicately and slowly to the viewer the mythic nature and imaginary of a premodern China. The filmmaker makes use of the liminal space and sign of the feminine as the site and mode of subversion. As Ang Lee notes about the initiative in working in this genre: "My team and I chose the most populist, if not popular, genre in film history—the Hong Kong martial arts film—to tell our story, and we used this pop genre almost as a kind of research instrument to explore the legacy of classical culture" (7). The exploration of classical culture is inevitably intertwined with the history and discourse of Chineseness as a form of cross-cultural commodity and transnational gaze. When the "East" looks at itself through an imaginary China, which is a cross-cultural construction, opportunities for different perspectives in critical understandings emerge. A Chinese, Taiwanese, and American coproduction financed from all over the world, the film redraws the map of international cinema in terms of transnational capital.

As a transnational *wuxia* film, *Crouching Tiger, Hidden Dragon* creates an impressive cinematic space that can be entered, touched, and "embodied," and as a global box office hit, it exemplifies "a miracle of cultural commodity with its *qing gong* flight of transcultural circulation and consumption" versus *The Matrix*'s disembodied flight (Chiang 105). Comparing *Crouching Tiger, Hidden Dragon* and *The Matrix* films reveals the difference between Lee's cosmopolitical consciousness and the double consciousness embedded in *The Matrix*. Double consciousness, as Peter Feng indicates, can be used to analyze films such as *The Matrix* made by American filmmakers. *The Matrix* becomes an allegory of how global Hollywood imagines its borderlessness and how transnational capital aims at restructuring local and global economies. When protagonist Neo, played by Keanu Reeves, and other resistance fighters are hijacked into the Matrix, their agility "derives from their awareness of themselves as existing simultaneously in two worlds" (11).

Lee's cosmopolitical consciousness is different from W. E. B. Du Bois's famous formulation of "double consciousness." Du Bois's "double consciousness" indicates the racialized subject's awareness of both how he sees himself and how the others see him. In comparison, *Crouching Tiger, Hidden Dragon*'s transnational trajectory shows that Lee's cosmopolitical consciousness is a result of the subject's multiple displacements and tactical negotiations with or resistance to hegemonic power structures. Lee's work provides an example that "we must go through in order to arrive—not at the new destination of the truth of an 'other' culture but at the weakened foundations of Western metaphysics as well as the disintegrated bases of Eastern tradition" (Chow, *Primitive* 201). Instead of creating an individualistic/messiah-like Hollywood superhero who assimilates difference and transcends borders, Lee redefines the *xia* hero and heroine who problematize the common justice and righteousness in martial arts movies and question the social ideals that govern *xia*'s justice within the Confucian society.

Thus, the spectacle of the martial arts can be read closely within the hegemonic apparatus of global Hollywood. In *The Language of New Media*, Lev Manovich makes the historical comparison between the project of *Jurassic Park* (1993) and Soviet Social Realism in art that depicts current social problems along with some symbols of hope for the future. The Soviet Socialist artists would never imagine a future without concomitantly addressing the contemporary political condition that frames their imagination. *Jurassic Park* employs the same rationale as the computer-generated dinosaurs present the possibilities of a synthetic future but remained tied to a photographic tradition of the past. In this way, the computer-generated image fails to realize its perfection, for "its perfection is undermined by every possible means and is masked by the film's content" (204). Thus, the photorealistic approach circumnavigates the possibilities of a "perfectly realistic representation of a cyborg body yet to come" (202). Similarly, by inscribing synthetic possibilities onto the Orientalist fascination with embodiment in Asian martial arts performance, *The Matrix* trilogy employs the same kind of vision in its use of special effects and suggests that the computer-generated images of virtuality exist in the world of the Matrix, embodied by the martial arts.

In *The Matrix* trilogy, the "real world" of Zion is set against the digital reality of the Matrix. Yuen Woo-ping, choreographer for *Crouching Tiger, Hidden Dragon*, is also the choreographer for *The Matrix* trilogy. The use of Hong Kong martial arts choreography enables actors to accomplish amazing stunts—with computer-generated imagery—in the trilogy. Thus, the digitalization of martial arts is perceived as a superhumanist feat in the Matrix. It represents the Orientalist preconception of martial arts as the technology of the embodied Other that the self both fears and desires. The logic is acceptable because the reference points of embodiment (martial arts) and disembodiment (CGI) induce the audience for the moment to accept as truth that martial arts permeate the world of the Matrix but not reality (Zion).

In *The Matrix* films, martial arts function partly to constitute the individual unitary subject as an ideal of masculinity. The main protagonist, Neo, is transformed from an ordinary human to a martial arts superman, a lone computer hacker into the universal messiah. His mission to save and free humankind mainly revolves around his unique ability to engage and destroy his superhuman and machine opponents, albeit with the assistance of his small cohort of sidekicks, led by the Laurence Fishburne character Morpheus. *The Matrix* trilogy reinforces the humanist/posthumanist binary by positing the last human city of Zion as the ultimate reality and Neo as the messiah able to lead the human race to battle the machines and liberate humanity from a mere illusion of existence generated by artificial intelligence. His supernatural power grants him a tragic ending rather than a blessing and leaves him alone because of his godlike, fearful supernatural ability.

The transnational visibility of wirework and stunts as well as the popularity of themes such as revenge in the *Kill Bill* films and of heroism/salvation in *The Matrix* films reflect Hollywood's appropriations and reformulations of Hong Kong martial arts cinema, to which *Crouching Tiger, Hidden Dragon*'s martial arts spectacle has revealed a critical edge. In contrast to the human heroes in the fantasy *wuxia* tradition, Hollywood productions envision globalization with computer-generated special effects and with American superheroes who dissolve national, cultural, and economic boundaries as they spread free-market corporate capitalism, individual entrepreneurship, and democracy to the world. In *The Matrix*, as Peter Feng notes, "The absorption of Hong Kong style into Hollywood's melting pot was noted by many commentators. . . .

[T]he film introduces the Asian cinematic technique of wire-fighting into an American action film" (15). Multiracial Keanu Reeves becomes the primary conduit for the Matrix's assimilation of Hong Kong action filmmaking. As David Palumbo-Liu argues, for most of the twentieth century, American modernity "is inseparable from historical occasion of real contact between interpenetration of Asia and America" (2). *The Matrix* is considered an example of assimilation of the Other as it is marked by Hollywood's efforts to modify Asian bodies and psyches on the screen representation and to think locally and not globally.

The Matrix's tactics of assimilation are different from what Lee demonstrates as a cosmopolitical filmmaker. Ang Lee has noted that Chinese cinema at this point cannot top Hollywood in other genres except through martial arts films (M. Berry 359). In the context of global Hollywood, *Crouching Tiger, Hidden Dragon* has kept alive the vibrant, sumptuous martial arts spectacle that Hollywood has not fully developed. Hollywood reasserts a familiar teleological narrative of globalization and assimilation, where *Crouching Tiger, Hidden Dragon* explores the martial arts film genre's close relation to theater, choreography, and cinematic spectacle. Chinese cinema, particularly martial arts film, is able to break through the Hollywood dominance. As a renewal of the *wuxia* film, *Crouching Tiger, Hidden Dragon* is an attempt to imagine alternative tactics and modes of representation in a global film market. Martial arts are a form of technology, a technology of the body. The film negotiates the imposition of the assimilation agenda of mainstream Hollywood as a global enterprise by combining the knowledge of technology and body.

Jen's "Taoist Leap" and Feminine Agency

Crouching Tiger, Hidden Dragon demonstrates the ways that the hero or heroine's physical abilities are mostly human rather than superhuman. In the Taoist tradition, both men and women can be extremely skilled in their techniques, which are the results of training over time. In its incorporation of both *wuxia* and Taoist philosophy, *Crouching Tiger, Hidden Dragon* provides a cross-cultural response to Hollywood's appropriation and hybridization of martial arts traditions, including thematic, philosophical, and technical concerns.

Crouching Tiger, Hidden Dragon embodies a cosmopolitical perspective of the feminine that is inspired by both Taoism and feminism. Taoism suggests the feminine ways that break down traditional norms and conceptions of man and woman and the individual's merge with the nondichotomous universe and nature. Tao emphasizes the complementarity and harmony of *yin* and *yang*, the female and male cosmic principles. By recommending the feminine ways to the male sage as the way to govern the empire, Laozi's *Dao De Jing* advocates a non-dichotomous universe that breaks down traditional inscriptions of man and woman. It is the feminine aspects of Tao that target Confucianism's masculine values of moral righteousness, feudalism, and patriarchal thoughts as the sites of contestation.

The feminine positions pose this contradictory gesture, which leads to the question of ethics in which the experience of the impassible and impossible is what the feminine represents. Luce Irigaray introduces the notion of a "female imaginary" based on a critique of the Oedipal narrative and its exclusion of the female infant (in terms of the analyses of Freud and Lacan) (30). As Irigaray comments:

> How, then, are we to try to redefine this language work that would leave space for the feminine? . . . We need to proceed in such a way that linear reading is no longer possible: that is, the retroactive impact of the end of each word, utterance, or sentence upon its beginning must be taken into consideration in order to undo the power of its teleological effect, including its deferred action. (79–80)

Thus, Irigaray sees the feminine as characterized by "duality" and "disruptive excess" (77, 78). The feminine becomes a category that inaugurates a kind of future within language and intelligibility that is not yet known. This utopian dimension that is beyond articulation and endlessly breaks up the existing symbolic order renders this feminine position continuously transformable and, therefore, unforeclosed to a radical future.

In *Crouching Tiger, Hidden Dragon*, the woman warrior image and the martial arts genre that set Jen Yu off from traditional femininity have become broadly received signs in global consumption. The gender significations and geopolitical meanings reveal the feminizing "China-as-spectacle" in cross-cultural transmissions. In the end, the evil female warrior Jade Fox dies. Jen jumps off the mountain with ambiguous possible meanings: Does she literally fly off the mountain? Does she transcend into another world? Does she die? Jen is an ambiguous figure, a "Dragon Lady" who enjoys the brief adventurous freedom as a *xia* in *jianghu*. While Li Mu-Bai fails to attain Tao through meditation in the beginning, Jen is able by the end of the movie to make the Taoist leap (allegorical for the language of the "feminine" in the film narrative). Reading Jen's story in the novel is different from watching Lee's film adaptation. In the novel, Jen jumps off Miaofeng Mountain to perform ritualistic filial piety to bring about the recovery of her father. As Jen has planned, she survives her jump and later gives birth to a son. The screenplay has Jen jumping off Wudang Mountain, leaving open the question of whether she has freed herself from all relationships/social obligations or whether she has sacrificed her life for Mu-Bai's resurrection. The ambiguous ending also forever suspends Jen in her flight into the mist and refuses to suggest her death.

The ambiguous ending is also due to the fantasy nature of the *wuxia* genre that enables its heroes and heroines to have the ability to survive from such daring endeavors. As Fran Martin notes, Jen's final leap is similar to "the death defying drive off the cliff at the conclusion of the American pop-feminist classic *Thelma and Louise* . . .—another film that refuses visually to imply the deaths of its heroines, who seem to remain forever suspended in their ultimate trajectory" (159). Soaring defiantly and eternally into the mist, Jen the rebellious girl refuses to submit herself to any of the social systems that structure the world of living, following only what her nature and temperament lead her to do. Earlier in the film, Lo tells Jen a story about a young man who wishes for his parents to be healed; by jumping off the mountain, his wish is granted. In the end, Lo makes the wish to return to Xinjiang with Jen, but Jen, by choosing to leave the world by jumping off Wudang Mountain, denies Lo's wish. As Jen finds liberation from the role that society has dictated for her, the narrative has left the ending multivocal; she may have died or not.

In comparison to the novel, Tze-Lan D. Sang notes that the film reduces Jen

> to a woman who occasionally cross-dresses but is firmly locked in a normative female position in a heterosexual romance. Her anatomical sex is female and so is her social gender, but her sexed embodiment is masculine with female specificity—constituted differently from the bodies of ordinary women that lack the charm of the novelist's heroine that keeps his readers' enthusiasm for this gender-queer body in the sharpest of focus. (110)

Indeed, Sang's dissatisfaction with Jen's characterization reflects the binary argument about a woman's identity as either being the sexualized female body who uses her sex as power or a masculine or androgynous figure with a "gender-queer body" that is a socially outcast. The question is not about which agency defies patriarchy and mainstream expectation. In fact, woman is presented to us with two modes of alienation. Evidently, to play at being a masculine or androgynous figure will be for her a source of frustration; but to play at being a woman is also an illusion: to be a woman would mean to be the object, the Other in a heteronormative narrative.

Although as a woman Jen finds herself in a situation dominated by men's imaginary, she does not succumb to the parameters of this imaginary. To be transcendent would be to construct her own imaginary, knowing that it is grounded in nothing other than her commitment to herself. Rather than subduing the feminine, the effort to read Jen as a particular discursive formation resists its marginality. However compelling as a figure for a radical feminine alterity, the unruly Jen must not preclude either the feminine or the masculine nor obscure the conditions of her own desire. Only with the double-edged conclusion does Jen's presence rupture the realm of discourse and politics of the linear narrative. A fantastic construction, Jen reveals the difficulty of isolating an Other's agency or experience outside of (or at least prior to) its cultural manifestations. The multivocal ending envisions a paradoxical scenario that the positionality of the feminine provokes. The Other's multivocality reveals the feminized subject whom mainstream ideologies have subordinated and who has yet to be recovered.

The feminine signals the ultimate basis of Tao as *wu* (nothing or non-being), the site of nothing that is forever evolving and beyond language. James Schamus discusses the ways in which the aspect of the feminine in *Crouching Tiger, Hidden Dragon* is an intervention in the *wuxia* film genre. He notes: "So the irony is that at the end of the movie, really it is the woman who's following the Dao [Tao], she's the one who takes the Daoist [Taoist] leap. It's not the man. . . . He's nowhere near it. . . . And the tragedy that ends that process of cultural transmission is that it's the woman who figures it out . . . who gets there" (qtd. in Teo, "'We Kicked'" par. 38).

In *Crouching Tiger, Hidden Dragon,* Lee targets the conceptions of the feminine both in Taoist and Western feminist ideologies that in turn reflect his cosmopolitical consciousness. The Taoist philosophy takes the feminine or the marginal in the patriarchal society as a metaphor for the force field of nature. It emphasizes what is considered, as part of nature, non-dichotomous and therefore can also be accessible to all individuals without discrimination. While Confucians stress the subordination of the individual emotion to collective forms and behaviors, Taoists suggest that individuals break loose from social duties and obligations and merge with the genuine life of nature and the universe. Taoism is considered not necessarily opposite to but rather a complement to Confucianism.

Taoists do not inhibit the individual's wishes and desires that are excluded from the framework of familial and sociopolitical relations. In explaining "Tao," Zhuangzi comments: "The Way [Tao] has never known boundaries; speech has no constancy. . . . Let me tell you what boundaries are. There is left, there is right, there are theories, there are debates, there are divisions, there are discriminations. . . . The Great Way is not named" (43–44). Tao is the alternative, nameless, and ever-changing nature of reality. It is nameless, but if one has to name it, it alludes to the feminine and as ever-evolving. Laozi referred to Tao as the feminine and alludes to the "Mother" (*Dao De Jing* 3, 41, 51, 107, 121):

> There was Something undefined and yet complete in itself.
> Born before Heaven-and-Earth.
> Silent and boundless,
> Standing alone without change,
> Yet pervading all without fail,
> It may be regarded as the Mother of the world.
> I do not know its name;
> I style it "Tao";
> And, in the absence of a better word, call it
> "The Great."
>
> (51)

Feminine difference is the site where the imaginary is kept alive. The feminine in the context of *Crouching Tiger, Hidden Dragon* is allegorically *wu* (nothing), the void that bypasses the conventional division of the self and the Other, and breaks open the ground of fundamental concepts, reasoning, and perceptions that comprehend the dichotomy. A feminine figure, given its unique access to the feminine, unleashes the imaginary domain in both new and old identifications. The position of the border, the symbol the feminine originally embodied, now takes on a different meaning and dwells in the interstices or the overlapping spaces of transnational filmmaking.

In *Crouching Tiger, Hidden Dragon*, Ang Lee uses the female figures and the subject positions of the feminine as the sites of transnational "cultural transmission." *Crouching Tiger, Hidden Dragon* complicates the kinds of "reductivist" feminist constructions of Chinese woman or Oriental Other as a monolithic object of oppression and makes use of multiple positionalities within the narrative itself to engage in heteroglossia and to negotiate different female subjectivities. The film deploys the woman's ambiguousness and the feminized Other's liminal position (effeminate Asian male). It brings forth the (in)visible intonations of Jen's name as female dragon (Jiao Long), the embedded discourse of language and its accented differences, and the "Dragon Lady" cross-cultural intonations as sites of reversal.

The martial arts genre, with its visualized style of action, is a transnational genre that is most recognizable for world audiences. In *Crouching Tiger, Hidden Dragon*, the Asian actors and actresses perform not only martial arts but also their feminized ethnicity as stereotypical images of martial arts practitioners transnationally. Yet the context that enables the visibility of martial arts film is not unilateral but multiple. By engaging with different geopolitics, gender and ethnicity become the domains where discourses of subjectivity can be constituted and contested. In the film, the issues of gender and ethnicity are carefully crafted within the realm of a utopian and fantastic fiction of imaginary China. Ang Lee projects his own cultural heritage, identifying himself with the female *xia* who is able to engage in the cultural transmission between East and West. He creates a new version of a classic Chinese myth of woman warrior by making the female protagonist refuse to perform the traditionally patriarchal role of a *xia* heroine or to compromise as a bride/wife/daughter in a patriarchal society. In fact, the mixing of West and East is not only a result of global media commodity. Lee's strategy of synthesizing and hybridizing East and West is cosmopolitical as he targets femininity and feminine agency as the sites of contestation and collusion with mainstream ideology.

In the introduction to the issue on "Cosmopolitanisms" in *Public Culture*, Sheldon Pollock and others comment on the future of the "cosmofeminine." They write: "The cosmofeminine could thus be seen as subverting those larger networks that refuse to recognize their own nature as specific [universal] systems of relations among others" (584). Pollock and his colleagues' "cosmofeminine" challenges the universalism of feudalism and patriarchy; only this time the film *Crouching Tiger, Hidden Dragon* demonstrates that "the cosmofeminine as the sign" contextualizes and demonstrates what it means to "invite other universalisms into a broader debate based on a recognition of their own situatedness" (584, 585). In *Crouching Tiger, Hidden Dragon*, the positionalities of the feminine in the narrative evoke and take advantage of the multiple intersections and disjunctures of temporalities and spacialities to investigate the constructedness of gender and ethnicity.

Crouching Tiger, Hidden Dragon is made in the context of multiple historical trajectories and temporalities, in which the worlds are coeval and interlinked and the transactions among cultures are multifaceted. The film reveals how ethnicity and the interpellated positionalities of femininity serve as an intriguing and conflicting terrain for constituting ethnic and feminist subjects among national/culturalist discourses of the Chinese diaspora in Hollywood. The feminization of male heroes and the empowerment of female characters can be discursively transformed to represent the larger ethnic and national community. The bodies in the masquerade of femininity become the sites of a series of metaphorical regenerations of ethnic and bodily politics. Ang Lee portrays the female warriors each in conflict with the other's position and with the choice of whether she should remain in the confines of society or break free of her own inhibitions.

Lee does not engage uniformly with the stereotypes of the Chinese woman as a victimized Other trapped in the Confucian ideology and age-old Chinese civilization. In the film, he critically interrogates multiple positionalities of the different women warriors. In particular, the female *xia* Jen enters the fantastic world of *jianghu* to get knowledge and martial arts skills, and yet that does not necessarily help her family or the nation (as the myth of Fa Mu Lan and Hollywood's version of Fa Mu Lan did). In this light, the effeminate male *xia* heroes also intersect with the feminization of the male characters in the hegemonic traditions of Hollywood and American culture. The emotional warrior Lo is an instance of the effeminate male character whose representation collides and colludes with the images of Asian males in mainstream Hollywood.

The politics of representations, however, are more diversified as a cosmopolitical consciousness emerges among the multiplicities of accents and their disjunctions. The portrayal of the male character conforms to the mainstream ideology of Western culture that perceives the Asian Other as "primitive, infantile, carnal, effeminate, backward" (Marchetti, "America's Asia" 37). Yet, the effeminate male subject such as Lo, with his exile from the Sinocentric notion of China, enables a heteroglossial dialogism with language and representations that unveil the constructedness of ethnic ideology as hegemonic misrecognition of Otherness—be it American racial politics, Orientalism, imperialism, or Chinese nationalism.

Crouching Tiger, Hidden Dragon is a critical mode of reflection on the meanings of ethnicity and culture. Lee considers multiple positionalities in reaffirming, challenging, and/or conceiving the power structures that condition what his work represents and, therefore, in which it is enmeshed. Lee's cosmopolitical awareness reveals his geopolitical stances in the global film market as he navigates between both art and commercial cinemas. The exhibitionism of martial arts cinema attracts world audiences who are more used to perceiving the martial arts films as the commercial epitome of Chinese cinema. As a popular cultural tradition, the film also engages with issues such as individual expressions and feminist issues in art cinema.

As a cosmopolitical subject, Lee's geopolitical positionality can be read as expanding from a Taiwanese subject to an Asian American subject to a diasporic subject displaced from Taiwan, China, and the United States. The multiple dislocations of subjectivity call into question not only the determinacy of Chineseness but the ethnic marker as a signifier for identity. Multiple displacements also lead to the recognition of the heterogeneity of identity formation in which its meanings are not monolithic but constantly negotiated both within and outside a category, such as ethnicity, as a new form of transnational imaginary. The film underscores how a cosmopolitical framework offers us a reading practice that enables us to see differently and to identify where seemingly discrete ideological projects collide and collude with each other. Ang Lee demonstrates how he intervenes in the transnational historiography of martial arts films and how he manipulates his geopolitical knowledge of navigating hegemonic power structures in different cinematic contexts.

3

FACING OFF EAST AND WEST IN
THE CINEMA OF JOHN WOO

The critical intervention of cosmopolitical consciousness challenges the Orientalist conventions of treating Asia as either uniform and totally pure or traditional with authentic difference from the West. These issues have become more complicated and fascinating since famous Hong Kong director John Woo entered American mainstream film production and continues to produce hits in Hollywood. Woo's film trajectory demonstrates itself not as a one-way response to Hollywood but as a translocal existence and subjectivity that continuously remaps the East and the West beyond their geographical bases.

It seemed coincidental before and during the 1997 political changes, when Hong Kong transferred from British to Chinese sovereignty, that Woo began to seek a new career in the West. Woo's Hong Kong films intersect with the emergence of collective anxiety over the reunification with China (Hanke 43). Cinema becomes a particularly revealing medium for the examination of the disjunctures that Hong Kong represented culturally and politically with the end of British colonial rule. Woo's combination of massive bloodshed, choreographed gunfights, and honor codes based on *wuxia* traditions has given new life to the contemporary action thriller and gangster and war films.

In Woo's cinematic world of *jianghu*, individuals, instead of being controlled by the government, define their roles and relationships. These relationships exist outside of the law. The urban *xia* can be a member of the underground, similar to today's gangster or Triad society, but codes of honor such as trust and loyalty are the main values. The nostalgic longing for the *xia* values of the past provides the site for Woo to find meanings of self-definition in the colonial present (pre-1997) while facing the new political uncertainty (1997 handover). The intensification of male homosociality in his films reveals the destabilization of masculine identity in the face of social, ideological, and cultural changes. The recurring themes of male bonding, hyperviolence, and stylized action provide the speculative ground on which political anxieties are played out in both Woo's Hong Kong and Hollywood films.

Filmmaking is a crucial industry for revealing the mechanisms of contemporary transnational production and the global circulation of commodities, capital, images, and people. John Woo is a filmmaker who transcends the local and works across different cultural, economic, and historical contexts. Some of Woo's highly successful commercial works, such as *Face/Off* and *Mission: Impossible II*, are not simply examples of Americanization or Asianization. Woo reveals the renewals of themes and motifs such as *xia* heroism in a transnational context, targeting polities such as hegemonic masculinity, family, and nation. Even the film title *Face/Off* might allegorically indicate that the East and the West finally "face off" in the era of transnationalism.

To many, Woo's films show influences from Chinese film traditions, including the works of Zhang Che, Chor Yuen, and King Hu (Leong and Tsui 35; Shek Kei, *Shi* 13, 19, 33). Woo notes Zhang Che's effect on him, as he admits, "I use some of his techniques in the gun battle scenes" (qtd. in Havis 13). Zhang's "unrestrained way of writing emotions and chivalry" also influenced Woo's *A Better Tomorrow* (qtd. in Leong and Tsui 35). As Shek Kei points out, King Hu has also had an impact on Woo's works, and Woo's heroes resemble those in Chor Yuen's romantic film adaptations of Gu Long's 1970s novels (Shek Kei, *Shi* 13, 19). However, Woo himself also says in an interview, "I'm not very Chinese. My techniques, my themes, my film language are not traditionally Chinese" (qtd. in Reynaud 25). Woo has long acknowledged the influences of filmmakers from both the East and the West:

> Besides the latest from the Hollywood studios we also watched, in the first run cinemas, the latest from Europe, Japan, Hong Kong, China and Taiwan. Films from international masters (Melville, Clouzot, Kurosawa, De Sica) as well as new directors (Fellini, Truffaut, Demy, King Hu) were as commercially successful as their Hollywood counterparts. . . . This blending of East and West, commerce and art, molded Hong Kong films into an art form that is entertaining, unselfconscious and energetic. I am very lucky to be part of that current. (Preface 9–10)

Woo's list of directors embraces several major trends: American action films, musicals, Japanese samurai films, the French New Wave, and Hong Kong martial arts cinema. Woo combines the raw violence in such action films as samurai, gangster, Western, and Chinese *wuxia* genres and the advocacy of countertraditional spirits of the French New Wave. He artistically fuses East and West. Woo draws on Western and Eastern film techniques and themes to enrich the action genre. His concerns with techniques and themes parallel their use by other directors and in turn influence Hollywood action films ranging from *Reservoir Dogs* (1991) to *The Matrix*. Steve Fore explains: "This cultural cosmopolitanism is one of the reasons why Hong Kong film and filmmakers have been relatively accessible and attractive to Western fans and Hollywood brass in recent years, and it is also one of the reasons why Woo and other Hong Kong directors have been able to adjust successfully to Hollywood's professional and cultural norms" ("Life" 134). It is this "cultural cosmopolitanism" that leads me to reconsider the fact that Woo's films have continuously reworked and redefined styles and themes of filmmaking in the transnational contexts. The interconnections and intermingling of filmmaking practices across different national, cultural, and historical boundaries also lead to new understandings of the symmetries and asymmetries between Hollywood and Hong Kong action films.

In this chapter, I examine through the works of John Woo the cross-cultural flows that cannot be simply understood in terms of essentialized and normative notions of "East" and "West." Instead, the discursive and transnational contexts in which filmmakers negotiate and contest "East," "West," national, diasporic, gender, and ethnic differences must be examined. Woo also emerges from a local Hong Kong film history with close links to Hollywood and ties to its own local film traditions. He deliberately uses Western and Chinese film traditions, ranging from gangster to *wuxia* films. During the 1990s, Woo made the move to Hollywood to make action films and brought not only his signature style but also his embodied political awareness as a form of intervention into the Hollywood imaginary of masculinity and racial politics. In turn, Woo's cosmopolitical consciousness shows the complicated political contexts in interpreting screen violence and its social and cross-cultural implications from Hong Kong to Hollywood.

Transnationalization of the Gangster Film

Beginning in 1968, twenty-two-year-old Woo made four 8mm and 16mm shorts over two years (Fitzgerald 17). In 1969, at the age of twenty-three,

Woo landed his first job as script supervisor at Cathay Studios in Hong Kong. In 1971, he moved to the prestigious Shaw Brothers Studio and worked under the well-known martial arts director Zhang Che (Reynaud 25). In his first period martial arts epic, *Last Hurrah for Chivalry* (1978), Woo highlighted individual moments of heroism, grace, and chivalry in the genre. He made several more martial arts films, then directed comedies and a Chinese opera film. One exception was *Heroes Shed No Tears* (1986), in which he abandoned comedy and kung fu films and made an ultraviolent tale about mercenaries sent to capture a drug lord deep in Southeast Asia's Golden Triangle. In Christopher Heard's *Ten Thousand Bullets: The Cinematic Journey of John Woo,* Heard notes that *Heroes Shed No Tears* was actually made five years earlier yet remained on the shelf until 1986 (58). The film was out of sync with the popular film trends at the time; the studio thought the film was too violent and shelved it. The film was later released in 1986 after Woo's success with *A Better Tomorrow. Heroes Shed No Tears,* with its extreme violence, however, foreshadows the "heroic bloodshed" films he would make to succeed *A Better Tomorrow*.[1] The nonstop shootouts result in massive bloodshed, explosions, fire, and dead bodies piled up across the streets. Characters covered in blood and die for the code of honor as a *xia* in the *wuxia* traditions.

In chapter 2, I critically examined the way that Ang Lee in *Crouching Tiger, Hidden Dragon* uses strong female *xia* characters and effeminate male *xia* as a site of intervention in the hegemonic binary split between public and private, male and female, empowered and disempowered. Lee's strong female *xia* characters Jen Yu and Jade Fox are outlaws with uninhibited behaviors and excellent sword skills; they challenge the ideal moral codes of *ren* (forgiveness for all), *yi* (uprightness and selflessness), *zhong* (loyalty), *yong* (bravery), and *xin* (trust) that *xia* had embodied in the conventional historical and literary account. While Lee reveals the positionality of the feminine as the site of intervention and embodiment of histories and struggles, John Woo's works target the terrain of masculinity and the homosocial bonds that constitute it. Woo casts doubt on collective consciousness in such themes as loyalty, alliances, and brotherhood that constitute the patriarchal order and subjugates the fear of homoeroticism and the threats of the shifting grounds of social and political frames under the guise of bloodshed and violence.

The culture of the Chinese legendary *xia* has long fascinated John Woo, and he has noted Zhang Che's contribution to *wuxia* film in the form of male individualism, an innovation at the time in Hong Kong, since female leads were generally the trend during the 1960s. Shek Kei has suggested that Woo has renewed the martial arts film and has modernized it in the gangster film genre (*Shi* 13, 33). In Woo's films, the viewer does not see martial arts fights with swords but rather shootout scenes with machine guns. David Bordwell has noted that Woo's action style is anticipated in the floating fights of Hong Kong director Chor Yuen's *The Killer* (1972; aka *Sacred Knives of Vengeance*) (*Planet* 103). Woo worked as assistant director on Zhang Che's *The Boxer from Shantung* and *Blood Brothers* (1973). Zhang Che was an old master of the Chinese martial arts film genre, and his influence deeply resonates in Woo's later works, such as *A Better Tomorrow*.

Woo's time under Zhang Che had a long-lasting effect on him. The martial arts hero in Zhang's 1967 film *The One-Armed Swordsman*, Fang Gang, is a proud and strong-willed loner with extraordinary martial arts skills. He disregards his physical disability after his foster father's jealous daughter cuts off his arm. In the end, he rescues his foster father, whose life is in danger. Confucianism believes in the importance of hierarchical loyalty in relationships such as ruler and ruled, lord and servant, and father and son. The narrative demonstrates how Fang, a righteous-minded commoner, is devoted to the course of justice as defined by Confucianism, even though his foster father's daughter has severely injured him. The *xia* in the film, however, acts like a loner and appears to be individualistic and full of pride and rebelliousness; he is tied in fact to the social constraints of Confucian ideology. In *The Assassin*, released the same year, Nie Zhang is the most individualistic of Zhang Che's male heroes, demonstrated by his willingness to die for a cause and by his sense of destiny. A prince in distress treated Nie Zhang as an equal and convinced him of the justice of his cause. Impressed, Nie Zhang agrees to take up an assassination assignment. Nie Zhang has no regrets in offering his life for the prince, an example of their homosocial loyalty through their benevolent bond.

The severing of limbs positions bodies as spectacles of violence in Zhang Che's *wuxia* films. Zhang's heroes commonly have swords stuck in their stomachs or their bodies cut in half. John Woo's debt to Zhang is evident from themes and characters in his films. The ways Woo's heroes are riddled with gunshots and drenched in blood and his revision of Zhang's violent spectacles in the gangster film genre are astonishing. One example is Woo's *The Killer* (1989). The film crystallizes some of Woo's major themes, such as loyalty and brotherhood, that are extensions and revisions of the similar portrayal of *xia* characters in martial arts films. In addition, Woo also transposes the *xia* heroes from *wuxia* films into the particularly American-influenced gangster film genre and transforms it into a new version of *xia* in the city. Martha P. Nochimson discusses the differences between Hong Kong and Hollywood gangster films:

> [T]he modern relationship of the gangster, religion, and the law in Hong Kong movies is quite different from the representation of modern American gangsters, religion, and the law. In Hollywood movies, religion and law combine to condemn the gangster to punishment, even while he is moving toward a hard-won understanding about himself and the world that neither the court nor the church facilitates. In Hong Kong movies, the religion of the Triads provides the gangster something more stable than modern, impersonal, flawed civil law. (18)

The Hong Kong hero's act of benevolence toward the weak and the trust among non-blood-related brothers can form a sense of collective community that transcends the limit of family and nation. Thus, "men and women of Hong Kong gangster film are measured by their steadfastness to honor, loyalty, and their sense of Taoist valuation on balance between these moral values and the materialist values of the society in which the characters live" (Nochimson 2). For John Woo, the death of the hero in his films very often shows the dilemma of individual power (an individual's moral criterion) against the hegemonic forces of conformity.

The gangster culture in Woo's films is essentially feudal and anachronistic, separated from the political, legal, and economic structure of the mainstream society. In his films, Woo honors the homosocial loyalty and interpersonal bonds between men. Such an affective social force is governed by the *xia* ideology of trust and loyalty. In *The Godfather* films (1972–90), for instance, the patriarchy of the gangster culture depends upon the hierarchical relationships among the gangsters and their subordinates. The loyalty among the gangsters is governed by the threat of violence, as the transgressors are often severely punished in the *Godfather* films. But instead of using violence to gain loyalty, Woo romanticizes and idealizes violence to dramatize the characters' homosocial loyalty. Much in the same way, Woo uses the hero's violence, action, and martial skills to challenge the basis of law enforcement that in most cases fails to execute a fair moral judgment. Thus, the heroes in Woo's films are modernized versions of *xia* heroes who judge and challenge hegemony in the unique Hong Kong/Chinese context.

Woo modernizes the *wuxia* ethos with a transnational awareness of the difference between the Hong Kong and Hollywood contexts. In this way, violence no longer causes shock, but rather its excessiveness can reveal the powerlessness of the heroes (with the collapse of morality). Woo's heroes are hired killers in modern settings who are not only part of the plight of capitalism but also set against the background of Hong Kong's political transition of sovereignty from Britain to China in 1997. Di Lung, who plays Chow Yun-Fat's best friend, Ho, in *A Better Tomorrow*, was one of Zhang Che's favorite film stars and plays *xia* characters in Zhang's films. Chow Yun-Fat's role as Brother Mark is reminiscent of another Zhang *wuxia* film star, Jiang Dawei, especially in his romanticism and light-heartedness.

The iconography of the gunfire scene is central to Woo's *A Better Tomorrow*. On the choreography, Woo has commented, "When I shoot action sequences I think of great dancers, Gene Kelly, Astaire. In action I feel like I'm creating a ballet, a dance" (qtd. in Weinraub). The combination and mix of influences from gangster films, film noir, Westerns, musicals, and kung fu and *wuxia* films suggest Woo's crossover between Asia and America. Woo's choreography is not a total replica of gunfire scenes in gangster films or Westerns. The two handguns have become a signature icon in Woo's action films. While Woo's distinctive style is rapidly becoming fashionable in Hollywood contemporary action films, such as *Desperado* (1995) and *The Matrix*, it also can be seen in his own Hollywood works, such as *Hard Target* (1993), *Broken Arrow* (1996), and *Face/Off*, in which Woo personally introduces his trademark and plants it.

The interconnection of the transnational flows of this trademark is more complicated, because the icon of a gun in each hand was actually born out of Westerns, such as *Butch Cassidy and the Sundance Kid* (1969) and John Wayne films. In this way, Woo reintroduced this icon of the Western film into contemporary Hong Kong gangster films in 1986. In *A Better Tomorrow*, the character Mark fires two semi-automatic guns, one gripped in each hand, while exiting the room in the assassination scene. It has been a consistent part of the choreography used in Woo's Hong Kong films since *A Better Tomorrow*. Woo further explores this in a way best exemplified in *The Killer*. The assassination scene of a crime lord in the beginning of the film is a perfect example of Woo's hybridization of choreography and styles from Western, gangster, and *wuxia* films. The motifs of the gun in each hand, the *wuxia*-influenced heroes, and action choreography created the signature style of Woo's films. Such a transnational sensibility in film cultures informs Woo's cosmopolitical consciousness.

In Woo's films, however, he features male leads that fight for loyalty and friendship rather than for money or capital. Woo's camera always focuses on the male character and his strong, emotional reaction to the moment. The character's fate concerns the audience. The characters openly mourn their losses and sentimentally rejoice in their friendships. In *The Killer*, Woo has Inspector Li weeping at the loss of Jeff. Woo has an essentially romantic sensibility toward male friendship and homosocial bonds. He changes the accepted ways in which episodic fight scenes in *wuxia* films are included purely for the sense of spectacle and emotional arousal. The end is to express an individual's vision and moral judgment about an incident.

Woo's *A Better Tomorrow* is a remake of Hong Kong director Lung Kong's *Story of a Discharged Prisoner* (1967). *Story of a Discharged Prisoner*, one of Lung Kong's best works, is about an ex-convict, Lee, who tries to rehabilitate himself in society but is harassed by a police inspector and a crime boss, both trying to enlist him for their own benefits. Lung Kong is well known for dealing with social themes like prostitution and juvenile delinquency in his films. *Story* was set against the background of Hong Kong in 1967 with income disparity, little welfare for the lower class, widespread corruption, and dissatisfaction with the colonial government. The film shows that reform for grassroots and social outcasts was a difficult proposition in late-1960s Hong Kong. And Lung Kong tackles the social concerns of the 1960s with the gangster film genre. Also set against the backdrop of political and social uncertainty of pre-1997 Hong Kong, the comradeship among the male characters in Woo's *A Better Tomorrow* alludes to the intense bonding process in Hong Kong as a collective community faced the 1997 handover. While John Woo's remake follows quite faithfully the original plot in Lung Kong's film, he highlights the *xia*-like quality of the gangster character played by Chow Yun-Fat and focuses on his strong bond and friendship with Ho.

One of the most famous dialogues in the film is when Mark and Ho lament that they cannot imagine that something as beautiful as the night scene of Hong Kong will one day disappear. The film shows the undertones of political uncertainty the characters have to face. Woo's ideal portrayals of *xia*-like gangster characters are rebellious, independent, and at the margin of law and order. What binds the male characters together is the uncertain future of the post-1984 era. The character Ho is torn between his loyalty to his friend Mark and his need to reconcile with his brother Kit. Ho is situated in a liminal position, torn among issues of loyalty, brotherhood, friendship, and law, much like Hong Kong's contested position in between China and Britain in the post-1984 era. Woo clearly shows his strong belief in brotherhood and friendship instead of in the capitalism of traditional gangster films that undergirds hegemonic state power. Thus, the world in Woo's films is a utopia that centers on the strict order of honor, as the characters seek some semblance of justice in a world of betrayal and chaos.

The sequel, *A Better Tomorrow II* (1987), begins one year later; Ho is still serving time in prison while his brother Kit continues to rise in the police force. Kit's new assignment is to go undercover in a shipping company owned by ex-Triad godfather Lung, who happens to be Ho's former mentor. Matters become complicated when Lung, the retired godfather, is blamed for a murder. Fleeing to New York, Ken—Mark's twin brother (and also played by Chow Yun-Fat)—helps Lung when a group of hired assassins comes gunning for him. Back in Hong Kong, Ken, Lung, Ho, and Kit join together to take revenge. The movie focuses on Chow Yun-Fat's character, Ken, and particularly his relationship with the retired godfather, Lung. The film reworks the themes of trust and loyalty across the two different generations as represented by Ken and Lung. One of the most memorable action choreographies is in the film's last scene. The action sequences are more polished than its prequel, especially the movie's finale when the three heroes (Ho, Ken, and Lung) participate in a final death-duel. The film ends with the three soaked in blood, simply sitting amid violent shootouts, bloodshed, and explosions and self-consciously contemplating imminent death, as the cops are approaching. Woo places his characters in pre-1997 Hong Kong, which is positioned at the junctures of (neo)colonialism, globalization, and transnationalism. Hong Kong's cultural production during this period, as Rey Chow notes, is "in a negotiation in which it must play the aggressors, Britain and China, against each other, carving out a space where it is neither the puppet of British colonialism, nor of Chinese authoritarianism" (*Ethics* 157). The intensification of male bonding is a form of collective consciousness against the fate that looms over the community. Violence on-screen plays out the social instabilities inherent in the political transition of 1997.

Woo uses the themes and conventions in martial arts films and renews them in the gangster film genre, imbuing the gangster heroes with *xia* qualities. In Woo's films, the gangster closely follows the code of a righteous *xia* warrior while at the same time he is rebellious and independent in his actions. Woo's heroes are extensions of the kind of nomadic *xia* character, who prefers a wandering life instead of stability in the mainstream society. In his films, Woo criticizes the values of modern capitalistic society, mourns the passing of Hong Kong as a collective community, and destabilizes the polity of homosociality that governs the basis of community, nationhood, and belonging. By targeting the subversive aspect of *xia*/gangster in both Hollywood and Hong Kong film cultures, Woo politicizes homosociality that reveals his cosmopolitical perspective, a topic that I will discuss in the following section.

Politicizing Homosociality

Critics and scholars have noted Western influences, as well as Chinese chivalry, in John Woo's films (Hanke; Hall; Bordwell, *Planet*; Heard). Some examine and challenge the different interpretations of masculinities in display and the homoeroticization of violence (Sandell, "Better Tomorrow"; Stringer, "'Tender Smiles'"; Hanke; Gates).

In a 1994 article, Jillian Sandell suggests that the homoeroticization of violence underlines the male bonding relationship and encodes the unrepresentable and unacceptable homoerotic desire between men ("Better Tomorrow"). In a later article in 1996, Sandell reconsiders this thesis of violence as displaced homoeroticism and reinterprets Woo's themes of male bonding through violence in relation to the values of honor and chivalry in Chinese literature and martial arts films ("Reinventing"). Sandell suggests that the males in Woo's films occupy both passive spectacle and active narrative in the relationships ("Better Tomorrow"). Julian Stringer has provided a more historical and genre-based textual analysis of Woo's films that departs from the psychoanalytic models in the discussion of masculinities. Stringer points out that the moments of suffering or spectacle of Woo's male characters do not interrupt the narrative but in fact "provide the strength needed for the superhuman acts of heroism and violence" ("'Tender Smiles'" 32). For Stringer, Woo's films show the instabilities of masculinities responding to the historical crisis of Hong Kong's reunification with China in 1997.

Mikel J. Koven's article "My Brother, My Lover, My Self: Traditional Masculinity in the Hong Kong Action Cinema of John Woo" suggests that Western film critics have misread Woo's films as "homoerotic" (55). Koven indicates that Woo's films construct a certain kind of "Chinese masculinity . . . not the homoerotic per se, but something much more germane to a Chinese experience of masculinity" (59). He also notes that Woo's films are related to the concerns in "Chinese *wuxia* stories" (62). Although there is a predominance of the themes from *wuxia* and brotherhood in Woo's films, Koven's argument echoes Kam Louie's notion of Chinese *wu* or martial masculinity (23). Homosociality constructs the basis of male bonds in Woo's films. The significance of homosociality leads to the question of patriarchy as a structure of masculine bonds.

The theme of homosociality as exemplified in Woo's films reveals the particular historical function of the modernization of the male hero *xia* and the intrinsic structure of gender. In particular, it calls attention to the constructedness of identity that is related to Hong Kong's historical, political, and social contexts, both locally and transnationally. Wong Sum has analyzed the recurrence of twin heroes in Woo's films, drawing on Paul Radin's model of the Winnebago hero cycle. In Radin's analysis, the twin brothers are joined together in their mother's womb but separated at birth. Belonging to the same body, they seek to come together again, even though the process is difficult (qtd. in Law Kar, "Hero" 71).

The motif of twin heroes is an example of homosocial bonding and loyalty in Woo's films in the face of imminent threats of the Other. For example, in *The Killer*, Jeff accidentally blinds nightclub singer Jenny during an assassination assignment. Suffering from a guilty conscience, he soon befriends Jenny, tries to help her, and eventually falls in love. Jeff attempts to finish his final killing assignment in order to pay for Jenny's surgery. Another character, Li, is the police inspector on his trail. Soon Jeff and Li confront each other. At the same time, Jeff discovers that his longtime partner Fung has betrayed him, putting their relationship to the test. Meanwhile, unpaid by his boss, Jeff attempts to kill him. Jeff forgives Fung as an old friend, while Fung attempts to prove his loyalty and friendship to Jeff by fighting on his behalf for the boss to compensate him. The boss, however, finally kills Fung, and his sacrifice proves his *yi* to Jeff. Overwhelmed by such a loss, Jeff decides to take revenge.

The film shows a woman caught in the patriarchal logic in which she exists as the Other. Jenny in *The Killer* is the site of difference, and her presence diverts attention from the underlying homoerotic tendency between Jeff and Li and between Jeff and Fung. In this example, Jeff embodies the *xia* in the city, as he is a savior of the weak (Jenny and the little girl who is accidentally shot by the gang) whose actions are purely for the sake of justice. Jeff puts loyalty to his friends above all, to the extent that he is a virtual rebel against the established order. With his extraordinary strength and agility with guns, he can repeatedly escape capture until he dies in bloodshed and gunfire at the end. Woo completes his action choreography with extensive gunfire, explosions, and slow-motion shots of his heroes leaping or literally "flying over," as in *wuxia* films, to take cover. The background is 1980s Hong Kong but presented simplistically; the cityscape serves as a gangland for the action.

The Killer suggests the importance of homosocial male bonding relations through the oath of loyalty. When Jeff saves a little girl hurt during a shoot-out, the code of *xin* (trust) and *yi* (uprightness and selflessness) brings the two characters together: Jeff the killer and Li the cop. There is no clear-cut division between the killer and the cop, as both are presumably the good characters. The multiple stand-offs between Jeff and Li in the film dramatize the ambiguous division between good and evil.

Both Jeff and Inspector Li skew away from the strict definition of good and evil and are outsiders of society—one being an outcast of a gang and a hit man and the other a police officer whose boss does not respect the way he works. By joining forces, the two uphold the chivalric codes of *xia* heroes, such as *yi* and *xin*. Their homosocial bonding is based on the nostalgic longing for *xia* values and tradition; friendship between men is found at the margin of society (as *xia* are generally the outcast of the society), in opposition to the model of the heterosexual family, which is also the basis for the dominant ideology, marriage, family, and home.

The scene where the assassin and the officer discuss their fates in the church is the one that epitomizes their relationship. While they are on opposite sides of the law, they share a common bond of being outsiders in their respective social groups. Woo puts the final shootout scene in the religious setting of the Catholic church. As the flights of white doves punctuate the action sequences, the machine-gun battle in the church climaxes with its indelible image of an exploding statue of the Virgin Mary. In the end, Jeff is slain, his goals are left unaccomplished, and Inspector Li is arrested. The Christian motif leaves the audience in doubt as to whether there is an ultimate ideological closure for the heroic deeds of Chinese *xia* traditions. The moral ambiguity of Woo's modern *xia* characters also places the defining line of good and evil of Western Christian ethics in question. The homosocial bonding, rooted in the traditional code of Chinese *xia* heroism, unites the male characters who are outsiders to the civilized repression of law and society. The film emphasizes homosociality at a time when Hong Kong as a collective community was undergoing political change as it approached the date of the handover to China in 1997.

The homosocial bonding between people on opposite sides of the law, however, resists the incorporation into the dominant form of masculinity that is symbolized either by Chinese nationalism or by British colonialism. Woo's films reflect a Hong Kong society undergoing successive changes in which its subjects were navigating multiple displacements by hegemonic political forces, including nationalism and colonialism. Such experience of displacement shapes Woo's films as well as his cosmopolitical perspective.

Yet, homosociality is also the guarantor of patriarchal order. These outlaws live above law but can also be considered as enforcing it. Homosociality empowers the patriarchal hegemony in an indirect way and actually reinforces constitutional masculinity, such as the loyalty and face values that bind the social relationships and establish the individual's self-identity in his community. The Chinese notion of face entails respect and honor and has received extensive research attention (Hu; Hwang; Yu). The face in the Chinese context implies a level of politeness (Du; Mao; Chen, Ye, and Zhang). Face enhances an individual's value, and friends attend to each other's public self-image in achieving politeness and harmony, in keeping social relations intact, and in reciprocating someone's favor (Hwang). The latter notion of a social network, in Chinese, is *guanxi*. Face functions through a social network involving three major aspects: self (social identity), others (social relationships), and the specifics of the social events involved (Hwang).[2] Woo targets the *xia* traditions and the Chinese face values that consolidate homosocial bond and order.

The fact that audiences so widely admire *xia* and the rebels in films sets up a critical moral dilemma for hegemonic patriarchy. Heroic stories are attractive. These stories also glorify heroism and encourage strong personalities to ignore the law, to seek the autonomy of the hero, and to advocate or take up his unorthodox ways. The form of homosocial loyalty, in addition to the Confucian hierarchy of state and subjects, thus emphasizes and establishes the relation between prince and subject, lord and servant, father and son. The hegemony institutionalizes the heroic code of honor in the form of masculine bonds that is not detrimental to respect for family ties and authority. The stress and glorification of the oath of brotherhood and the homosocial bond and relationships between swordsmen can, in fact, be manipulated for reinvigorating hegemonic practices whose basis is the sameness of the subjugated. Thus, one of the ways to complicate, destabilize, and challenge the workings of masculine bonds—the homosocial bonds that may only in turn empower the hegemonic investment—is to question the basis of ideological and pedagogical instruction that governs loyalty, belonging, and collectivity in homosocial bonds.

Woo puts forth and questions the concept of *yi* as the only arbiter of morality in the action genre. Friendship becomes the ultimate test in *Bullet in the Head* (1990), which takes the themes of *yi* and *xin* to another extreme. It puts people in a context of war and tests the ways in which *yi* and *xin* operate. The film is set in 1967, when followers of the Cultural Revolution in the Mainland led riots that shook Hong Kong.[3] The story revolves around three childhood friends—Ben, Paul, and Frank—and how the war will change the meanings of their friendship. On the night of Ben's wedding, Frank borrows money from a loan shark but runs into Ringo's gang, who robs him. Frank is seriously hurt, and both Ben and Frank take revenge and have Ringo killed accidentally. Having to flee for their lives, Ben and Frank decide to leave for Vietnam. Paul also wants to seek his fortune in war-torn Vietnam. When they arrive in Vietnam, their possessions are burned during a Viet Cong suicide bombing. All suspects, including the three protagonists, are rounded up in a church schoolyard. One by one, they are questioned. The police beat Frank, Ben, and Paul when they do not confess to being part of the bombing, but soon the real suspect is found, who is executed with a bullet in the head, set against the backdrop of a statue of Jesus and Mary. At a time when the world is in chaos, disloyalty, betrayal, and violence bring values of trust and righteousness into question. The friendship is put to the ultimate test as the three are forced to play a fierce game of survival in order to stay alive in Vietnam.

In the film, there is a cross-reference to Hong Kong and Vietnam during the 1960s. In Hong Kong, there are demonstrations and riots; the same is true in Vietnam. In *Bullet in the Head*, Woo examines the dangerous and ironic situations that the characters face as they strive to survive, reflecting the situation of the people of Hong Kong. The three characters, born in an age of Western influence, as shown when briefly reflecting on their appreciation of popular music and dance, try to seek another life in diaspora (Vietnam) as an escape from the dilemma historically signified by the 1967 riots. Woo has mentioned that this film is in part a metaphor for Hong Kong's handover to China in 1997, noting, "I draw a parallel between 1967 and 1997" as political changes and wars have often forced people into flight and exile (qtd. in Law Kar, "Bullet"). The polarization of sentiment along ideological lines peaked in the Cultural Revolution of 1966–68 and erupted in fierce riots in Hong Kong in 1967. Soon after the impact of the 4 June 1989 Tiananmen incident, Hong Kong survived a series of demonstrations and psychological turmoil after which Woo made *Bullet*.

The 1967 riots that *Bullet* portrays, a battleground for contesting political (People's Republic of China and Republic of China) and colonial (British) ideologies, rival those that Hong Kong experienced after the 1989 Tiananmen incident in their complexity. The film tells a tale about betrayal in which the face values, such as *yi*, that bond people together—not necessarily by blood, but through allegiance to each other—are under a severe test. Hong Kong subjects are perpetually caught between China and Britain. *Bullet in the Head* was released in 1990 at a critical juncture when the people of Hong Kong experienced the powerlessness of being between Britain and China. This particular film reflected people's sense of rootlessness caught between the two sovereigns.

In *A Better Tomorrow*, the ironic and nostalgic longing for honorable *xia* qualities through the disguise of a gangster or killer is a kind of collective consolation, an escape from reality. This version of homosociality also accounts for the irony in the collective dream of an optimistic future. *Bullet in the Head* puts such honorable qualities of trust to the test when three close friends become involved in the cruelty of political turmoil and wars. Woo's *Once a Thief* (1991) of the same period is about three orphans—Jim, Joe, and Cherie—whom their foster father, a powerful crime lord, raises to be professional thieves. Abused by the evil foster father, the three come upon an alternative father, a kind police inspector who cares for them. The trio go to Paris to steal a valuable painting. Unaware that their own foster father has betrayed them, Jim and Cherie manage to escape with the painting, while Joe is presumed killed in a car crash. Three years later, Joe returns, crippled in a wheelchair, to reunite with his two siblings, and together they plot revenge against their foster father. *Once a Thief* portrays Hong Kong's political dilemma metaphorically. Hong Kong negotiates and contests its identities as it becomes enmeshed between Britain and China. Similarly, the characters in the film are placed between two fatherly figures and establish their identity based on trust among themselves instead of on the model of patriarchal order. *Yi*, the primary quality of a *xia*, becomes Woo's nostalgic dream and a collective longing for righteousness—righteousness that is embodied in the ideal *xia* figures in times of injustice. Such a dream is also deemed impossible, a point of no return as a result of Hong Kong's liminal status vis-à-vis the imminent return to China in combination with the colonial sublimation of politics under Britain.

In *Hard-Boiled* (1992), Chow Yun-Fat plays an inspector nicknamed "Tequila," a hot-headed cop who decides to take matters into his own hands when his partner is brutally killed in a shootout. He teams up with undercover cop Tony, who has infiltrated chief gunrunner Johnny's organization. The relationship between Tequila and Tony is reminiscent of the team-up of killer Jeff and cop Li in *The Killer*. Woo appears to abandon the concept of *yi* as the only arbiter of morality in the action genre. For the bad guys well versed in *yi*, the cops may be the ultimate enemy. And in a battle scene, the standards of morality, such as *yi*, do not apply. In the hospital scene in the end, both the police and the gangs kill innocent, sick, or disabled people who try to escape, and Tony accidentally shoots a cop. In the film, the intense site of identity struggle happens with Tony, who attempts to locate Johnny and the gun smuggler's secret arms cache. Johnny hires Tony and takes him to his first job, then orders Tony to kill his current boss (another arms dealer). As an undercover cop, Tony faces the dilemma of killing the boss who trusts his loyalty as part of the gang.

Woo undoes the attributes of Chinese face values as embodiments of *yi* and *xin* and unleashes them in ambiguous and multiple ways. The complex morality plays that dominate Woo's earlier works are magnified in *Hard-Boiled*, because the choices Tony and Tequila confront reveal that good and evil are not always clear-cut. As in the hospital killing scene, Tony's dual affiliations as a cop and a gang member reveal the gray areas of righteousness, loyalty, and benevolence in the face of emergencies and riots. *Hard-Boiled* reveals the ironic situations in which the fantasy of homosocial bonding and the defense of ultimately unchallenged values can be put under brutal scrutiny. The film does not romantically and idealistically dwell on the themes of honor and sentiment among gangsters or cops. It acknowledges the trend toward less romantic and more realistic representations, as it allegorically reflects on Hong Kong's situation and people's concerns about peace and security upon the handover in 1997.

In this light, the standard of morality, such as *yi* and *xin*, does not always apply as times change. When the collective dream for a nostalgic past is no longer possible, loyalty becomes an atrocity. Woo modifies the context in which he applies and contests the elements of *yi* and questions its morality in judging a hero's deeds and character. Woo's films and their themes of loyalty are related to Chinese knightly, or *wuxia*, pathos. In this way, Woo gradually transforms and contests the sense of belonging embodied in the homosocial ideal of the brotherhood of *xia*. He disputes the basis of the Confucian moral and face values of *yi*, *xin*, and *zhong* that had once deceptively bound the community together. The sense of collectiveness is challenged—either in the name of common culture and ethnicity, such as Chineseness, or as a politics of subjectivity that Hong Kong has to contest at both local and global levels, as colonizer and nations' Others whose identities are constantly subjugated and therefore excluded.

The "Westernization" of *wuxia* films in terms of the gangster genre or the "Orientalization" of gangster films with *wuxia* themes suggests the intricate path on which Hong Kong cinema negotiates and contests identities of the East and the West. In *A Better Tomorrow* and *A Better Tomorrow II*, Woo modernizes the *xia* heroes in the urban gangland.

In *Once a Thief* and *Hard-Boiled*, Woo begins to cast doubt on the very legitimacy of loyalty and righteousness that generally govern the sense of brotherhood, fatherhood, community, and nation and puts the traditional values of *xia* and face into question. In *The Killer*, the incompatibility of *xia* values and Christian morals points to the multiple awarenesses that the subject embodies. Disorientation and confusion ensue as cultural diversions and influences from the West contest the meanings of Chinese honor values of face, and vice versa. In *Bullet in the Head*, time spans from 1967 to the apocalyptic projection of 1997, and the location shifts from Hong Kong to Vietnam. The geopolitical consciousness across time and space results in the reconstitution of memory and identity that draws upon the various sociopolitical discourses of the local and the translocal, Hong Kong and Vietnam, which are in turn reconstituted in the continuous negotiation of self and Other.

Chow Yun-Fat commented to Kenneth E. Hall, the writer of *John Woo: The Films*, "[Woo] want[s] to show the audience, that right now the whole world is in need of discipline—even [if] you're a thief, a killer, you have your discipline. He wants to say that men must have loyalty, purity, and responsibility, must be loyal to family and to friends. They must have dignity" (22–23). The state of homosociality that sustains patriarchal hegemony requires collective themes such as loyalty to found its basis of community in order to construct masculinity as the norm. In the same manner, the brotherhood forged in Woo's earlier films, such as *A Better Tomorrow*, is a form of collective consciousness in the alternative or possible subject formation that strives against the significant Other, the ungraspable unknown future. Mark was killed in the end to restore the relations between the brothers Ho and Kit. This moment signifies Woo's use of hegemonic homosocial loyalty and brotherhood to consolidate relations between blood brothers, thereby utilizing gangsters' outsider status to establish an alternative view on community and Hong Kong's self-identity.

Woo's later Hong Kong films, such as *Bullet in the Head* and *Hard-Boiled*, contest the theme of loyalty that grounds the sameness of masculinity. Bordwell has noted the ways in which Woo uses the shots and editing in Hong Kong films, as Yuen Woo-ping has suggested, to make the audience literally "feel the blow" (qtd. by Bordwell, "Aesthetics" 90). Bordwell has pointed out that the choreography sequence and kung fu are part of only one side of a cinema thoroughly fascinated with bodies in extremis (*Planet* 7). Thus, he identifies one tradition of Hong Kong cinema as the exhibitionism of bodily excess. In fact, violence is more than an exhibitionism of bodily excess and has becomes the melodramatic excess that dramatizes and contradicts themes of loyalty and brotherhood in Woo's films.

The ground that governs collective consciousness in such themes as loyalty, alliances, and brotherhood in pre-1997 contexts is equally tentative and questionable, because it only reinscribes the sense of identification (community or kinship) that excludes the nation or colonizer's Others, that is, the unfound and excluded identities of Hong Kong. Woo made both *Once a Thief* and *Bullet in the Head* at a time when Hong Kong underwent radical political change (after the 1989 Tiananmen incident and before the 1997 handover). *Bullet in the Head*, for example, is set in overseas locations, expressing a diasporic consciousness that encourages a radical rethinking of homeland, nation, and culture alongside themes such as loyalty, allegiances, and collective belonging. *Ren* (benevolence), *yi* (uprightness and selflessness), *zhong* (loyalty), *yong* (bravery) and *xin* (trust), the primary ideal qualities of a *xia*, define the longing for justice and righteousness that Woo represents in the collective longing for the *xia* characters in modern Hong Kong. The historical and political transition of sovereignty systematically downplays the existence of many conflicts, contradictions, and silences in the formation of Hong Kong's subjectivity due to its particular sociopolitical history.

The theme of loyalty and justice that govern male bonding is not a stable motif in Woo's films but rather is constantly contested. There is no authentic Chineseness or Hongkongeseness for a Hong Kong subject to dream or claim, because its colonial history has already hybridized the subject and rendered any essentialized or normative notions of identity implausible. Instead, the situation of being between cultures, identities, and colonizers produced Hong Kong's own mode of expression—unresolved tensions between continuity and disruption and channels between centers and peripheries within wider international and regional systems.

The *xia*-like heroes and their homosocial bonds create an imagined wholeness for a displaced subjectivity. Woo's cosmopolitical consciousness emerges from such displacement by hegemonic forces and by transgressing the code of honor and face values across time and geopolitical locations. Woo's films exemplify the *xia*/gangster cultural connotations as the Other (to mainstream society, law, and order) to contest the totalizations of the monolithic notion of "Hong Kong identity" and the inscriptions into hegemonic and oppositional pro-Chinese or pro-British political praxis during the pre-1997 transition period. Woo combines East and West in his film aesthetics and ideologies. His films offer alternative conceptions of both Chineseness and of masculine identity that put traditional *xia* qualities and Chinese face values into question. Woo also moves beyond the monolithic understanding of face in an increasingly globalized/Hollywood context by incorporating his cosmopolitical perspective. The historical, cultural, and political embeddings lodged in the *xia*/gangster honor codes extend beyond the geopolitical boundary of Hong Kong and disrupt the mainstream ideology of American masculine, family, and national politics. Contained in Woo's cosmopolitical perspective itself is a geopolitical intervention that interrogates these values and ideologies.

"Other Who Is Me"/"Me Who Is the Other"

Woo's Hong Kong action films have long caught the attention of the West. Bordwell called Woo's *The Killer* "a triumph of sheer romanticism" (*Planet* 106). Michael Bliss commented that his *Hard-Boiled* was "apocalyptic" about the fate of Hong Kong under Chinese rule after reunification (71). Verina Glaessner labeled *Hard Target* "destructive mayhem" ("Hard Target" 42). Woo began his first Hollywood film, *Hard Target*, in 1993, then followed it with *Broken Arrow, Face/Off, Mission: Impossible II*, and *Windtalkers*. *Hard Target* and *Broken Arrow* exemplify the transnationalization of the Hollywood action movie, particularly with regard to filming action sequences, Woo's *wuxia* themes of loyalty and trust, and his recodings of male bonding. It is not until his third Hollywood film, *Face/Off*, that Woo manages to deploy and politicize themes of homosociality with the possibility of contesting hegemonic masculinity that consolidates kinship and family.

Many critics have suggested that Woo has been assimilated into mainstream Hollywood, has transplanted his themes of male intimacy, and has modified the "buddy film" formula and family and heterosexual themes. Critics have emphasized the importance of Chinese *wuxia* films in Woo's films and how he has transferred such themes as male bonding, loyalty, and honor to his Hollywood works. Sandell argues that in Woo's Hong Kong films, he represents masculinity, "which celebrates both strength and intimacy, and where male bonding can suggest an erotic charge without the associated anxiety such relationships often trigger within the Hollywood action genre," whereas in his Hollywood films, the representation of masculinity follows much more closely the tradition of the Hollywood buddy/action film ("Reinventing" 33). Pei-Chi Chung argues that Woo has replaced strong male relationships with heterosexual couplings in his American films and that he has done so in reaction to, and in appreciation of, Hollywood ideology (44).

Though these statements carry some truth, I suggest it would be worth examining how the governing mechanisms of hegemonic masculinity, reflected in genres and themes, underline similarity or difference in Woo's Hong Kong and Hollywood works. John Woo takes the themes of male intimacy in his Hong Kong films and advances and reestablishes them in light of the American ideological problematic difference of gender and the family. These differences do not necessarily point to an "Asian" difference. Rather, Woo seeks to deconstruct and demystify the classical texts both in the martial arts and American action genres by violating the various conventions and traditions, working between the gaps of agency and resistance from the position of marginality and the Other.

Most heroes in Hollywood action films, beginning with Sylvester Stallone in *Rocky* (1976) and *First Blood* (1982), emphasize physicality over emotional depth. Action stars ranging from Stallone and Jean-Claude Van Damme to Steven Seagal and Chuck Norris offer impressive bodies for visual display and in their films undergo physical torture in order to defeat the villains. Excessive physicality can be seen in Arnold Schwarzenegger's *The Running Man* (1987), *Predator* (1987), and *The Terminator* (1984). Susan Jeffords has discussed excessive masculinity in Hollywood action films as an expression of American gender and political ideology that reifies male power and privilege during and after the Reagan administration (*Hard Bodies* 24–25). Anneke Smelik calls the changes in the theoretical basis of gender representations "the crisis in which the white male heterosexual subject finds himself, a crisis in which his masculinity is fragmented and denaturalized, in which the signifiers of 'man' and 'manly' seem to have lost all their meaning" (141).

Woo's films are less invested in the male hero's excessive physicality as the upholder and advocate for heteronormative masculinity than in the extreme violence the action choreography portrays. The bodily excess of hyperviolence structures the melodramatic climax. This moment of excess is the moral polarization in the narrative. It plays out the primary contestation between the ideal moral/*qing* (emotional)-based qualities of a *xia* (that define the longing for justice and righteousness) and the rationality of modern, impersonal, and flawed civil law. In Woo's films, emotionality and violence counter anxieties produced by the decentering of moral values and the massive scale of changes in contemporary society.

In response to Chung and Sandell, who criticize that Woo's Hollywood films move toward a heterosexual conclusion, I argue that Woo's films have always leaned toward the socially acceptable conclusion of heterosexual coupling, even in his Hong Kong films, from *A Better Tomorrow* to *Hard-Boiled*. The primary difference is that the bond between the men has changed. Those once friends in Woo's Hong Kong films have now become enemies in Hollywood settings, including the characters played by Christian Slater and John Travolta in *Broken Arrow*, Nicholas Cage and Travolta in *Face/Off*, and Tom Cruise and Dougray Scott in *Mission: Impossible II*. On the surface, it would seem that Woo has sacrificed male intimacy and the homosocial bond to the heteronormative allegiance to family; however, the politics played out between different sexes and ethnic groups is in fact more complicated.

Hard Target, Woo's first Hollywood film, is a remake of the pre–World War II action film *The Most Dangerous Game* (1932) in which the Belgian-born martial arts star Jean-Claude Van Damme is cast as Chance Boudreaux, an ex–war veteran hired by the young woman Natasha to find her missing father. They soon discover that her father is the victim of a sinister organization run by Fouchon, a ruthless businessman who arranges high-stakes hunting games for the rich with humans as prey. Many of these targets are Vietnam veterans who live in the streets of New Orleans. In contrast to the major villain, Fouchon, who capitalizes on the veterans, Boudreaux embodies the ideals of loyalty, honor, and trust that run through Woo's Hong Kong films. Woo places these ideals within a context that the American audience can identify with, that is, the love of country. Patriotism as a discourse is contested as the film reveals how the country has forgotten its veterans and their physical and psychological needs.

Broken Arrow, Woo's second Hollywood film, is about Vic Deakins (John Travolta) and Riley Haley (Christian Slater), military pilots as well as good friends who become rivals during a trip to carry two live nuclear weapons across Utah. Haley learns that Deakins plans to use the nuclear weapon to hold the country for ransom. *Broken Arrow* tells the traditional tale of conflict between two men, one good and one bad. The action takes place on the frontier, cut off from civilization, reminiscent of the Western landscape in John Wayne movies. The film deviates from the standard cowboy mentality insofar as the hero and the villain represent two sides of the same coin. *Broken Arrow* continues Woo's recurring preoccupation with the ambiguous boundary between good and evil, self and Other.

In 1997, John Woo's *Face/Off* (his third movie in Hollywood) became a great summer box office hit. *Face/Off* is pivotal in Woo's transnational repertoire of works. In portraying and transforming meanings of heroism through emotion, sociopolitical complexity, and moral ambiguity, *Face/Off* shows that Woo's transnational aesthetic and his recoding of masculinity were then transplanted to Hollywood. From the very beginning, Hollywood inspired Woo, but he has been able to fuse this with his training in the Hong Kong popular film genres and to transform genres such as the gangster film into a new breed.

Identity transformations and role reversals fascinate Woo. In *Face/Off*, John Travolta stars as Sean Archer, a FBI special agent whose life revolves around his pursuit of a villain called Castor Troy, the murderer of Archer's beloved son. The film begins with Troy's capture at Archer's hands. Troy is seriously injured in the capture, and Archer discovers that Troy is planning a terrorist attack. In order to trap the rest of Troy's gang and retrieve the secret plan for the attack, Archer undergoes an experimental surgery in which he has Troy's face placed on his body, so that he may infiltrate the gang in the guise of his worst enemy. The plot is complicated further when Troy wakes up from his coma and forces the medical staff to place Archer's face onto him. In one major shoot-out scene in *Face/Off*, Archer-as-Troy saves Troy's son Adam from the FBI agents who launch an attack at Troy's base.

In one major shoot-out scene, the gunplay includes double-fisted shootouts and midair acrobatics that are pillars of the kinetic martial arts–influenced choreography of Woo's previous works. The scene's choreography is reminiscent of the opening scene in *The Killer* when Chow Yun-Fat's character, Jeff, flies over space in elegant leaps to save Jenny from gunshots. The scene in *The Killer*, composed by choreographer Ching Siu-tung, incorporates martial arts work. The choreography is used to highlight the heroic and benevolent act of the character toward the weak and the innocent, whom he does not need to be related to or even know. In *Face/Off*, Woo similarly employs the acrobatic choreography to emphasize the hero's grace in saving the child. The scene contradicts the melodramatic excess of the fatherly love/loss of a son and the multiple meanings of being a patriarchal figure (Archer to his dead son/Archer as Troy to Troy's son).

In *Face/Off*, Woo complicates the choreography of male heroism by contrasting violence with the song "Somewhere Over the Rainbow" from *The Wizard of Oz* (1939). Robert Hanke interprets the gunfire scene in *Face/Off* and the use of the famous and gentle song:

> [T]he ensuing shoot-out, which juxtaposes ballistic ballet with shots of the innocent Adam (while "Somewhere over the Rainbow" is heard on the soundtrack), emphasizes Archer as Troy's heroic effort to protect Adam as if he were his own son. The bullet wound which Archer receives at the beginning of the film is a reminder of

his lost son, and both his wound and the narrative is closed, so to speak, when the Archer family adopts Adam. (53)

Instead of emphasizing Archer-as-Troy's heroic effort, the juxtaposition of violence and the song reveals the contradictions in the melodramatic excess of heroism. Hanke has described the melodramatic elements in the film: "In generic terms, *Face/Off* exemplifies the infusion of Woo's 'male melodrama' and the 'doing and suffering' heroes into the Hollywood action film, where the male body, its wounding, surgical transformation, and restoration, is a condensed signifier of masculine subjectivity in crisis" (54–55). In the scene when Archer-as-Troy tries to save Troy's son from the FBI agents, he covers the child's ears with headphones playing the song, which is the diegetic sound the child character experiences. The viewer not only takes on the child's perspective but is also temporarily alienated from the scene's action. The gunfire sound effect and therefore the excitement of the violence are muted. The viewer is left gazing at the choreography of the violence. Only the general chaos of the battle remains. It is a scene of continuous weapons fire with the sentimental song set against the brutal and physical sensation of the action. The melodramatic excess of the moment is an act of intervention, an uncanny interstitial state of dialogism with multiple cultural texts and interpretations. It is also in the melodramatic moment of excess that the cosmopolitical implications of screen violence between Hong Kong and Hollywood are unleashed.

Action and violence become an outer symbolization of inner emotions in Woo's films. Philippa Gates asserts:

[In Woo's] scenes of hypermasculinity and violence lie the more profound thematic concerns with male heroism, emotionality, and bonding that escape through the moments of excess and give Woo's films a complexity and intensity most often lacking in the Hollywood action genre. It is the moments of excess and the readings made possible by those moments that distinguish Woo's films from even the best of Hollywood's action films and that draw audiences seeking the pleasures of his male melodrama. (74)

As examples of "male melodrama," Gates suggests, Woo's excess in emotion and violence enables alternative readings and gratification for audiences that they do not usually find in Hollywood films. Gates proposes that audiences find pleasure in male heroes who can be vulnerable as well as heroic. In fact, transgressive meanings and ideological contradictions underline the moments of emotional excess and hyperviolence.

After all, the attackers are the FBI agents. And the savior is the FBI agent Archer wearing Troy's face. In a linear reading taking Archer as the focus, the film's melodramatic excess of the loss and restoration of the nuclear family unit signifies the heart of the film. Archer in the end adopts the orphaned child, restabilizes the American bourgeois family/home (literally, the nation's basic structural unit), and masters the role of the family patriarch. The face-off between Archer and Troy, good and evil, and their interchangeable roles as father in each other's situation point to the dual dynamism that Woo builds into the film. Woo upholds the mainstream ideology of fatherhood and white masculinity in its melodramatic excess with sound and action as a facade, only to disassemble such themes within the hegemony. The facing-off works tactfully within the field of power, and yet simultaneously its unsettling perspective remains outside dominance, because the interchangeability of identities, good and evil, subverts hegemonic values. The performative relationship between self and Other places one character in the Other's positionality.

In *Face/Off*, both main characters feel pity for those who belong to the close, interpersonal circles of their enemy's lives. The child whom Archer later adopts symbolizes this transcendence. The moment of melodramatic excess symbolizes the surreal juxtapositions of fantasy, violence, and chivalric codes. It transgresses the moral codes of good and evil, the *xia* value in Chinese culture or family values in American contexts. The themes of family, benevolence, and honor (as a *xia* figure) underline Woo's cross-cultural film trajectory. Face is the center of significance in national, gendered, ethnic, and culturally specific identity politics. It is the performativity of face that reveals this subjugation of subject to identity.

In *Face/Off*, Troy is the villain, the site of alterity, in the narrative. When Troy wakes up without a face, it also represents the moment when hegemony is un-facializable. Troy puts on Archer's face and assumes Archer's identity. In this case, the face hijacks the body and the hegemonic hijacks the face. Rather than reading the face as a material expression that extends to the body, the face according to the logic in *Face/Off* represents a system. The hegemonic notions of the face have intercultural implications. As an instance of transnational filmmaking, Woo's notion of face in *Face/Off* does not offer an alternative framework as empirically Chinese or Western but rather crosses over the sociopolitical contexts of the Chinese diaspora in Hollywood. Face becomes the site of intervention that Woo uses to question the aspect of honor (*xia* traditions and family values) and the common practice of identification according to skin, face, and race in the American context.

According to Gilles Deleuze and Félix Guattari in *A Thousand Plateaus*, the obsession with faciality is primarily a Western, especially Christian, phenomenon: "The face is not a universal. It is not even that of the white man; it is White Man himself. . . . The face is Christ. The face is the typical European" (176). The dominant identifying marker with which humans are primarily obsessed is the face, and, in fact, the face and its features deceive us into believing we know the subjectivity underneath. Societies stratify through the mechanics of facialization. This assemblage of variations of the same entirely occludes any potential for a body to be unique, different, or even itself. The body neither conforms to nor expresses the face. The system of the face overcodes and annihilates the body.

Face/Off's spectacle of masculinity, the performativity of faces, and the fusion of film cultures and values of East and West remind us that external violence executed onto the face and internal violence overcoded onto the body are not opposites but are always implicated with each other. Deleuze and Guattari state: "Faces are not basically individual: they define zones of frequency or probability, delimit a field that neutralizes in advance any expressions or connections unnamable to the appropriate significations" (168). This system works like a machine, constantly defining and delimiting the subject it presents.

Woo uses the performance of Archer-as-Troy and Troy-as-Archer to indicate that masculinity is a constructed identity, a performative act, and that the Chinese face values demand the context of social relations to exist. The Chinese face values are no longer bound to the code of honor that sustains the Chinese context of social relation or *guanxi*. The Chinese *xia* qualities of *yi* and *xin* are based on the acts of benevolence toward the weak or needy and the face values that establish the individual place/recognition within the community. Such values are translated to the context of family relations that emphasize the father/son relations.

The performativity of self and Other unsettles the conventional fictional planes that are generally breached with the synchronizing of *xia* values and family themes, ideology and artifice. The action choreography punctuates the emotional moral excess in the film's melodrama. The insertion of the sentimental song "Somewhere Over the Rainbow" contradicts the visual and melodramatic excess that accompanies the linear interpretation of violence as heroism and plays out the ideological contradictions related to hegemonic masculinity, identity, family, and code of honor in East/West contexts. *Face/Off*'s protagonists embody dialectical tensions within masculinity and codes of honor (Chinese *xia* traditions and the transnational values of family and dignity in both Chinese and American cultural contexts).

In *Face/Off*, Archer passes as Troy, and Troy passes as Archer. During a gunfight scene, Troy-as-Archer points his gun at Archer-as-Troy on the other side of a mirror, and vice versa. They must confront "the Other within the self" at the climax in Woo's trademark standoff. Each character begins to inhabit the subjectivity of the Other, so the binary logic of the self and Other, violence and emotion, is dissolved into both the intersubjective spaces and correspondences in negotiations and confrontations. By the end of the film, the narrative allows several resonating interpretations as Archer represents a new and improved husband and father. At the same time, the fact that Troy has appeared as Archer in the domestic sphere earlier in the narrative also represents the inherent threat of domestic violence against Eve, Archer's wife, and their daughter. Woo's vision takes us to its emotional and narrative conclusion with the complexity of "Other who is me" and "me who is the Other." Being the Other and in the Other's shoes, the father-terrorist or the terrorist-father in turn initiates a blurring that occurs about the dichotomous nature of good and evil.

By the end, Archer represents the loving and understanding father and husband. Fatherhood and other patriarchal discourses in the name of nationhood, for instance, represent variations of hegemonic masculinity. But the faciality of Archer in the narrative has suggested the potential violence that can be enacted on the family and society in general. Thus, *Face/Off* shows how masculinity seeks to preserve its hegemony by being fluid and open to definition.

As one of the major cosmopolitical directors to make his own distinctive mark in Hollywood, Woo is hoping he will be able to smooth the way for others to follow. "When I arrived, there were a lot of stereotypes and a certain bias against Asians," he says. "I hope that through my films people will see our true nature" ("Cinema"). *Face/Off* is a manifestation of his personal statement. In this way, Woo displaces the obsession of race/ face of the American context and the honor/face of the Chinese context. It is through this, along with the heroic bloodshed and extreme violence, that Woo opens a door to reinvent not only the gangster film genre but also the facing-off of values in cross-cultural encounters.

The performativity of the faces in *Face/Off* reveals the disciplinary power it enforces onto the body and the failure of traditional identity politics in which difference (governed by the face in ethnic or gender differences) grounds sameness (stereotypes and inscriptions in the name of honor). It reconceptualizes identity as a process of self-creation and offers a way out of the traps of identity politics and the fixed notion of identity. Woo fuses elements from various film cultures and uses styles and motifs that include excessive violence, gang relationships, the opposition between good and evil, the respect of *xia* values, and the code of honor, along with new elements in his Hollywood filmmaking, that is, issues and contexts specifically American. The value of face (from the Chinese to the American context) is manipulated and played out in its fullest. The deconstruction of the wall that separates the villains from the heroes and the critical intervention of one cultural context with a cosmopolitically conscious counterpart are Woo's major contributions. He has helped to change the face of transnational filmmaking.

Similarly, *Mission: Impossible II* (2000) brings IMF (Impossible Missions Force) agent Ethan Hunt (Tom Cruise) back to his mission, as he is to retrieve a genetically created deadly virus called Chimera. To complicate matters, renegade IMF agent Sean Ambrose (Dougray Scott) has stolen the cure for Chimera, code-named Bellerophon, and now needs to get the virus in order to complete the plan of infecting the whole world. To help recover the virus and the cure, Hunt enlists the aid of a beautiful thief named Nyah (Thandie Newton), who coincidentally used to date Ambrose. Matters become more intricate and difficult as Hunt falls in love with Nyah and she gets caught between two men at war against each other. In the midst of the action, Nyah injects the virus into herself. And Hunt must race against time to save the woman he loves. Woo has already shown the contestation of such themes of reverberant ideas of honor and morality in his later Hong Kong films such as *Bullet in the Head* and *Hard-Boiled*. In his Hollywood works, he complicates themes of belonging and betrayal to the more fluid and complex multiplicities that showcase struggles and disparities between different political and cultural boundaries.

The performativity of identity is also a main motif in *Mission: Impossible II*. Former agent Sean Ambrose, disguised as good guy agent Ethan Hunt, intercepts the transportation of the deadly new virus Chimera. He plans on selling the bio-weapon to the highest bidder. Later, as Nyah talks to her beloved Ethan, "Ethan" suddenly rips off his latex mask and turns out to be Sean, the terrorist. By the end of the film, Ethan is captured and tortured to death—but then we find out it was Sean's partner wearing "Ethan's" mask who was actually the victim. The face change is one of the major motifs in the film; it leaves viewers wondering if the Ethan Hunt they see is the "real" one or just someone else behind his faciality.

The constant replay of themes, such as the interchangeability of faces and their perceptions, loosen boundaries between self and Other. An adversary may turn out to be part of a coalition; the glowing opponent peels off the smiling ally's face.

In Woo's Hong Kong films, only trust in justice and loyalty can bring the two heroes on opposite sides of the law together, sharing similar ideals in the code of honor. The jousting duel on the motorbikes between Ethan Hunt and Sean Ambrose and the kung fu finale are ballistic battles. These choreographed encounters in *Mission: Impossible II* recall the equally deadly gunfire scenes in Woo's Hong Kong films. In the 2000 film, though, the two male characters fight in violent gunfire and resolve their differences, dramatizing their divergences and similarities at the same time. The film targets hegemonic heroism in white masculinity, focuses on the performative aspect of identity formations, and expresses the ambivalent distinction between the hero and the villain, the self and the Other.

Mission: Impossible II puts on a show of triangular heterosexual romance between two men and a woman. The cultural value of face is based on a context for interpretation, and Woo translates the benevolent act of *xia* heroism in the interpretative context of romance and sacrifice in the American context. The site of action conflict is the ethnic woman, Nyah, the racial and sexual Other. As Nyah injects the virus into herself, Hunt must save her from death, and Ambrose must capture her in order to get the virus. In *Mission: Impossible II*, the love triangle theme is no different from many film narratives in which the traffic of the woman between the two men is used to indicate masculine intimacy (rivalry). Cynthia J. Fuchs notes that homoeroticism would inevitably be invoked by the male bonds in cinematic representations. She writes, "[T]he exclusion of women compelled overt condemnation of implicit and even explicit homoeroticism" (196). Thus, the inclusion of Nyah in the narrative displaces homoeroticism onto the gendered and racialized Other, the black woman. Yet, the interchangeability of the identity of Ethan Hunt and Sean Ambrose points to the homophobia below the surface.

Whereas in *The Killer* the two male characters bond, in *Mission: Impossible II* the bonding is transformed to a male/female relationship. The roles of hero and villain are clear-cut in *Mission: Impossible II*, as they do not engage in the cross-pollination of good and evil that is present in Woo's Hong Kong action films. Woo contests the white male's self-identity within the radical shifting social and political frames by confronting the male with the racialized and gendered Other. The film stages intimacy and vulnerability associated with the recuperation of the racial and sexual Other. The relationship between white males (the interchangeability of Hunt and Ambrose) in the film shows how the masculine hegemony has to subsume such tensions and, at the same time, indicates how the Other results in a feminizing effect that destabilizes self-identity.

In the film, Ambrose initially believes Nyah's sincerity, but small tests and disguises monitor her loyalty. She is not what she seems. Her location is the shifting ground of identification. Her situation may just work to address the ethical imperative and codes of morality for the conflicts. Nyah's gender and race (biracial in origin and may well be read as African, Anglo-American, or African American) generate multiple positions of marginalities and Otherness. In relation to her difference from the masculine and to white racial supremacy, the gendered and multiracial Other is stranded between the contested notions of race and gender. Her positions as multiplicities in a way disengage fixed and static readings from the dominant discourse. The sexual and racial Other's position generates ideological tension that structures white masculinity. Woo targets the convention of buddy politics in American action films, and the performative white male hero/villain relationship in *Mission: Impossible II* problematizes homosociality by recuperating racial and sexual Otherness in the love triangle relationship.

The first *Mission: Impossible* (1996), directed by Brian De Palma, ends with Ethan Hunt reuniting with his African American buddy—the only person he can confide in after the labyrinth of setups and chases. The representation of African Americans is typical; he is a token, "background" technical expert, one-dimensional and emotionless. The safe, nonthreatening image of an African American team member helps the white male to negotiate crises of masculine identity centered on questions of race, class, or sexual orientation. Thus, Woo turns male bonding into antagonism and inserts into the traditional erotic, triangular relationship narrative a theme of loyalty and disloyalty that Nyah embodies so as to contest and destabilize the racialized black/white dichotomy. In this way, Woo contests the hegemonic ideology in homosocial bonds.

In Woo's film, the two male characters fall for Nyah and also shift between the sites of empowerment and disempowerment. As an action hero, Ethan Hunt fights primarily on a personal level, to save Nyah, rather than due to a masculine code of honor, though his overall mission is to save the world. From the patriarchal perspective, Hunt's character is emotional, effeminate, and romantic insofar as the reason for his espionage is not only to stop the virus from spreading but also, and more important, to save Nyah, the woman he loves. Woo fully manifests the traditional themes of shifting loyalties in spy films and deploys these themes in the duplicity (and the performative nature) of masculinity that in turn reflects his cosmopolitical perspective. The power dynamic of the erotic triangle of two men and one woman, as in Woo's *Mission: Impossible II*, generates new meanings, as Woo takes gender and ethnicity into consideration in the historical function of patriarchal power and white masculinity. The performative relations between the white males transgress boundaries between self and Other. The racial and sexual Other ruptures the recuperation of homosociality within the national imaginary.

Woo's next work, *Windtalkers*, is a World War II drama starring Nicholas Cage as Marine Sergeant Joe Enders assigned to protect the Navajo-language military code during the war against Japan. In an earlier battle, Enders had refused to retreat before a Japanese assault, and all the people under his command, except himself, are killed. He recovers in a Hawaii hospital, and with the help of a nurse, he resumes duty. During the war, the United States employed the help of Navajo Indians, including Yahzee and Whitehorse, who would pass secret information via the Navajo language as a military code that no enemy country could translate. The Marines Enders and Anderson have to protect the code and kill the Navajo men rather than allow them to be captured by the Japanese and expose the code. Enders remains distant from Yahzee until Yahzee saves their lives by impersonating a Japanese soldier and penetrating the enemy's lines. The scene in which Yahzee poses as a Japanese soldier and Enders pretends to be his captive is one of the significant moments of standoff in the film. The final action climax cannot match the intensity of the preceding sequence, in which Enders must perform a deed that almost totally embitters Yahzee toward him: Enders kills Whitehorse before the Japanese capture the latter. Yahzee is angry at Enders's act. In the final stage of the battle, Enders rescues the injured Yahzee but is mortally wounded carrying him to safety. Enders dies in the end.

In *Windtalkers*, Woo frames hand-to-hand combat and choreography, including the depiction of the pyrotechnics of the staged battles. The carnage of combat allows Woo plenty of room to stage long action set pieces, physical duels, and the propulsion of human beings through space via explosive concussion. In Steven Spielberg's Academy Award–winning picture *Saving Private Ryan* (1998), he shows the barbarous horrors of war in his depiction of the D-Day landing at Normandy Beach during World War II, emphasizing with handheld camera the graphic realism of the war. Ridley Scott's *Black Hawk Down* (2001) carefully alternates traveling shots with perspectives, such as that from inside the head of the ox, and places the viewers in different standpoints from godlike to subjective. Woo is no different from Spielberg and Scott in the ways he brings new combat and filming styles into the war film genre. Though *Saving Private Ryan* and *Black Hawk Down* incorporate different graphic techniques and various camera points of view to depict the war, the films do not change their basic hegemonic perspective and fall back into the conventional patriotic ideology of bravery and glory. The cruelty of the war in the end only preserves hegemonic masculinity by confessing its anxieties about destruction and mutilation at every turn. In *Windtalkers*, what happened to Enders and his fellows in the war severely disturb him. There is no mistake that the cause for the action in the film is the brutality of the enemy, the unknown Other. The militaristic comradeship and the intense male bonding in war films work to integrate the individual male to the corporate military identity.

In *The Remasculinization of America: Gender and the Vietnam War*, Susan Jeffords analyzes the ways in which patriarchal social forms are evident in male bonds by examining the image of the Vietnam veteran that dominated American popular culture in the 1980s. Jeffords suggests that the significance of the masculine bonds of the Vietnam veteran serve as a unified buffer against the feminizing influences of the distrustful American government and the Viet Cong enemy. Jeffords notes:

> As structure, the masculine bond insists on a denial of difference—whether black or white, wealthy or poor, high school or college-educated, from north or south, men are the "same"—at the same time that the bond itself depends for its existence on an affirmation of difference—men are not women. The motif of this structure is thus one of exclusion, and its primary shape is a hierarchy defined by participation in/exclusion from the experience of war. (59–60)

Thus, the emphasis on male sameness through homosocial bonds, as in Jeffords's discussions, functions as a site of empowerment for patriarchal hegemony in the face of threats from disruptive differences in race, sexuality, class, and gender. She observes that the postwar mythification of masculine bonds not only serves as the recuperation for the national imaginary and collectiveness after the traumatic loss in the war but also acts as a response to the feminist, civil rights, and gay rights struggles that challenged the structures upon which power hegemonic practices had depended.

Windtalkers not only inserts new filmic styles and choreography into the war film but also engages the moral ambiguity of ethnicity and loyalty in American war films. The action embedded in the film includes the point at which the American combat unit implodes and the troops kill each other instead. In *Windtalkers*, the moral dilemma that the white male has to face if he follows the military order to put a bullet in the ethnic Other's head disrupts the homosocial process in the corporation of military identity. Woo's *Windtalkers* is a different take on the polarity of self and Other in the war film genre. Woo portrays the polarities of self and Other in the war film as evidently unstable and the ideological assumption upon which they rest as untenable.

In Woo's earlier Hong Kong war films, such as *Bullet in the Head*, he uses the portrayal of brutality in wars as the background for the ultimate test of the characters' friendship (*zhong*, *yi*, and *xin*) and trust in each other. In *Windtalkers*, Woo uses the war as a background to dramatize the theme of *yi* and reveals the mixture of jingoism and ambivalence in white masculinity through themes such as loyalty and allegiance in light of ethnic differences. As an example, Yahzee at one point poses as Japanese, because from an American perspective his Native American looks allow him to pass for the enemy. Yahzee pretending to be a Japanese soldier and Enders posing as his captive proves to be the film's most exciting scene. It allows Woo to revisit some of his favorite dramatic and moral conflicts and leads us to examine the changing meanings of Woo's standoff sequences.

Woo neither elaborates on the coalition between Yahzee and Enders at this standoff, nor does he portray Yahzee as a frenzied killer of the enemy, the Japanese, which is what the ideology of an American war film will allow and celebrate. The rigor and verisimilitude in directing action films entitles Woo to engage in moral ambiguity and contest the ethnic and racist prejudices in American war history. The insertion of Native Americans into the Pacific war has rich and multiple possibilities, especially for a war that has much history of foreboding racism connected with it. Simmering in the forefront is the moral dialectic of the Allied campaign against Nazism and later of the Japanese attack of Pearl Harbor. The racist cast of the Pacific war also led to the home-front internment of Japanese Americans and the atomic bombing of Hiroshima and Nagasaki in 1945.

Notably, Woo's *Windtalkers* includes the Native Americans as patriotic participants in a war so much clouded and fogged with prejudices and racism, narrating the history of the minorities' roles in war that is generally neglected in the mainstream ideology of war films. Part of the generic structure of the buddy film formula is the inequality in the way the two protagonists are depicted within the narrative. The presumed normative masculinity is defined as different in terms of ethnicity, as in the case of the Native Americans. The Other's role is to marvel at the hero's achievement and to support him as a loyal figure. The male bonding is always a threat to a conservative and patriarchal Hollywood as it at the same time implies homosocial bonding and therefore homoerotic inflections.

The subject positions and dimensions of masculinity in *Windtalkers* do not diverge from the buddy movie format that is constructed on the basis of ethnic difference or inequality. In *Windtalkers*, the two Navajo men, Yahzee and Whitehorse, are paired up with the white guards Enders and Anderson respectively. Enders and Anderson have the order to kill the Navajos in order to prevent disclosure of the code to the Japanese. In *Windtalkers*, unlike most mainstream buddy films, there are two buddy pairs instead of one. Anderson and Whitehorse develop an open and congenial relationship. At the same time, Whitehorse shows bitterness when he comments that the Marines are "covering our Navajo asses," a grim sign of the Native American resentment of their white bodyguards in a country that displaced them and rendered them Other from the very beginning. Racism erupts in *Windtalkers* with the other pair, as Enders tells Yahzee, "You do look like a Jap." As soon as Anderson is dead and Whitehorse is captured, Enders kills Whitehorse before he can be interrogated. Enders later asks Yahzee to kill him, but Yahzee holds back. And at the end of the film, Enders saves Yahzee on the battlefield but is himself mortally wounded.

The film also is weighted with religious symbolism that, in fact, relates to the judgment of Enders's morality. In the midst of the war, Enders draws a Catholic church on a flour-covered table and remembers his past as a Catholic schoolboy, "a soldier of Christ. Somewhere along the way I must have switched sides." The interchange of alliance and positions suggests that the moral judgment of *yi* and *xin*, and the Christian belief of good and evil, is never fixed. Woo uses the twin buddy pairs to explore the shifting meanings and multiple possibilities in interracial bonding, rather than simply recuperating and empowering dominant positions for white heterosexual men. *Windtalkers* is about the struggles and assimilation of the Others, the windtalkers or code transmitters, and the tensions between Navajo and Marine warrior cultures. From the very beginning, the film narrative suspends the fate of the Navajos. Finally, the execution of the military order at the critical moment makes the fantasy of the Marines, like Enders and Anderson, as a symbolization of bravery and glory in the name of honor and in the conceit of war, questionable. The film reflects Woo's cosmopolitical perspective on race, honor, and war in Hollywood cinema.

Based on Philip K. Dick's story, Woo's *Paycheck* is a sci-fi movie about an advanced engineer named Michael Jennings (Ben Affleck) who voluntarily has his memory erased by his employer after a special project. Jennings is capable of building new machines the likes of which define the future. He is willing, thanks to a sizable paycheck, to have his memory erased by the corporation that hires him to design new products, which have far-reaching consequences, so that he will not be able to redesign them at the end of his contract. The compensation money is large enough to induce him to ignore the downside of his amnesia and look the other way about any ethical issues that may be involved. While his intellectual capability is erased, Jennings shows his physical potential by training with a baton and basic martial arts techniques. After he finishes his latest project, Jennings receives in the place of a large paycheck an envelope with nineteen items that he has no recollection of sending himself; he soon learns that he must use these items to discover why he was double-crossed. With the help of his lover and a former coworker he has no memory of, he retraces his past and finds out why he is being hunted.

The idea of a machinery of premeditation that would in fact see into the future is a central part of the premise of *Paycheck*. More, the representation of masculinity (self) depends on an active forgetting (the Othered or alienated self), which is also a crucial part of remembering. The representation of masculinity is predicated on the amnesia about the dangerous technology of premeditation; the remembering of the self is portrayed as a cruel moment of trauma and oppression from which the subject is liberated. Notably, Jennings resurfaces as a subject who, because of his amnesia, does not remember who his allies and enemies are. However, he has the intellectual capacity to leave traces for himself to search for his identity, thus transforming the actual threat of amnesia into the active path of remembering—a heteronormative masculinity that is reinstated by the reunion with his lover.

Paycheck shows memory's susceptibility to manipulation. Mieke Bal calls cultural memory "something you actually perform" by invoking Judith Butler's theory of performative identity (vii). Butler argues that identity categories such as sex and gender are not fixed or natural but are constructed through performance governed by social condition and expectation. Thus, insofar as identity is enacted, it can also be intervened in for the purpose of change. Likewise, cultural memory is not something fixed but involves active performance, which can be intervened in to alter an apparently fixed future in a global context. Woo's cosmopolitical consciousness about the performativity of memory brings out the contemporary relevance in a global context and can be seen as an allegory or metaphor for the political question of transnational subjectivity and the notions of deterritorialization and reterritorialization that emerge in their complexity and power.

Woo's two-part epic films *Red Cliff* and *Red Cliff II* can be considered the Chinese equivalents of *The Lord of the Rings* trilogy (2001–03). The films are about the mythical and legendary history related to the establishment of the Three Kingdoms in China. *Red Cliff* and its sequel are the most expensive Chinese-language projects ever and feature dramatic spectacle and visceral action. The $80 million historical epic mixes elements from history (as recorded in Chen Shou's *Records of Three Kingdoms*) and Luo Guan Zhong's fiction *Romance of the Three Kingdoms*. The films are Woo's romanticized accounts of actual historical events that are inspired by his interpretation of homosocial bonds and martial attributes of masculinity/femininity in a Chinese setting. The films became box office hits, sweeping across Asia.

The epic focuses on the major battle, the Battle of Red Cliff, in the account of the history about the Three Kingdoms. The films open in the summer of A.D. 208, with prime minister and general Cao Cao asking permission from Emperor Xian of the Han Dynasty to lead an expedition south to take on southern warlord Liu Bei. In order to resist Cao Cao's massive army, Zhuge Liang (main advisor to Liu Bei) formulates a small but resolute coalition between Liu Bei and Sun Quan, another warlord. The coalition is led by Zhou Yu (counselor to Sun Quan) with the assistance of Zhuge Liang. But the journey south is not easy for Cao Cao's massive army, and before long the soldiers are suffering from lack of water and sheer exhaustion. In the sequel, when typhoid breaks out among Cao Cao's troops, Cao Cao tactically infects Zhou's army with the disease. Subsequently deserted by Liu Bei, Zhou prepares to lead an army of approximately 30,000 men against Cao Cao's massive force of several hundred thousand. The battle drawing near, Zhuge Liang resorts to some clever tactics in order to undermine Cao Cao. The undercover princess Sun Shangxiang succeeds in delivering secret messages from Cao Cao's camp. As violence erupts on the Yangtze River, Zhou Yu's wife, Xiao Qiao, heads toward Cao Cao's camp alone and in secret, hoping to persuade Cao Cao to give up his plans, but she fails. She decides to distract Cao Cao instead to buy time for Zhou's army. In the nick of time, Zhou Yu manages to reverse the situation by rescuing Xiao Qiao with a surprise attack and puts Cao Cao at the mercy of the allied forces instead.

Violence, which is the basis of war, as with *Windtalkers*, is not the ideal in the *Red Cliff* films. Kam Louie argues that Chinese masculinity has been structured by the archetypes of *wen* and *wu* that operate in a productive relation. Ideal *wen* masculinity, associated with the gentlemen-scholar or *junzi* by Confucius, aims at maintaining civil order, hierarchy, and filial piety. *Wu*, the martial masculinity, represented by Guan Yu, is associated with the outlaw space of the *jianghu* and emphasizes the bonds of brotherhood (1–21). These two archetypes of *wen* and *wu* masculinities operate together, although *wen* has been more highly valued in Chinese culture. It is the coordination between the two prototypes of *wen* and *wu* masculinities that operate in the complementary principles of *yin* and *yang* and define the moral standard in the *Red Cliff* films. This principle allows the filmmaker to present to the audience his moral code very clearly, as there is no moral ambiguity in the film.

The moral code that Woo promotes is overall a Confucian one. Honor and dignity are prized highly, even when Zhou deals with his subordinates. Guan Yu represents the ideal of *wu* masculinity, and he would attack only in plain sight from the front. Woo shows that *yi* is a important trait for being a leader, so Liu Bei orders his troops to defend the peasants, even though this will thin out the troops and ruin his chances of victory over Cao Cao's forces. *Red Cliff* and its sequel's most memorable qualities lie outside the battlefield. Woo shows Zhou Yu's chivalry and fair-mindedness, demonstrating that mercy is commendable. Zhou runs his troops through the mud so that the men who stole the peasant's buffalo can have a second chance.

In *Red Cliff* and its sequel, lust and obsession with women is considered a despicable trait. Women also represent temptation and the threat of loss of control for both *wu* and *wen* masculinities. Thus, Cao Cao's lust for Zhou Yu's wife is an example. Cao Cao is portrayed as a selfish individual who starts a war for a woman whom he has met one time and wishes her to belong to him. Cao Cao demonstrates aspects of martial masculinity, but he is discounted as a defective model because of his egotistic nature. He is seen metaphorically as the tiger, a silent predator that will attack someone in the dark from behind. He governs his subjects, including soldiers, commanders, and generals, by fear as he eliminates all those who oppose him or whom he distrusts. For example, Cao Cao kills the naval commanders Cai Mao and Zhang Yun because he rules by fear instead of by trust. The difference between Cao Cao and Liu Bei and Zhou Yu's coalition lies in the strategies they use to consolidate homosociality. In the *Red Cliff* films, instead of honoring the notion of "rule by fear" (like Cao Cao), as in most of the Hollywood gangster films, Woo revisits the themes of *yi* and loyalty in homosocial bonds, developed in his early Hong Kong films.

The biggest difference between Woo's version and the widely accepted novel *Romance of the Three Kingdoms* is that he does not focus so much on the legitimacy of Liu Bei's reign.[4] Instead, Woo focuses on the joint effort between Liu Bei and Sun Quan during the Battle of Red Cliff. In the films, Woo develops the relationship between Zhuge Liang (Liu Bei's advisor) and Zhou Yu (Sun Quan's counselor). In the novel, Zhou is portrayed as a very narrow-minded person, so jealous of Zhuge's talent that he eventually dies of jealousy. Woo, however, thinks it was unlikely the two could have united and achieved victory if they were so hostile to each other ("Preparing"). Historic records such as *Records of the Three Kingdoms* support Woo in this assumption (Huang 58–59). In Woo's interpretation, therefore, Zhou and Zhuge admire each other, and their friendship helps the alliance win the war. In *Red Cliff* and its sequel, Woo also depicts the male friendship and homosocial bonds between Zhou Yu and Zhuge Liang. Zhou Yu and Zhuge Liang make plans on how to eliminate Cao Cao's naval commanders Cai Mao and Zhang Yun and produce 100,000 arrows respectively. They agree that whoever fails to complete his task will be punished by military law. The multiple intellectual duels between Zhuge and Zhou during the battle reveal the homosocial bonds, appreciation, and competition between the two male characters. The similarities and differences between the two are also based on the traditional definition of *wen* and *wu* masculinities.

Wen masculinity, demonstrated by scholar-gentlemen, is considered feminine in Hollywood films, as justice is achieved only when cowboys, policemen, and soldiers break the set of rules, demonstrate their adequate masculine physique, and resort to violence. In *Red Cliff* and its sequel, Woo uses the contested site of homosocial bonding to reveal the different nuances of Chinese masculinities that are different from the Hollywood model. Zhuge, in Woo's films, is a scholar-intellectual figure that represents *wen* masculinity as he can shrewdly apply ingenious strategy in war. Zhou Yu is the major hero in the film. He is married to a gentle wife, and his association with music and swordsmanship makes him an admirable hero in the film. He represents an ideal balance of *wen* and *wu* masculinities. Zhou also emphasizes the knowledge that comes with learning as a means of abiding by civil code and avoiding the use of violence.

The films show how the homosocial bondings are destined conditionally by the alliance. Homosocial bonds between Zhou and Zhuge are the site for homogenizing competing and contradictory subjectivities that Woo explores in his Hollywood films such as *Face/Off*, *Mission: Impossible II*, and *Windtalkers*. In *Red Cliff* and its sequel, Woo revisits the theme of homosocial bonding established in his early Hong Kong films such as *A Better Tomorrow*. Both Zhou and Zhuge realize that as the war against Cao Cao ends, they may be at the opposite side of a battle one day. In *Red Cliff* and its sequel, Woo reveals that male homosociality is subject to destabilization in the face of social, ideological, political, and cultural changes, a reality in a global environment.

In *Red Cliff* and its sequel, Xiao Qiao is a gentle wife to Zhou Yu and a motherly figure; when the audience first meets her, she helps to deliver a newborn foal into the world. She is easily settled in being a wife/motherly figure who shows her femininity. Shangxiang is a woman warrior character, taking on a more independent role in choosing her potential mate and fighting off those she finds unworthy of her affection. Shangxiang undertakes the challenge to go undercover in Cao Cao's military base. Xiao Qiao represents the ideal femininity, as even the opponent Cao Cao desires her, and Shangxiang demonstrates martial ability in Woo's masculinist narrative. Whether feminine or masculine, both women adhere to the principle of maintaining their independence from Cao Cao. Thus, Woo demonstrates the conventions of *wu* attributes in the definition of femininity and masculinity.

The battle scene shows not only the spectacle of action choreography but the tactics behind them. As Woo notes: "For me, the *Red Cliff* battle is a story of the weak winning out over the strong, which cannot be achieved without Chinese intelligence, courage and, most importantly, unity. . . . But these Chinese virtues are rarely seen in today's *wuxia*, or martial arts movies—the best perceived genre of Chinese films in international cinema" ("Preparing"). Woo makes the films reveal the Chinese culture and tradition through the *wuxia* genre, deploying the visual effects to demonstrate Chinese symbolism and its visual metaphors. The film also emphasizes the philosophy and strategy of war. Aided by longtime collaborators Corey Yuen, stunt coordinator, and assistant director Patrick Leung, Woo uses computer graphics and spectacular stunt work for his astounding battle scenes, matching the grandeur of Hollywood epics with the poetic intensity of his early films and those of his mentor Zhang Che.

In *Red Cliff*, assembling an impregnable fortress and a vast, unstoppable armada of 2,000 ships, Cao Cao mounts a naval attack to conceal his true intent to invade by land. In response, Zhou and Zhuge design the "Eight Diagrams Formation," an ingenious battle formation drawn from Chinese mythology and war strategy. Massed shields slide open like trap doors as soldiers are dragged to death. The "Eight Diagrams Formation" sequence shows how Cao Cao's army is trapped within the labyrinthine formations of the coalition forces. In *Red Cliff II*, Woo portrays another famous battle scene. After examining the weather that predicts a heavy fog, Zhuge Liang uses an ingenious strategy, known as "borrowing of arrows with straw boats," involving merely a small fleet of twenty boats loaded with straw, hay, and scarecrows under the cover of the thick fog. Cai Mao and Zhang Yun (of Cao's camp), believing enemy forces are attacking, order a barrage of arrows to be fired at the boats. Zhuge Liang fulfills his goal, bringing in over 100,000 arrows.

These battle scenes reveal how the marginal defeats the powerful by using tactics that include deception, timing, positioning, and strategy. In *The Art of War*, Sunzi notes, "Warfare is the Way (Tao) of deception" (168). The coalition outsmarts Cao Cao. Rather than using sheer force, the alliance wins a battle that depends upon strategy of deception instead of size or force, reflected in the essence of *The Art of War*. *The Art of War* is a book of military strategy. Such strategy is affected both by objective conditions in the physical environment and by the subjective opinions of competitive actors in that environment. It requires quick and appropriate responses to changing conditions. Planning works in a controlled—but competitive—environment, opposing plans collide, creating unexpected situations. *Red Cliff* and its sequel retell the David versus Goliath story as the coalition uses tactics and strategy to create ways to crack Cao Cao's forces. The coalition defeats Cao Cao's army physically, mentally, and (most of all) strategically.

Thus, with a vested interest in the relative power between the margin and the center, Woo destabilizes the monolithic subjective position of hegemonic masculinity, including physique and force. Woo in turn contests the ideal masculine model in Hollywood cinema from the subject positions of the Other. In this way, Woo's films show the contested relation between assumed normal masculinity and homosocial bonding in the shifting terrains of politics. His films also demonstrate how with the use of strategy the strong power is defeated by forces that, although they are smaller and weaker, have used tactics and possess high moral ground. These are qualities by which the marginal overcomes the stronger force.

In employing his intellectual capacity for the Hollywood machinery, the two-part epic can be seen as a metaphor for the globalized reality in which filmmakers like Woo live and work. Woo has to equip himself with the skills and knowledge necessary for being a commercially successful filmmaker in a transnational reality. Very often, the filmmaker has to strategize about incorporating his sense of geopolitical difference in his work, and his cosmopolitical endeavor often collides and colludes with the economic and market ideology of blockbuster films.

Face-Off: East and West

Jillian Sandell redefines Steve Neale's argument about "spectacular masculinity," not as homosexual repression or sadistic voyeurism but rather in terms of intimacy and friendship, as Woo's films show ways of reinventing masculinity for the male characters so they are able to express their emotions ("Reinventing"). In fact, Woo has not only invented male characters capable of showing their emotions but has introduced a politics of representing masculinities and stresses the instability and decenteredness of subjectivities in the encounters between the self and the Other in the examples from *Face/Off* (Troy and Archer), *Mission: Impossible II* (Hunt/Ambrose and Nyah), *Windtalkers* (Enders/Yahzee, Anderson/Whitehorse), and *Paycheck* (the narcissistic reflection of the self and its alienated/Othered self).

To many, Woo has brought to Hollywood the possibility of portraying vulnerable, failing, and destroyed male characters (Gates; Sandell, "Reinventing"; Bordwell, *Planet*). Such multivalent representations taken together also dramatize the inequality of races and genders. Hollywood films largely reify the hegemonic construction of gender and sexuality (white heterosexual masculinity as the norm) by subordinating racialized and gendered Others. John Woo's films differ from the generic tradition of war films in mainstream cinema that communicate a dominant ideology of masculinity. Woo targets the terrains of masculinity and the homosocial bonds that constitute histories and struggles; he marks hegemonic masculinity, contests it with Otherness, and makes it visible and problematic.

Gender and ethnic relations are often multidimensional, diverse, and contradictory. It is a system of unequal power relations. White masculinity is constructed and legitimized in the discourse of difference. These differences are often constructed and conventionalized in terms of ethnicity and gender as in *Mission: Impossible II* and *Windtalkers*. The inclusion of the Other results in the destabilization of hegemonic identities, and the manipulation of cosmopolitical knowledge loosens the binary boundaries between self and Other, allowing for multiple sites for the contestation of self-identity and positionality to coexist. In *Red Cliff* and its sequel, Woo reinterprets a famous Chinese battle from the perspectives of homosociality, tactics, and honor and problematizes the Hollywood masculine model as natural, normal, and self-evident. Woo continues to make films produced by Hong Kong/Chinese or Hollywood studios in which the reexamination of popular action genres, including *wuxia*, martial arts, gangster, war, sci-fi, and adventure films, as a cross-cultural marketing strategy is only one strain of his cosmopolitical awareness.

In this chapter, I have examined the ways Woo's films construct heroes from *wuxia* traditions. And I have looked at the seeming naturalness of masculinity in homosocial bonding and at the ways Woo has contested such constructions to challenge the prescriptive norms that contain contradictions within and between a variety of identities and differences. I have investigated the interconnections between martial arts choreography and Woo's action films and also the ways in which Woo has incorporated pathos and styles from different action films, both from the West and from the East, and has manipulated filming techniques, narratives, and styles transnationally. Woo's action films are already a hybrid genre, combining film traditions from different Eastern and Western films, thus fundamentally transforming the style, content, and potential of contemporary action cinema. Are Woo's films the examples of Americanization or Asianization? How do we reimagine these rigid classifications when the two film industries are constantly in the process of cross-fertilizing each other and reinventing themselves? These questions also lead to a larger reconsideration of what it means to be American or Asian. Moreover, the interconnections and intermingling of filmmaking practices across different national, cultural, and historical boundaries also reveal new understandings of self and Other in a global context.

The diverse and different cross-cultural and transnational boundary crossings between Asia and America indicate one example of the many possibilities the subject has to defy the prescriptions of the local or the global. It is therefore important to note the emergence of cosmopolitical consciousnesses, to examine the ways they rework or contest the dialectics of hegemony and counter-hegemony and unearth the ways in which they define and redefine identity politics in the Chinese diaspora and Hollywood. Woo tries to find working power from Hollywood, incorporates his training from film practices both of the East and of the

West, and, more important, unearths the contradictions in mainstream representations. So is Woo a Hong Kong or American director? Is he a director from the East or a director of the West? He is neither and all at the same time. His works have forever transformed the ways *wuxia* films can be imagined, and they contest the ways mainstream Hollywood has portrayed white masculinity in its engagement with the Other. His film practices blur East/West dichotomies and contain within them the contesting and multiple boundaries of history, identity, space, systems of polity, and good and evil.

The ability to know and engage with the intense experience in the paradoxes of home and location is the major attribute of the cosmopolitical consciousness. The need of continuous self-defining and self-revealing is a political means of survival and existence in the changing geopolitics of transnationalism. The subjects question geographical location and the ideological boundary that gives structural and symbolic significance to the subject and his or her human condition. The political subjects embody critical insight, aesthetic inspiration, and a heightened sense of awareness, which are results of the process of taking the knowledge of being at home in the world. They are cosmopolitical in their roots and belonging.

4

JACKIE CHAN AND THE POLITICS
OF COMIC DISPLACEMENT

This chapter examines how transnational martial arts filmmaker and star Jackie Chan embodies and deploys a cosmopolitical perspective in his work. Chan possesses several important qualities that distinguish him from other popular media personalities, including comparable action film figures such as Chow Yun-Fat, Jet Li, and Michelle Yeoh. Since the 1980s, Chan has consistently and dramatically grown in popularity in international media markets, initially in Asia, the United States, and Europe, then the rest of the world, thus indicating his broad appeal across national and cultural lines. Indeed, he is the most commercially successful Asian film personality since Bruce Lee. Largely due to this success, Chan also has asserted a high degree of creative control over his film projects, not only as a star but also as a director, producer, choreographer, and/or writer. This control has enabled him to shape his public image in ways that include engaging with and undermining dominant ideologies involving such categories of identity as Asianness and hegemonic masculinity. Related to these qualities, Chan also exhibits various forms of knowledge and action that are cosmopolitical. Together, these qualities demonstrate that Chan is not an ordinary star, martial artist, or comedian. His complex persona is a significant commercial and ideological force in today's global media landscape.

Chan's cosmopolitical perspective emerged from experiences of displacement in his native Hong Kong and continues to develop in an increasingly transnational environment of media production, distribution, and consumption. His cosmopolitics show how British colonialism, Chinese nationalism, and Western Orientalism and imperialism—along with their associated patriarchal discourses—shaped his complex identity and film persona. Chan has not been a passive victim of these forces but instead has deployed cosmopolitical consciousness strategically in navigating through them, with an inventive flexibility that has enabled him to succeed both commercially and ideologically. His ideological success is not static and absolute but always subject to the complex transnational context where political agency must act with tactical expediency and at times must confront or cooperate to achieve strategic goals. Jackie Chan's transnational filmmaking career provides an opportunity to develop a more nuanced model for human identity, including how agents navigate multiple temporal, spatial, historical, and geopolitical positions, particularly in the global capitalist system, and allows us to examine the paradoxes or contradictions these may engender in colliding and colluding with mainstream ideologies and institutions. With attention to Chan's film trajectory from (neo)colonial Hong Kong to global Hollywood, I address his efforts to achieve and maintain commercial success and to disrupt power inequities, locally and internationally.

Comic Displacement

With displacement as an ongoing condition, Jackie Chan's personal and professional backgrounds have shaped his cosmopolitical consciousness, and vice versa. In Hong Kong, he grew up in a society enduring the legacy of a long history of successive changes: from a fishing village to a British colony, a diaspora of Mainland Chinese immigrants, a global financial city, and then, after 1997, a Special Administrative Region of the People's Republic of China. His early film work in Hong Kong was in an industry that likewise has endured multiple dislocations through globalization, capitalism, colonialism, and the Chinese diaspora. Since the 1980s, he has worked with one significant participant in these dislocations, the Hong Kong film production and distribution company Golden Harvest, which has become a successful exporter of Chinese-language movies throughout Southeast Asia and around the world. Golden Harvest fostered and benefited from Chan's international success as he starred in several top-grossing Asian-produced action movies beginning in the 1980s (Fore, "Golden Harvest" 41, 45). Chan's popularity spread overseas, first in early to mid-1980s Hollywood/Golden Harvest projects including *The Big Brawl*, the *Cannonball Run* series, and *The Protector*, then later with the 1996 American release of *Rumble in the Bronx* (released in Asia in 1994). Chan's comic vision emerges from these experiences of transnational displacement. Overall, culture- and language-based comedy has been a less successful export, largely due to social and cultural differences; however, physical comedy has achieved some success, most notably in Chan's films.

For Chan, comedy is a primary form of expression extending back to his directorial debut, *The Young Master* (1980), which was among the first martial arts films ever to blend action and comedy. In this and subsequent work, Chan has practiced what I would call a "comic displacement." His films make great use of one common trait of comedy, namely the flouting of logic or the laws of probability, with humor often arising from various forms of disparity or displacement. As Geoff King notes, "Comedy can result from a sense of things being out of place, mixed up or not quite right, in various ways. One set of examples is found in films that derive much of their comedy from temporal, geographical or other forms of displacement" (5).

Following King, I argue that a key part of Chan's cosmopolitical perspective and film practice is his comic displacement of hegemonic notions of identity, an approach that capitalizes on his transnational "always both inside and outside" status and his style of action, which is at times active, passive, ambiguous, subversive, creative, and disarmingly playful in relation to hegemonic power and ideologies. Chan constructs transnational humor based on a physical and comedian-centered performance style and contributes to the popular tradition of Chinese comedy, though that tradition has been trivialized by the orthodox and mainstream scholarly/ literary culture (Rao 8). Chan's characters often deviate from hegemonic masculinities displayed by Bruce Lee's stoic heroes, Wong Fei-hung, and John Wayne cowboy figures. His martial comedian personae have crossed various ethnic/national boundaries, both blending ideological sensibilities and playfully critiquing them, sometimes playing one against the other. Chan's comic displacement of hegemonic practices is integrated with martial arts, a form that has a close cross-disciplinary relationship with both theater and film.

Chan's northern kung fu fighting style derives from his rigorous theater training at the China Drama Academy, which began at age six and was accompanied by music and dance instruction. His martial comedian persona can be traced back to the theatrical tradition of the *wu-chou*, or martial clown/acrobatic comic role, in which action heroes perform a combination of acrobatics, stage fighting, and comic acting (Liu 191). As with the *wu-chou*, Chan embodies the skills of comic acting, takes pleasure in breaking dramatic stage conventions, and "plays at being the 'other'" to standard hero roles (Riley 270). He creates comical fights that are more flexible and acrobatic than the straightforward martial arts practice of traditional stoic martial hero figures such as Bruce Lee. As Lee described this traditional sensibility, "The application of the theory of Yin/Yang in Gung Fu [kung fu] is known as the Law of Harmony, in which one should be in harmony with, and not against, the force of the opponent" (82). The notion of *yin* and *yang* as a reciprocal interchange (*bian*) is a major theme in Asian philosophy and martial arts, as a way to both view the world and act in it, in the latter case by consolidating one's force while knowing when and how to attack or evade opponents. In his films, Jackie Chan does not simply deploy this philosophy but instead practices a more complex form of *za-shua*, or mixed acrobatics:

> While making films in Hollywood during the 1980s, the American directors commented that I did not appear to be as powerful and invincible as Bruce Lee, because Lee usually one-punch defeated his opponent. My character falls down, gets hurt, and fights back. I incorporate people and objects in my choreography so as to attack and defend. When making films in Hong Kong, I learned to adapt my fighting skills and use the camera to capture motion under any circumstances. I am not only a martial artist, but a choreographer, director, producer and editor. [Comedy] is what makes me different. (personal interview)

Chan's adaptability and comic sensibility have not only contributed to his commercial success but also yielded a more complex alternative to Bruce Lee's fighting style and exploration of themes of masculinity and Chinese nationalism in films such as *The Chinese Connection* (1972) and *Return of the Dragon* (1974). Mark Gallagher notes that, "[p]hysically, Chan incorporates into action-oriented narratives the burlesque body fundamental to comedy. His body's continuous motion, feminised through its implied vulnerability, calls into question conceptions of the ideal male body" (119). However, Chan problematizes conceptions of masculinity not simply through feminization but also through the broader approach of displacement. Chan's fighting style displaces Lee's idealized masculinity with a more complex and dynamic model that includes momentarily being in feminized/vulnerable situations in order to ultimately overcome, control, and strike back more powerfully.

As Yvonne Tasker observes, "Chan's 'softness' does not consist of a lack of masculinity or an inability to fight, but more in a refusal either to take the male body too seriously or play the part of the Oriental other" ("Fist" 334). This occurs, for example, in the *Drunken Master* films (1978, 1994) in which Chan plays the kung fu hero Wong Fei-hung as a troublesome youth. The incorporation of women (such as the female fairy Ho) and Chan's comical drunken fighting style in these films undermine the cultural and political discourse of the folklore hero as well as the idealized masculine persona of Lee and other martial film heroes. In *Drunken Master* and its sequel, Chan's character strives to pass as a woman and drunkard not only to trick his opponents but also to distance himself (and audiences) from the rigid norms of heroic masculinity governed by fatherhood and patriarchy embodied by the likes of Kwan Tak-hing and later Jet Li (during the 1990s) in their famous Wong Fei-hung personifications.

Chan's Wong Fei-hung character is a performative transgression and mimicry of the traditional kung fu hero. The powerless young man (the oppressed), rather than submitting himself completely to his father or to authority, subverts the father figure's role by becoming a drunkard. Chan's Wong Fei-hung uses the grotesque style of the drunken body to undermine the typical constitution of a kung fu hero as a patriarchal and fatherly figure, the essential guide to a heroic notion of Chineseness. The fatherly figure becomes the object of mimicry and transgression. The love/hate relationship with the patriarchal father figure is therefore foregrounded in the *Drunken Master* movies in the disguise of drunkenness. Chan fleshes out an image of compulsory masculinity imposed on the disobedient child. Chan's performance derives from a series of improvisations incorporating kung fu and acrobatics. The training process shows physically how a mischievous young man learns the master's skills and accedes to his master's position by preserving and subverting the full range of movements in the kung fu tradition with a repetitive difference. Although the symbolic order induces patriarchal masculinity as the norm, parody and improvisation might subvert it. Chan not only stresses his determination in his torturous apprenticeship to train his body but also endures the suffering with comic relief and good humor.

With the popularity of *Snake in the Eagle's Shadow* and *Drunken Master*, Chan successfully established himself as a new kung fu action film star and also created the genre "kung-fu comedy" (Shek, "Development" 35–36). Chan, who displayed pain and weakness, contrasted with the already recognized images of Bruce Lee as the indomitable, undefeatable martial artist whose injuries only gave him more strength. For example, Chan would wince when facing an opponent triple his size and would risk injuries in his daring stunts. In what would be the two major trademarks of his films, Chan would act out death-defying stunts, drawing on his opera training and stunt work, and outtake sequences in which various mistakes in the stunt work were shown would play during the end credits. The mimicry and contestation of hegemonic masculinity is intrinsic to Chan's later works, as he destabilizes and disrupts the general expectation of the kung fu patriarchal, masculine figure and subversively undermines it with parody and laughter. Chan's boundary crossing and indirection comically destabilize the more serious or hegemonic masculinity embodied by his opponents in the *Drunken Master* films and his cinematic forerunner, Bruce Lee. Chan's martial clown persona and parodic masculinity make for a comical displacement that disrupts rigid notions of identity.

Almost sixteen years after his initial success with *Drunken Master*, which helped launch his career, Chan revisited the role as young Wong Fei-hung in *Drunken Master II* (aka *The Legend of the Drunken Master*), which is about British colonialists and their Chinese associates stealing and smuggling valuable Chinese artifacts and treasures to Britain.[1] This was at the height of Jet Li and Tsui Hark's popular collaborations in the Wong Fei-hung film series (1991–93). Whereas Jet Li's empowering Chinese martial arts in the *Once Upon a Time in China* series merely affirmed "Chinese-ness as a 'national style'" in the face of imperialist oppression (Teo, "Tsui Hark" 153), Chan used the drunken style to find the best position to attack his opponent in a comical manner and undermined such inscription of patriarchal masculinity and the Jet Li character's strong association with Chinese nationalism. In this regard, Chan's character, with his adoption of animal gestures, drunken postures, and comic personae that mock even his own father, symbolically and comically contests fatherhood, hegemonic masculinity, and Chinese nationalism that would have been unlikely in Jet Li's version.

Chan's Wong is a mischievous son who, while traveling with his father, gets in trouble when the evil Chinese associates dressed in Western-style suits steal the national treasures to export to the West. Wong Fei-hung gets involved when he accidentally acquires a jade seal in a suitcase mix-up. The sequel to *Drunken Master* was made ten years after the Joint Declaration in 1984 between China and the United Kingdom that decided the future of Hong Kong. At this time, more Hong Kong films began to deal with the uniqueness of Hong Kong's culture and identity, since many filmmakers, including Tsui Hark, for instance, modified the use of monolithic allegories of "nation" and "Chineseness" to grasp the accelerated social and political change before and during the 1997 transition.

In *Drunken Master II*, Chan's Wong Fei-hung uses the drunken fist to fight his opponents. Although Chan in his drunken style seems to be in a sleepy, half-awake state, his skills in martial arts are not to be underestimated. In fact, "drunken fist" in this sense is a disguise. With faltering steps and stumbling body, Chan raises a jar and pours out wine for himself, wriggling and staggering along, as if on the verge of falling. In the fight, Chan lights fire with his alcohol spit and smashes crates to reveal his excess energy. He fights in a loose, fluid style that is the foundation of drunken boxing. The sequence is acrobatic, as Chan's Wong Fei-hung moves swiftly from childish inebriation to delirious madness. In comparison to the first *Drunken Master* film, Yuen Woo-ping's choreography and Chan's performance show more clearly the inspiration of the drunken style with a mixture of acrobatics and action choreography that helped launch their success.

In *Drunken Master II*, the drunken style has become more a part of the choreographic style. In the fight scene in the steel factory, Chan's character accidentally drinks grain alcohol instead of wine, and his fighting style becomes furious. Chan moves with extreme dexterity, power, and coordination, although his style and his bodily movements are grotesque in appearance. Instead of finding the most vulnerable spot to hit his opponent, Chan's fight choreography unfolds with rhythmic precision, coordination, and continuity. He attacks his opponent from unlikely positions, such as when he falls to the ground and launches an attack with his leg to the back of his opponent's head. Chan, as if drunk, impersonates females, children, and madness, winning the last battle. It is in this interpretive shuffle between innocence and mischief, drunkenness and the performance of drunkenness, that countertexts of disguise and consciousness are enacted. The drunken style becomes a form of reflexive consciousness, a "drunken consciousness," in which Chan chooses not to reveal his own identity as a martial artist fully aware of his environment and only pretending to be drunk.

Drunken Master II is Chan's statement on the uniqueness of Hong Kong's culture and identity. Set in 1913, Chan stops the British, along with their Chinese associates, from stealing artifacts and saves the nation from losing its treasures to the colonialists. Chan does not present a nationalist figure of Wong Fei-hung as Jet Li's version does; instead, Chan's Wong navigates his role within the Chinese nationalist formations of masculinity circulating at a time when China had a semicolonial status with the advance of Western imperialist interests. Specifically, in comparison with other more serious patriarchal representations of Wong Fei-hung, whose love interest is Aunt Yee and whose fighting style is the heroic exponent of "no shadow kicking" and lion dancing as exemplified by Jet Li, Jackie Chan draws on the deceptively laughable drunken style with its bilateral attack and defense disguise, Chinese opera training, and acrobatics to transform his portrayal of Wong, but he ultimately retains a deep ambivalence toward him.

Jackie Chan's Wong Fei-hung initiates different ways in dealing with such notions of nationalism and Chineseness. In discussing the film's identity politics, Steve Fore notes: "*Drunken Master II* is a contradictory film in that it is simultaneously Chan's last unambiguously 'local' film to date (in terms of the geographical setting and the incorporation of somewhat culturally specific values and narrative threads) and implicitly a denial of the Hong Kong identity 'movement' of the past decade and a half" ("Life" 137). Even though Fore suggests that *Drunken Master II* is unambiguously "local," it is culturally specific to Chinese tradition, unlike Chan's other films, such as *Project A* and its sequel, which pay tribute to Harold Lloyd's *Safety Last* (1923), Buster Keaton's *Steamboat Bill, Jr.* (1928), or *Police Story III: Supercop*, set in transnational locations. *Drunken Master II* is fixed in a local Chinese geographical setting. Rather than arguing it is a denial of the Hong Kong "identity movement" in an attempt to be international and global, however, I suggest that what is considered "culturally specific" is itself continuously contested, and the binary of the local/global at the basis of Fore's argument is not rigid but extremely fluid.

At the end of the film, the British ambassador does not fight for the treasures the British stole but rather flees before the final confrontation. Chan is left to fight with the Chinese associates who work for the British. The Chinese associates, dressed in Western suits, provide a visual symbolization of their Westernization, in contrast to Chan, who dresses in traditional Chinese clothes as he fights the British colonialists who have tried to steal parts of the Chinese cultural heritage and take advantage of the Chinese people. Drunken style in this film has merged boxing, wrestling, drunkenness, and acting skill (comical moves and expressions) into an organic whole. Chan's investment in the cultural dimension of Chineseness can be seen in his drunken style–inspired fight-dance to protect the national treasures of China. However, Chan also negotiates with the regulatory forces of cultural identifications with playfulness, revealing the contrasting positions of nationalism, belonging, and ideas of citizenship. In this case, Chan's playful, drunken style of martial arts reflects his comic displacement of multiple cultural inscriptions as well as his cosmopolitical perspective toward hegemonic forces.

Chan does not actually fight with the British colonialists in a simple anti-Western form of narrative; rather, he displaces a generalized,

Westernized notion of Chineseness that the Chinese associates embody and impose on Hong Kong. Chan's character finishes his combat and demonstrates his masculinity mixed with a mimetic refinement of the patriarchal figure. His comical portrayal of a kung fu hero is parodic of patriarchal codes and national identity. The fight between images of "local" and "translocal" Chineseness generates more contrasts and ambivalence, because Hong Kong was historically an emblem of the British imperialist invasion of China in the 1880s and was going to transfer from British to Chinese sovereignty in 1997.

Rather than indulging in the allegory of nation as the ultimate ground of deterritorialization and reterritorialization, the transformation of Jackie Chan's screen persona from kung fu hero in a historical setting to the hero Wong Fei-hung, who tries to situate himself in a web of social forces, shows the ideologies that permeated and surrounded the film at the time of its production. Hong Kong was to be handed over to China in 1997. The territory was at once too local and too global to be assimilated into official Mandarin Mainland culture. Another example of such disparity between local/global and national identity can be seen in Chan's *Supercop*. In a notable fight scene in this film, Jackie Chan is sent as a Hong Kong "Supercop" to work with the Mainland police force targeting a Mainland/Hong Kong drug operation. Chan's partner in this film, a Mainland woman cop played by Michelle Yeoh, accompanies him undercover to infiltrate the drug gang and destroy the operation from the jungles of Thailand to the city of Kuala Lumpur in Malaysia.

In the first encounter between Chan and the Mainland police force, a casually dressed Chan walks into a meeting with the officers who wear neat, official uniforms. The officers tease him as a "Supercop" from Hong Kong. The contrast in dress is a visual symbolization of Chan's different values as a "hybrid" Chinese from the British colony. As a Hong Kong policeman under British rule, Chan symbolizes a subject too hybridized and therefore too delocalized to be considered and included in the official account of Chineseness.

In the film, Yeoh's character as a Mainland cop is able to strike both strong and fluid martial arts poses in her fights. Yeoh represents the inversion of the common gender category with her presentation of an official and military drill style of Chineseness. Moreover, Chan's agile masculinity enables the emergence of such a strong female character as Yeoh to appear alongside him and allows the more complex discourses of historical and political struggle to emerge. In one scene, Yeoh puts Chan to the test and asks him to fight a *qigong* (a form of Chinese martial arts as well as physical and mental training for health) master in the Mainland police force. The *qigong* martial artist in the Mainland police force in *Supercop* also embodies a harsh fighting style in comparison to Chan's alternately feminine and masculine style. Aaron Anderson comments on the different fighting styles: "The dual nature of this movement [*yin* and *yang*, feminine and masculine] is further amplified through other elements in the scene codified as Chinese yang aggression against Hong Kong yin agility. Thus, these movements may also be read as transmitting aspects of an underlying anxiety about the then impending 1997 return of Hong Kong to communist China" (par. 57). Instead of seeing China as *yang* and Hong Kong as *yin*, Jackie Chan adopts at times "masculine" (harsh, fierce hits) and at other times "feminine" (agile, seemingly unintimidating strikes) styles, as he does in the drunken style, in order to find the best positionality to launch an effective attack in the moment. Being the object of awe and laughter, Chan uses his dexterous movements to displace the rigid norms of patriarchal masculinity embodied by the Mainland officer. He is continuously transgressive, becoming a constant reminder of his own displacement and that of his body's liminality. Chan contests the symbolic figure of a harsh masculinity that the naturalized patriarchal system depends on to maintain its nationalist ideological structures. His eclectic and comic transgressions generate multiple meanings regarding cultural citizenship, belonging, and Chineseness. Chan disrupts the general expectation of the kung fu patriarchal, masculine figure, undermining it with a humorous persona and comic actions. In this and other films, his comic personae perform alternative models of masculinity, and his cosmopolitical endeavor challenges notions of what Chineseness and Asianness mean on the local and transnational landscape.

The Performative Body

Jackie Chan's comic displacement of hegemonic paradigms relies upon the body as an instrument of transgression. Expanding upon the work of Linda Williams, Leon Hunt calls martial arts cinema a "body genre," or a form that is like pornography, horror, and melodrama in that it emphasizes the "display of sensations that are on the edge of respectable [as] the body of the spectator [is] caught up in an almost involuntary mimicry of emotion or sensation of the body on screen" (2). As with Williams and Hunt, I also take the "low" genre of the martial arts film seriously for its ability to offer visual and kinesthetic pleasures as well as ideas and images that can explore and challenge social norms. However, a problem with Hunt's view of the martial arts film as a body genre is that the statement risks being ethnocentric in the minimization of cultural and historical specificities, including the pre-cinematic origins of martial arts as well as how they have been translated into and developed in different national and regional cinemas.

The body in Hong Kong–produced kung fu films is not only a device of spectacle but also the physical enactment of the philosophy of martial arts as a discipline of self-defense and confrontation. Martial arts action films may typically offer the "universal fantasy [of] an escape from gravity and 'the real of flesh,'" but Hong Kong–produced films are distinct in their tendency to foreground the uniting of mind and body in heroic fantasies of the body equipped with mental/spiritual techniques to fight against profound national, political, and social inequality and oppression (Bordwell, *Planet* 220). Such distinctions matter, though so do the overlaps. Martial arts films have generally depicted performance styles that are highly transnational, created to appeal across diverse cultural borders, especially with Jackie Chan, whose fighting techniques freely combine East and West in what he has termed "an international body language" (personal interview). Chan's range of performance styles is grounded not only in his theater training but also in martial styles including hapkido, judo, and karate as well as sports more commonly associated with the West, including boxing, skiing, and motorcycling—thus giving him the versatility necessary to appeal to global audiences (personal interview). Rather than being simply a "body genre," Chan's films deploy the body as what I consider to be a "site of performative enunciation," in which he combines varied performance styles with a knowledge of Asian philosophy and the body's signifying potential to enunciate a cosmopolitical sensibility that entertains diverse audiences while also providing a model of creative and expressive agency. In *Shanghai Knights* (2003), for example, when Chan's character uses an umbrella to fight his opponents with fluid acrobatics as the melody of "Singin' in the Rain" plays in the background, he is not evoking the famous song and dance number simply for its own sake but performing a creative act of improvisation that uses immediately available resources to achieve tactical and ultimately strategic goals.

Like the slapstick comedians to whom he often pays homage, Chan's characters use settings, objects, and costumes as devices that serve their interests while also eliciting awe or laughter from audiences. Chan's skills in stunts and martial arts, however, move beyond the fact that the slapstick comedians often were, as Peter Kramer indicates, "the victims of unintentional physical mishaps involving other people, treacherous objects" (104). Chan shows contemporary audiences how one may act cosmopolitically, manipulating—instead of being manipulated by—technologies and institutions, whether they be physical objects like automobiles or ideas and practices like nationalism and patriarchy. In *Police Story IV: First Strike* (1996), Chan turns a ladder into a weapon to fend off opponents, while in *Mr. Nice Guy* (1997), he battles behind the wheel of a 120-ton mining truck, finally driving the truck over an enormous fleet of cars, including Rolls-Royces, before destroying an entire mansion—thus both literally and symbolically confronting capital, if in a playful manner that is nonthreatening for audiences. In each case, Chan's body is a tool that links his ingenuity to his surroundings so as to further his cosmopolitical goals. Thus empowered, his body cannot be contained but instead becomes a vibrant site of performative enunciation that exercises agency and mediation within and among dominant structures.

Another example is *Project A II* (1987, written and directed by Chan), a sequel that revisits Chan's role as Sergeant Dragon Ma, this time in a nostalgic story set in Hong Kong's colonial period during the 1890s (prior to the 1911 revolution that overthrew the Imperial Qing Dynasty in China). The final scene evokes Buster Keaton's *Steamboat Bill, Jr.*, in which Keaton as a deadpan yet humorous victim narrowly escapes the collapse of a house. In *Project A II*, Dragon not only (and miraculously) outruns a falling ceremonial wall structure but also uses it as a weapon to destroy his opponent, a British loyalist and corrupt cop. Soon, when another ceremonial wall falls, Dragon just misses getting crushed by passing through a paper window as the rest of the facade falls around him, thereby generating dramatic and comic relief as he narrowly escapes. It is ideologically provocative when the film first depicts Chan's character turning the imposing infrastructure to his advantage as a weapon, then evades the potential affirmation of patriarchal masculinity by depicting his body in a situation vulnerable to his opponent and over which he has little or no control. In this and other films, Chan effectively navigates between different political and social forces while his comic persona retains a deep ambivalence toward them by playing one power against the other. Perpetually adept and flexible, Chan's body performatively enunciates its displacement of political constituencies that try to categorize and hence limit him. Chan's inventive and resilient cosmopolitical sensibility successfully navigates multiple ideological, political, and physical forces, allowing his films to appeal to diverse audiences.

Established as a martial arts hero in Hong Kong films, Chan temporarily put aside his subversive comedian persona when he made the transition to Hollywood projects in the 1980s. His first wave of such projects included *The Big Brawl* by Robert Clouse, who also directed Bruce Lee in *Enter the Dragon*. Clouse, determined to find the next Bruce Lee, placed Jackie Chan in 1930s Chicago. Chan plays Jerry, a new immigrant to old Chinatown in Chicago, who helps protect his father's restaurant. Domenici, a mobster, forces Jerry to represent him in a battle in Texas. Unlike Chan's other roles during this period, Jerry is tough and not particularly comical. Clouse presents Chan in the Bruce Lee mold, having him mimic Lee's trademark scream in his fights.

Chan also has a white female love interest in the film (played by Kristine DeBell), which is common for the Caucasian hero in films but in sharp contrast with the many portrayals of asexual Asian males in American cinema. This "Americanization" of Chan's image follows the model of conventional white male action stars such as Sylvester Stallone and Jean-Claude Van Damme, who generally have female love interests in their films.

If the image of the Asian martial arts fighter is generally considered only at best "asexual," without heterosexual love and sexual relationships in Hollywood films, Chan's 2005 Hong Kong project *The Myth* confronts such a notion with a cross-national paradigm shift, destabilizes the workings of the asexual martial artist stereotype in a global Hollywood context, and redefines the definition of martial masculinity in the Chinese setting. In this film, Chan plays a warrior/archaeologist who has a romantic relationship with a princess.

In Chan's Hong Kong films of the early 1980s, however, there is rarely a female role or oversexualized figure. Instead of dominating heterosexual love relations with physical, economic, or political power, Chan defines masculinity through empowerment of the body. His transnational stardom represents a geopolitical intervention that tackles the representations of Asians in Hollywood and the discourses surrounding masculinity in American and Hong Kong action films. His character in *The Big Brawl* strongly contrasts with his image established in *Drunken Master* that manages to face defeat only to manipulate his flexibility and strike back tenfold stronger.

Later, Chan took part in the Hollywood projects *The Cannonball Run* (1981) and *Cannonball Run II* (1984), appearing only briefly as a Japanese racecar driver. The two films allow him to showcase his martial arts skills but not his more ambiguous and subversive rendition of the martial comedian character in action film. Chan plays the foreigner who cannot speak English. He appears only as one of Burt Reynolds's sidekicks who is soon forgotten. But while Hollywood tries to put Chan into roles that reinforce the perceptions of Asians as immigrants or foreigners, his screen personas in Hong Kong films diverge from such Orientalist stereotypes. In Hong Kong, Jackie Chan's films transform from the early kung fu works set in late-nineteenth-century China to later films set in colonial Hong Kong. Such transitions are significant, since historical China was the generally preferred background for kung fu films, but later the background changed to modern Hong Kong in Chan's *Police Story* films (1985–2004).

Jackie Chan successfully changed his image of a kung fu fighter to that of a policeman when he appeared in Sammo Hung's *Winners and Sinners* (1983). His next project in Hollywood was *The Protector*, in which he plays an Asian American cop (Billy Wong) teamed up with Danny Aiello; the two embark on a mission to Hong Kong in search of a rich business-man's kidnapped daughter, in the process uncovering and squashing a drug trafficking ring. Although the film is packed with action and stunts, it downplays Chan's martial arts skills and his acting ability, compared to his Hong Kong work of the same period. In his early films produced in Hong Kong, Chan performed without having to prove or deny his Asianness to audiences. His transition to Hollywood projects in the 1980s caused him to temporarily collude with power, as he was compelled to play traditional roles that merely reinforced perceptions of Asians as immigrants or foreigners.

The repertoire of additional Asian male stereotypes in American cul-ture includes coolies, turn-of-the-century laborers, bachelors, laundry men, gardeners, bellboys, houseboys, grocers, and restaurant workers. The martial artist is another stereotype, which extends historically at least back to *Mr. Moto's Last Warning* (1939), in which Peter Lorre plays a yellow-faced Japanese detective able to defeat strong white men with his martial arts combat skills. This stereotype became widely popular in the 1970s with the success of Bruce Lee's movies and has been per-petuated in films such as *Dragon: The Bruce Lee Story* (1993) and most of Jackie Chan's work.

Where possible, when Jackie Chan has played stereotypes, he has done so in ways that undermined their most reprehensible qualities. When he played a cop in *The Protector*, for example, Chan was dissatis-fied with director James Glickenhaus's action sequences. By the mid-1980s, however, Chan had achieved enough clout to re-shoot and re-edit many sequences for a version to be distributed in Asia, thus providing a more palatable version for this audience and a form of resistance to Hollywood's stereotyping and condescension (personal interview). In the

American version, the white fighter is privileged in his subjectivity as well as in his physical stature, appearing giant-like compared to Chan, who is portrayed as a tiny Asian male running for shelter. In the end, Chan's character wins mostly due to luck, as his opponent is electrocuted when he punches an electric saw into a power circuit. Chan's revised version depicts points of view from both Chan's character and the white fighter that express a relative equality in subjectivity. When Chan knocks down his opponent, slow motion is used to emphasize the power of his strike. And the eventual victory of Chan's character is more deserved, as he is more resourceful, using available objects and bouncing off a wire fence to attack his opponent.

Though Chan still is portrayed as a relatively tiny figure, he wins because of his better wits and skills in a sort of David and Goliath scenario, which diverges from common portrayals of white masculinity dominating through size and brutality, as in the American version of this film and other Hollywood action films from *Rocky* to *True Lies* (1994). Presented with a condescending source text, Chan was able to soften and in some ways reverse its ethnocentrism. In this and other productions, Chan has applied a sophisticated knowledge of both the techniques and politics of fight choreography in ways that please audiences while also challenging dominant ideologies. Though lacking the comic displacement and subversive performances of Chan's Hong Kong films, such as *Drunken Master* or *Project A,* his Asian version of *The Protector* is an instance of cross-boundary transgression and resistance to Hollywood's traditional film narrative and style. The ability to shift and take the best positionality as a point of intervention and resistance reflects his cosmopolitical cinematic consciousness.

Jackie Chan also made a statement by filming his own version of cop action in Hong Kong with his *Police Story* (1985), a nonstop action thriller with humor that he directed and choreographed and in which he stars, and many more sequels. Chan as the director for *Police Story* changed the action genre represented by *Dirty Harry* (1971) and *The French Connection* (1971) in the combination of martial arts, stunt work, and humor never before seen in Hong Kong and Hollywood action films. *Police Story* begins with the spectacle of Chan ripping through Hong Kong's hillside shantytown and tearing it down. The drug baron Chu Tao flees capture, but Chan stops his runaway bus by standing fearlessly in front of the approaching vehicle. As the bus resumes its movement, Chan hooks onto it with an umbrella handle. The film makes use of the familiar characters of drug dealers and corrupt cops with intricate fight sequences.

In *Police Story*, the spectacular stunt work includes Chan sliding down a high pole covered with electric lights in a shopping mall. Battling huge machines that impose the threat of the violence of modern technology on the body is a common theme in Jackie Chan's films. Chan's knowledge and bodily skills always triumph. His body becomes the weapon that confronts machinery, technological threats, and catastrophes. But the idea of the battle is not limited to high-rise buildings and large vehicles. He interacts with the establishment of modern technology that produces high-rise buildings, skyscrapers, and machines or with such vehicles as motorcycles, buses, trains, and helicopters. Chan's agility and his body's liminality cannot be contained by the boundaries of his own body; rather, he embraces and exploits every object in his environment.

In the filmmaking process, the transnational in fact permeates the local in *Police Story* and its sequels, and Chan's heroes are no longer from the early colonial period but live in modern times. Chan is a police officer who believes in honor and selflessness instead of personal gain. His character is not unlike the wandering *xia* in search of adventure living by a set of morals different from society's. He disregards the values imposed by the authority and instead chooses to follow his own conscience. Thus, in *Police Story* he insists on completing his case, even though he is expelled from the police force.

Similarly, in *Police Story II* (1988), he intervenes in terrorist bombers' plan to blow up a mall, even though he is no longer a police officer. In the film, Chan continues to experiment with death- and gravity-defying stunts and combines martial arts skills with cop action. Chan developed his own version of a policeman and extended the film from the usual gunfire and explosions of American action films to martial arts stunt work. This role then brought him entry into the American market in 1996 in the Hong Kong film *Rumble in the Bronx*.

Jackie Chan's comic personae playfully work against power and hegemony. Stanley Tong's *Rumble in the Bronx* was Chan's first major theatrical release stateside in the 1990s. Chan plays Keung, a Hong Kong cop excelling in martial arts, who travels to New York to help his uncle Bill with his Bronx grocery store. After Keung arrives, he finds out his uncle is getting married, retiring, and selling his store to a lady named Elaine. Once Elaine opens the store, a gang in the area demands protection money from her. Keung helps Elaine fight off the gang, but this leads only to more vandalism of Elaine's property and also gets her mixed up with a mobster's diamond smuggling scheme. Keung is a typical *xia* character who fights honorably against a motorcycle gang, protects a store, helps a girl and her wheelchair-bound little brother, and pilots a hovercraft. In the film, Keung fights his opponents, including a gang led by Tony in the ghetto.

Scholars have long related kung fu films to the ghetto. Stuart Kaminsky, for example, describes Bruce Lee's success as a "ghetto figure" and sees Lee's films as "ghetto myth" (137–45). Verina Glaessner talks about the ghetto roots of the genre in the lower-class poverty and social unrest of 1960s Hong Kong in the book *Kung Fu: Cinema of Vengeance*. Gina Marchetti notes that Jackie Chan transformed himself into a Hollywood star with *Rumble in the Bronx* and *Rush Hour* without severing his ties to Hong Kong, Japan, and non-Asian fans by creating a "ghetto myth" of transnational multiculturalism. Jackie Chan represents "the new American Dream of 'flexible citizenship,' and, as an icon, he symbolizes a white washing of ghetto culture for global, postmodern consumerism" (Marchetti, "Jackie Chan" 157). Drawing on Michel Foucault's notion of subjectification, Aihwa Ong uses the notion of "flexible citizenship" to understand the different regulatory forces that set the criteria for belonging and an idea of citizenship in both the nation-state and the global economy (*Flexible Citizenship* 6, 112–13, 117). Ong's "flexible citizenship" alludes to the mobility of the groups she examined under the disciplinary forces that different social, racial, or gendered categories exert and to which they subject citizens. Marchetti uses the example of Jackie Chan to make a connection here between the multiculturalist perspective on cultural diversity in the American context and transnationalism. Laleen Jayamanne also notes that in *Rush Hour* and *Rush Hour II*, Chan has "the kinship ties" with African Americans and "proper Asian sanction of an elder to cross phobic ethnic boundaries and tap diverse markets at the same time" (155, 159). However, instead of "flexible citizenship" that alludes to American multiculturalism and "kinship ties" that "tap diverse markets," I argue that Chan continues to make films produced by Hong Kong/Chinese or Hollywood studios in which the cultivation of a martial arts subculture with ties to the African American community as a cross-cultural marketing strategy is only one strain of his cosmopolitical awareness.

If Jackie Chan had to struggle and compromise with ethnocentric sensibilities in his earlier Hollywood work, by the 1990s, with films like *Rush Hour*, he could act more decisively, knowing that "I am on the same level with the biggest Hollywood stars because of my international success. Tom Hanks even coined my films as 'Chan-tastic!' I am the co-producer for my Hollywood films which gives me control over my screen image as well as influence during the editing process" (personal interview). *Rush Hour* updated his image as a Hong Kong policeman from the highly successful *Police Story* series of films with a character who worked with a clear mission in the United States. In *Rush Hour*, Chan plays Lee, a cop from Hong Kong, who partners with Carter, an African American policeman.

As with other popular mixed-race buddy films, the humor in *Rush Hour* often derives from cultural misconceptions and miscommunication, as when Lee imitates Carter and gets into trouble by greeting an African American as "nigger." In another scene, Lee pretends that he does not speak or understand English. Chan's character plays with the stereotypical misrecognition of Asians as perpetual foreigners, first through self-imposed silence and then by making fun of Carter's presumptions about Asians. *Rush Hour II* (2001) picks up where its prequel leaves off, with Carter traveling to Hong Kong for a vacation, and reverses the situation, with Carter now lost in the "Pearl of the Orient," put in the similar comic circumstances of being the foreign Other. Just as Lee tried to understand the ways of America, Carter now experiences culture shock as he fumbles through the streets of Hong Kong. In a massage parlor, for example, he unknowingly insults a Hong Kong gang leader, which leads him and Lee into a fight with the gang. The film allows an alternative perspective on the issue of ethnocentrism that makes Carter the clueless Other in an unfamiliar location. The latest entry in the series, *Rush Hour III*, transposes the action from Hong Kong to Paris, which becomes a transnational site of comic transgression. In one scene, a French cab driver refuses to drive Carter around Paris because he reviles Americans' violent behavior and participation in the wars with Iraq and Vietnam. Later, the cab driver abandons his anti-American attitude and, like an American superspy, revels in the glory of "shoot[ing] strangers for no reason." The film self-consciously pokes fun at Hollywood's action genre and its violent messages.

One aspect of Chan's cosmopolitical sensibility manifest in the *Rush Hour* series and other films involves the end credits sequences. End credits featuring outtakes have become common in Hollywood comedies and action films, at least since *The Cannonball Run*. But Chan's films famously show outtakes of stunts that went wrong, with all their stumbles, whacked arms, and twisted ankles. Audiences often look forward to these credits sequences in order to see outtakes that are entertaining and that also, in a sense, undermine and critique what came before them. Kwai-Cheung Lo notes that "it is precisely the outtakes of the flubbed stunts that create the myth of Jackie Chan. Portrayed as a comedian, a common man in the films, Chan becomes a superhero in his outtakes" (Lo, "Muscles" 117). In fact, Chan's outtakes are more complex, not simply signifying a super-heroic performer but also disrupting easy identification with his screen persona by revealing the carefully constructed performativity of his feats along with other paradoxes of his persona. Thus, his body becomes the performative site of enunciation and contests inscriptions of superhuman skills or fixed knowable identities affirmed in the film narrative.

Rush Hour's end credits, for example, show Chan's stunt work blunders as well as verbal wordplay that counters notions of Asians as inarticulate perpetual foreigners. When Chris Tucker tries to pronounce a line in Chinese and first forgets and then mispronounces it, Chan teases him by saying, "Now you can see how difficult it is for me to speak in English. He [Tucker] cannot even say three words in Chinese! Ha! Ha!" Chan's trickster-like persona humorously reveals Tucker in the awkward situation of attempting a foreign language. *Rush Hour II*'s end credits reverse the situation and reveal that Tucker mispronounces "gefilte fish," and Chan teases him by saying that Tucker cannot even speak English. In the end credits outtakes of *Rush Hour III*, Chan mispronounces "secret service." Tucker engages in an endless and fruitless struggle with the name of the fast-food chain "El Pollo Loco," and eventually Chan out-smarts Tucker by pronouncing the words correctly. Such moments reveal Chan's cosmopolitical consciousness as the performative identity of an Asian actor, director, and producer in Hollywood, having to be aware of and to negotiate with different ethnocentric contexts and to speak English in order to appeal to audiences and gain access to mainstream film productions.[2] The end credits also destabilize verbal wordplay and mispronunciation as the essentialized attributes of Asian subjects. The now-famous end credits sequences in Chan's films create space and po-tential for unanticipated commentary in *Rush Hour* and its sequels. The multiple nuances reflected in the end credits of Chan's films enable such suppressed narratives to return and converse with the major film texts.

Jackie Chan's films engage with different national and transnational contexts that do not confine identity to a singular frame of race, ethnicity, or nation. The cosmopolitical subject travels in the transnational arena, often signaling discrepancies and traversing gaps among different social, political, and cultural contexts in the Chinese diaspora, Hollywood, and beyond. As a filmmaker and star who is identified with transna-tional practices, Chan emerges as a cosmopolitical subject who applies the tactics of comic displacement to traverse normative national identity geopolitically, culturally, and commercially.

Mimetic Politics

As we already have begun to see, Jackie Chan's cosmopolitical approach to cinema includes mimicking or parodying oppressive forces, often contesting them. In Homi Bhabha's discussion of the colonial context, mimicry can serve as a political instrument for provoking contradictions through a kind of parody that calls attention to and undermines the power of the original (*Location* 105). As he notes, "The *menace* of mimicry is its *double* vision which in disclosing the ambivalence of colonial discourse also disrupts its authority. [It] is a desire that reverses 'in part' the colonial appropriation by now producing a partial vision of the colonizer's presence, a gaze of otherness" (88–89). Bhabha argues that the subversive mimicry of oppressors can expose their weaknesses and illegitimacy while also empowering and valorizing the mimic and those with whom he or she identifies. This is significant in light of Chan's comical and physical modes of expression. Combined with his mimetic tendencies, these aspects of Chan's work call attention to and question hegemonic norms of race, nation, gender, and class. This is perhaps strongest in his parodying of famous Hollywood action heroes, which not only is funny but also reveals and critiques the male subject's constitution along multiple ideological lines.

For more than forty years, British spy James Bond has been among the most significant action heroes on the transnational landscape. Such spoofs as *Casino Royale* (1966), *From Beijing with Love* (1994), and the *Austin Powers* series (1997–2002) have parodied the Bond character. In his Hong Kong films *Police Story IV: First Strike, Who Am I?* (1998), and *Accidental Spy*, Jackie Chan takes such transgression further when he plays a diasporic James Bond who tries to make sense of his situation and gain some political control.

First Strike uses Chan's transnational adventures based on the James Bond myth in the service of nationalist politics and heteronormative ideology. In the film, Chan plays the role of a Hong Kong cop (also called Jackie) who becomes a spy and helps to break up a smuggling ring that steals nuclear weapons from Ukraine. Inspired by some of the chase scenes on skis and snowmobiles in James Bond movies, Chan performs his breathtaking stunts in the snowcapped landscape of Ukraine and underwater in Australia on the other side of the globe. The current James Bond character played by Daniel Craig would never end an action sequence curled up as Jackie Chan's "Hong Kong James Bond" with teeth chattering after falling into a frozen lake.

James Bond's masculinity is perceived as so natural that one never questions its constructedness. James Chapman in his book *Licence to Thrill: A Cultural History of the James Bond Films* has charted the social, cultural, and political changes that Britain experienced from the 1960s to the 1990s and traces out historically and politically a new perspective in looking at the whole range of James Bond movies. Although he points out again the examples in which anti-Soviet sentiments are less obvious than in the original novels, the James Bond films, however, cannot evade their cultural backdrop of British and American national diplomatic and military policies, both domestically and internationally. Some of the examples of the James Bond movies with the Cold War backdrop are *From Russia with Love* (1963), *Goldfinger* (1964), and *You Only Live Twice* (1967), together with those produced in the early 1980s: *For Your Eyes Only* (1981), *Octopussy* (1983), *Never Say Never Again* (1983), and *A View to a Kill* (1985). In a way, the films also show how much the images of James Bond and the representation of white masculinity are also a form of social and historical construction shaped by historical changes in Britain and also by the political and social climate of the British and American nation-states.

In *First Strike*, ex-CIA man Tsui comments that Jackie's position working for both the CIA and FSB (Federal Security Service of the Russian Federation) is rather complicated. Jackie replies that his role/identity is very simple—just a Hong Kong policeman taking on a special assignment. Jackie first works for the CIA and then the FSB. The Chinese title for the film means "simple mission," but it turns out that going on a transnational mission has complicated consequences. In the film, Jackie is forced to strip naked and put on a puffy clown outfit in order to evade all aural surveillance devices. Both the United States and the Russians suspect and scrutinize Jackie the spy. Different from typical James Bond movies in which Russia is generally portrayed as the villain and Britain/the United States as the hero, sustaining the Cold War mentality, Chan's figure engages in a project that involves both the American and Russian governments. It shows openness to differences not necessarily framed by Anglo-American political ideology. The irony is that both sides distrust and doubt the dual openness of a cosmopolitical mentality. In the film, the FSB bugs him, while he tries to follow the suspects to track down more details.

Arriving in Australia and boarding a Russian submarine, Chan tells his Hong Kong supervisor that the mission makes him "feel almost like James Bond, only without the Bond girls." Although there is a charming heroine called Annie for Chan to rescue, there is never so much as a hint of romantic interest between them. Referring to Chan's *First Strike*, Sheldon Hsiao-peng Lu comments: "One of the most self-reflexive moments within the diegesis of the film is when Chan says that his adventurous career is very much like that of James Bond but without the company of pretty girls. He casts himself in the role of something resembling an asexual, Chinese/Hong Kong James Bond" (24). Lu interprets the lack of sexual adventure as asexual. In fact, social ideologies determine conceptions of the body as asexual or straight. In this case, Chan's body on a transnational landscape is read and perceived as asexual in comparison to the heteronormative model of James Bond. Jackie Chan's model of masculinity enables alternative habits and ways of seeing, reconfigures the normative assumptions about relation between sex and gender, and disassembles the normative James Bond cultural discourse that weds sexuality to masculinity and thinks about masculinity only in the register of the sexual and racialized Other. As Kam Louie notes, the "unproblemati[z]ed incorporation of Western models of male sexuality previously applied generates the inadequate conclusion that Chinese men are less than 'real men'" (20). Chan's comic persona mimics James Bond and contests the unproblematized Western models of male sexuality in Hollywood films. Chan's image is a parody of white heterosexual masculinity and undermines the white masculine identity through sexual conquest.

Chan's screen persona, as I have discussed earlier, is constructed in relation to the conventions of his parody of idealized Chinese martial masculinity. Chan's agency lies in the experience of struggle in constructing the local itself, as the Hong Kong film industry waned and had to find new possibilities after the 1997 political transition. His unbound and undefined identity collides and colludes with the global flow of capital and traditional notions of gender and heterosexuality. In *First Strike*, Chan's comic persona displaces hegemonic white masculinity as a social-sexual norm. His comical superspy/kung fu hero playfully displaces dominant and idealized notions of masculinity in both Anglo-American and Chinese contexts.

Jackie Chan's pluralistic persona across borders speaks critically to the dislocation of diaspora, the transnational journey of travel, the status of the rootless migrant, and a history of struggle. While Chan was filming *Rush Hour* in the United States, he also made the action comedy *Who Am I?* with Hong Kong's Golden Harvest Company. In this film, Chan is a member of a commando group under the CIA whose purpose is to travel to South Africa to kidnap scientists working on new energy sources. However, a backup plan requires the whole group to be demolished in a plane crash upon the completion of their mission. Chan is the only survivor but suffers from amnesia in a tribal village, losing his identity. His question "Who am I?" becomes his name, "Whoami." Recognized by CIA agent Morgan, Whoami learns that covert operatives have sent assassins to eliminate him, and it leads Whoami to Rotterdam in hopes of recovering his memory. Certain action sequences, like the usual car race and helicopter scenes in *Who Am I?*, are reminiscent of James Bond movies of the same period, such as *Tomorrow Never Dies*. Beautiful women and exotic locations are common components in James Bond movies. Such a fantasy world of erotic relations bolsters the male subjectivity of the British spy who embarks on transnational missions in which the British empire appears never to have declined.

Filmed mostly in English, *Who Am I?* was produced by Hong Kong's Golden Harvest, a studio that wants to promote Jackie Chan's films to a greater world market with transnational settings. Chan has carried the concern for the quest for self-identity in Hong Kong cinema into a James Bond–type of action adventure. As an internationally renowned action star, he asks "who am I?" in his movie of the same title. What makes Chan, who has gained international recognition, feel insecure about his identity? With the film's James Bond style of globe-trotting adventure and Chan's character's confusion in his postcolonial and transnational quest for identity, his screen persona points to a new paradigm that cannot be contained within East/West dynamics. In *Who Am I?*, Jackie Chan's Hong Kong/Chinese James Bond also goes on adventures to exotic locations from South Africa to Holland, but unlike James Bond, Chan's masculinity does not depend on the assumed normativity of sexuality but on the knowledge of martial arts as bodily weaponry. Chan's mimicry of the James Bond image intervenes in the practices of hegemonic masculinity as embodied by the white hero while locating the possibilities for men to challenge their constitution as men. Unlike the typical James Bond, certain of his identity—"Bond, James Bond"—Chan finds himself lost, a "whoami" in South Africa. We know only that he works for a CIA special mission. "Whoami" is not related to a particular geographical place in the story, and he has at least six passports with him when the CIA searches his backpack. The central character of the film never recovers from his suffering, weakness, or amnesia.

The journey beginning in South Africa is the major plot holding the film together, a point of reference that is beyond the framework of Hong Kong or North America. With the aid of stunts, the journey leaves Chan as baffled and confused as in the beginning of the film, instead of solving his problems. His trauma is that he is not connected to a political or psychological place of origin. The amnesia leaves him vulnerable in terms of his history, but his body remembers well who he is in performance. Martial arts prowess comes in handy when Chan has to save himself from trouble. He wears the costume and makeup of an African tribesman and speaks English. It is apparent that, despite the loss of memory, he performs martial arts well and demonstrates *yi* (uprightness and selflessness) along the way. Chan shows brilliant skills as he climbs up the coconut tree and in a pinch saves Yuki's brother by using coconut water as blood plasma. With the comical street scuffle in which he fights in clogs, Chan even saves a puppy and runs away from the agents in pursuit. His body provides the traces of who he is, although he suffers from amnesia. Chan strives to find a place in the labyrinth of the post-1997 political situation when Hong Kong people, after the immediate transfer of sovereignty, were troubled (and still are troubled) by who they are. A Hong Kong person's individual identity is in a state of continuous flux and change, like the character Chan plays in his excursion from South Africa to Rotterdam, in a never-ending search for his identity. The film ends with Chan still not knowing his identity but with the CIA telling Chan it will help him to rediscover it. *Who Am I?* creates the image of a homeless exile who escapes an untenable past that seems to entrap him and who at the same time searches to create a new identity.

Hong Kong's colonial history under British rule gave it a "port" mentality as a place of transience, as Rey Chow notes, complemented by an identity vis-à-vis Mainland China after 1997 (*Ethics* 176). *Who Am I?* indirectly addresses the local and transnational socioeconomic forces and (neo)colonialism operating before and during its 1997 handover to mainland China. In his Hong Kong films, Jackie Chan plays a diasporic James Bond who tries to make sense of his situation and gain some political control in *First Strike* and *Who Am I?* While playing with the Bond persona, *Who Am I?* also alludes to concerns specific to Hong Kong following the transfer of sovereignty in 1997, articulating the anxieties of a people troubled by their identity and their future. Jackie Chan as a transnational film star, producer, and filmmaker encompasses a form of cosmopolitical subjectivity from the very beginning, a form of diaspora and alienation from any host culture or identity, be it Chinese, Asian, Western imperialist, or American.

Nevertheless, Chan's characters' cross-border personae speak to the dislocation of diaspora more generally, not just conditions in Hong Kong.

The Accidental Spy (produced by Chan) mimics and contests the James Bond myth with Jackie Chan playing an orphaned sporting goods sales-man, Buck Yuen, who discovers that he might have a Korean father who is a double spy for Korea and Japan. Yuen inadvertently engages in the spy business without knowing whether the Korean man is actually his father, as the intelligence agency chases Yuen from Hong Kong to Korea and finally to Turkey. Yuen's vague memory of his parents in his early childhood and his accidental adventure as a spy leave us uncertain as to his origins, as the purpose of the adventure is in fact to prevent the character from maintaining a stable identity. The adventure leads him to an international journey, as he struggles and battles with the regulating discourses that prescribe the states of subjecthood on a transnational level.

In *The Accidental Spy*, after Yuen's espionage from Hong Kong to Tur-key, it turns out that his vague memory of his parents in his childhood happens to be the result of Liu's hypnosis, as Liu tried to dupe Yuen to work according to his plan. Liu works for a special agency in the United States, and they find Yuen, who possesses good intuition and martial arts skills, to be a great asset in helping discover the Anthrax II virus. The film acknowledges that the individual can have a memory of his or her historical identity and yet questions the fact that the very practices of remembrance and identity can easily be the product of inscription. Jackie Chan's mimicry of James Bond challenges international espionage with the uncertainties of nationality, roots, memory, and belonging. As an accidental spy and martial artist in the film, Chan mimics and destabilizes the transnational spy image of James Bond. In turn, the hegemonic synthesis of nationalism and imperialism that initiates James Bond's international espionage is thus disputed. The seeming natural-ness of hegemonic masculinity, heterosexuality, nationhood, fatherhood, family, and citizenship can be revealed as a set of prescriptive norms of identity, history, memory, and inscription that contains potential contra-dictions within and between subjects. Chan's personae comically displace Hollywood's rendition of masculinity and subjectivity as hegemonic inscriptions. The unquestioned formula of the James Bond narrative and his transnational adventure can well turn out to be a practical joke constituted by the multiple lines of social and political inscriptions.

The Hollywood action comedy *The Tuxedo* (2002) also engages with the Bond myth. Chan plays Jimmy Tong, a cab driver and then a bellboy/chauffeur to a white master named Devlin, roles that can be considered stereotypes about Asian males in servile professions. The secret to Devlin's success as a spy is his trademark tuxedo, which is loaded with special gadgets that turn him into a high-tech fighting machine. When Devlin is hospitalized, Tong has to replace him and deploy this tuxedo and its associated technology in order to perform martial arts. If the tuxedo symbolizes the myth of James Bond as an ideal of white masculinity and Chan's character as a servant embodies Asian stereotypes, his character's adoption of the tuxedo becomes an act of subversive appropriation and comic spectacle. As Judith Butler notes regarding a different context: "Performativity describes this relation of being implicated in that which one opposes, this turning of power against itself to produce alternative modalities of power, to establish a kind of political contestation that is not a 'pure' opposition, a 'transcendence' of contemporary relations of power, but a difficult labor of forging a future from resources inevitably impure" (241). Applying Butler's discussion to Chan's film, I argue that by donning the tuxedo in order to perform martial arts, Chan pokes fun at Asianness and himself as well as at hegemonic white masculinity and draws attention to the performative nature of identities. Chan's comical treatment of James Bond, Asian stereotypes, and his own image as a martial artist destabilizes Asianness/Chineseness and hegemonic masculinity.

Because of fight choreography's overt associations with performance and corporeality, *The Tuxedo*'s use of special effects choreography opens up possibilities for disrupting normative identities. Although *The Tuxedo* is a martial arts–inspired Hollywood film, its virtual interface with computer-generated effects further undermines the general identification of Asianness/Chineseness with authentic martial arts and the body. The liberating potential of mimicking both Asian and white masculine stereotypes is epitomized in *The Tuxedo*, as Chan performs traditional stunts in his films, but at the same time he reworks the conventions of both the "authentic" martial artist and James Bond constitutions to suggest the performativity of these screen personae and identities. With the technological and corporeal interface in the tuxedo, multiple layers of symbolic contestations and subversions emerge in the film. The tuxedo gives the Chan character mechanical, but still super, powers; this incorporation of special effects denaturalizes the conventional perceptions of Asian martial arts stars and choreography. The deployment of special effects choreography valorizes defamiliarization precisely by making the accustomed interpolation of identity and subjectivity visible. Chan makes use of his transnational stardom as well as the transgressive quality of comedy to challenge the localized notions of identity politics and problematizes the preconceived identification of corporeality with the Asian Other.

Besides James Bond, Jackie Chan also has parodied the iconic American Western cowboy image of John Wayne, most notably in *Shanghai Noon* (2000) and its sequel, *Shanghai Knights* (both executive produced by Chan). This figure has often been parodied, but less frequently by nonwhite actors whose racial/ethnic status might introduce new questions, complexities, and contestations. The Western/kung fu comedy *Shanghai Noon* stars Jackie Chan (as Chon Wang) and Owen Wilson (Roy O'Bannon). The title is a pun on the classic Gary Cooper Western *High Noon* (1952). Chon Wang is an imperial guard of China. After Princess Pei-Pei is abducted to the United States, three of the emperor's guards, along with Chon Wang, are sent to retrieve her. Chon Wang (which puns on "John Wayne") is the "Shanghai Kid" who mimics and playfully alludes to Wayne's "Ringo Kid" in *Stagecoach* (1939) and Robert Redford's "Sundance Kid" in *Butch Cassidy and the Sundance Kid*.

Shanghai Noon's comedy derives from conflicts between Chon and Roy's different cultures and personalities. Roy is an American cowboy who is timid, constantly fools around, and gets himself into trouble—that is, a comic reversal of the idealized masculinity embodied by Wayne, Redford, and Clint Eastwood. In contrast to Roy, Chon stands for discipline, loyalty, and honor—an idealized Chinese martial hero displaced into the American West. *Shanghai Noon* not only refashions the cowboy-buddy prototype in *Butch Cassidy and the Sundance Kid* but also undermines Wayne's stoic masculinity in *Stagecoach*. In *Stagecoach*, ethnic Others include Native Americans and a Mexican, while Wayne plays the strong and likable outlaw who asserts his masculinity on behalf of the gendered Other, an ostracized woman with a scandalous past who leans on him for support. Chan's comic persona in *Shanghai Noon* facilitates his assumption of the lead cowboy role previously reserved for Caucasian dramatic actors such as Wayne, Eastwood, or Redford, free from the potential threats posed by ethnic difference, hypermasculinity, and stoic seriousness. Jackie Chan's global marketability and his cowboy/martial artist image transnationalize both the Chinese martial arts and American Western film genres, bridging and commingling them.

While Chon is a fish out of water in the American West in *Shanghai Noon*, the British backdrop of its sequel, *Shanghai Knights*, turns both Chon and Roy into strangers in a strange land, testing their buddy relations and displacing racial tensions from America to a transnational context. *Shanghai Knights* manipulates the kung fu/Western genre and the buddy formula established by *Shanghai Noon* and transposes fight choreography to a transnational setting other than America, namely the

Old West's antithesis in London, as the site of transgression. In *Shanghai Knights*, Chon Wang's name (in Chinese characters) appears as "Jiang Wen" in a parcel sent from his sister.[3] In addition to making fun of Wayne's idealized masculinity, *Shanghai Knights* reveals a translingual double pun by alluding to the Mainland Chinese actor and director Jiang Wen, whose roles, such as the First Emperor (*The Emperor's Shadow*, 1996) and an ancient warrior (*Warriors of Heaven and Earth*, 2003), question yet reinforce patriarchal masculinity in a local/national context. Chan's Asian sheriff/Chinese imperial guard/kung fu fighter character is introduced to Victorian Britain; the tourist landscapes of Covent Garden and Big Ben are the new transnational locations for his stunts and action. The film's comedy derives largely from Chon and Roy's temporal, geographical, and situational dislocations.

In *Shanghai Knights*, the American Western is displaced onto the global landscape where issues of race, masculinity, and nation that constitute the basis of John Wayne's iconic cowboy image are raised and contested. Such transnational crossovers challenge the nationalist politics of race, in this case with the transnational Asian star who works in the global Hollywood context. The ambivalence of rootedness for both Chon and Roy in *Shanghai Knights* destabilizes the social and political marginality of the Asian/Asian American representations in Chan's earlier projects, such as *The Big Brawl* and *The Cannonball Run*, and points to a new paradigm that cannot be contained within East/West dynamics because it encompasses a cosmopolitical subjectivity.

Chan once again took up the roles of actor/choreographer/producer in *Around the World in Eighty Days* (2004), a title that immediately announces its transnational identity. Not only are Chan's movies increasingly set in cross-boundary settings ranging from Hong Kong, Mainland China, Japan, Korea, India, Australia, Russia, France, South Africa, Turkey, Britain, and the United States, but Chan himself is also a constant world traveler and presence around the globe. Chan's next Hollywood project was *The Forbidden Kingdom* (2008), in which he and Jet Li come together on-screen. The film is a time-traveling take on the Chinese Monkey King fable that finds an American teen transported back to ancient China after wandering into a pawnshop and discovering the king's fighting stick. Once there, the adventurous teen joins an army of fierce warriors who have sworn to free their imprisoned king at all costs. In addition to appearing as the mythical Monkey King, Jet Li assumes the role of a silent monk, and Jackie Chan appears in the role of drunken kung fu master. Action choreographer Yuen Woo-ping presides over the fight sequences. *The Forbidden Kingdom* is basically a cross between *The Karate Kid* (1984) and *The Neverending Story* (1984), drawing upon cross-cultural references of both Hollywood and Hong Kong/Chinese martial arts films including Bruce Lee's works, Chan's *Drunken Master*, Li's *Shaolin Temple* (1982), and others of the 1970s and 1980s. As Chan notes, "People know about the story of King Arthur. But Chinese stories and legends are less known among the world audiences" (personal interview). *The Forbidden Kingdom* is an attempt to transnationalize the well-known Chinese story of the Monkey King and the martial arts icon of drunken master by engaging with popular cultural texts of both East and West.

One of Jackie Chan's recent Hong Kong films, *Rob-B-Hood*, mimics and playfully alludes to *Three Men and a Baby* (1987), an American remake of the French comedy *Three Men and a Cradle* (1985). *Three Men and a Cradle* and *Three Men and a Baby* focus on three bachelors who attempt to adapt their lives to fatherhood when a baby arrives at their doorstep. In *Rob-B-Hood*, Chan recreates the comedy formula by incorporating action choreography, playing a burglar and compulsive gambler. In *Shinjuku Incident*, Chan plays an illegal immigrant and gangster in Japan. In *Rob-B-Hood* and *Shinjuku Incident*, the images of burglar and gangster undermine Chan's idealized Asian (Hong Kong/Chinese) masculine persona as "Mr. Nice Guy" in Hong Kong–produced films and the stereotypes of emasculated Asian males in Hollywood cinema. These films return Chan to the spectacular physical stunts that Hollywood no longer will allow him to do because of concerns about safety and insurance premiums.

Rather than seeing Hollywood as a final destination in his career, Chan uses his Hollywood success to enhance a new phase in his transnational trajectory, continuing to make films in Hong Kong, Hollywood, and elsewhere. Chan's example shows how transnational film practices and the global marketability of star images can provide tools for mapping and remapping the terrain of transnational capital, but not necessarily only from the logic of Hollywood dominance. Here again, the mobility of Chan's star persona and directorial efforts translates across borders, and his critical reinventions of films multiply the channels and potentials of filmmaking in and out of Hollywood. Chan's film trajectory demonstrates his cosmopolitical endeavors, and his transnational humor continues to engage with multiple and often conflicting geopolitical sensibilities.

Jackie Chan as actor, director, producer, and choreographer brings and weaves together the possibilities of intervening in the political threads of oppositions and tensions between Asian, Asian American, and other racial and gender politics. Hong Kong cinema has long aspired to be the Hollywood of the East, to resist Hollywood's global imperialist project and the ambition to conquer the world market. Such a dream may be doomed with the recent decline of the Hong Kong film industry but has continued with China's burgeoning campaign to build a new global film industry that can compete on equal terms with both Hollywood and Bollywood (O'Hehir). As China opens itself to a continually changing awareness of its filmic representation and visibility on the global stage, cosmopolitical film artists such as Jackie Chan problematizes Orientalist perspectives of the East by playfully integrating the geopolitical knowledge of body, power, and discourse to create films in a transnational world.

In addition, Jackie Chan's cosmopolitical consciousness occurs as a result of the Hong Kong film industry's history of (neo)colonialism and transnationalism. Such consciousness of challenging the mainstream has to be conceived as finding the working potential from a transnational "always both inside and outside" status—as Jacques Derrida has noted, "This inside must also enclose the spectral duplicity, an immanent outside or an intestine exteriority, a sort of evil genius which slips into spirit's monologue to haunt it, ventriloquizing it and thus dooming it to a sort of self-persecuting disidentification" (62). Now, the outside does not return, like the repressed, as the force of haunting disruption within reiterative identification that shows the failure of conformity to symbolic ideals of the "inside." The multiple flows of people, capital, images, and ideas have now trespassed the boundaries of the nation-state, undermining its geographical and ontological security, disrupting the inside/outside dichotomy, and contesting the geopolitics of insider/outsider splits by destabilizing even the "spectral duplicity" of identification and disidentification that is generally governed by a geographic sense of identity and location.

Jackie Chan is fighting for an individual body, an almost impossible task, as the body has become incidental, synthetic, and mute by compulsory political economies of identities as a colonial subject, a national subject, an Orientalized martial arts fighter (Other), and an Asian asexual bachelor. His battles against machinery (modern technology and symbolic economies of race, gender, and nation) continue to be controversial as a way of imagining the political agency and cultural identity of the individual body—its possible intervention and reworking of the heteronormative logic through which a racialized or marginalized subjectivity has been formulated. Despite such political inscriptions, the body is also the site of performative enunciation, as Chan's body and its liminality turn its dexterity into weaponry. Chan's characters range from Japanese car racer, Chinese immigrant in the United States, Hong Kong police-man from the colonial period to post-1997, and Chinese kung fu hero like Wong Fei-hung, to the mimicry of James Bond and John Wayne's cowboy figure. Chan chooses multiple positions to announce his identification and the proposition that identities are imposed and enforced by Others.

Jackie Chan is a significant filmmaker of the transnational era. He par-ticipates in more than one cultural, economic, and sociopolitical system and simultaneously allows for the formation of transnational affinities and resistance. Agency and resistance are not premised on the idea that subjectivity is engaging with one hegemonic cultural-political system; rather, in the age of transnationalism, resistance has to be considered and achieved not within the bounded territory of the nation-state. Chan's comedy of displacement has been shaped by factors including the history of colonialism; Chinese nationalism; the geopolitics of race, masculinity, and power; and the experiences of transnational filmmaking in global capitalism. Through comedy, physicality, and parody, his works actively and creatively reflect his cosmopolitical intervention in these hegemonic discourses and practices.

CONCLUSION: COSMOPOLITICAL THINKING

Today's world is interconnected. Each challenge facing us is interlinked with others. Hollywood's cultural, economic, and political influence on the world film industry, as an example, cannot be addressed without considering its cross-pollination by Hong Kong/Chinese martial arts film traditions. Yet, the Chinese-language film industry's relations with Hollywood cannot be informed without taking notice of Hong Kong's specific sociopolitical contexts and examining its film industry's transnational dynamics. The recent interflows of film artists, styles, and genres in Hollywood and the Chinese diaspora, particularly through the transnationalization of Hong Kong/Chinese martial arts films, are examples of how East and West meet in the conjunction of local dynamics and global forces.

The applications of martial arts in cinema are forms of knowledge and power. The development of martial arts cinema in Hong Kong uses the notion of martial arts to express the concept of *xia*, a warrior who takes action in the public sphere. The concept of the *xia* and martial arts choreography manifest themselves in cinema as *wuxia*, kung fu styles, and contemporary action thrillers. The Hong Kong/Chinese martial arts cinema was always already a hybrid genre combining traditions from Chinese martial arts, novels, theater, and culture, as well as traditions from different Eastern and Western films. It has fundamentally transformed the style and the content not only of martial arts performance but also contemporary action cinema, both "East" and "West." Action, such as chases, stunts, fights, crashes, and explosions, is an important component of cinema. The martial arts film traditions from Hong Kong not only expand the potential for action in films but also have embodied the concepts, philosophy, and ideas of the martial arts hero and the concept of *xia* in contemporary action cinema.

The incorporation of honor and loyalty in the public sphere from *wuxia* traditions and martial arts choreography has reworked the multiple conventions of filmmaking "East" and "West." Audiences now know Jackie Chan and have seen films by John Woo. They are familiar with Ang Lee's *Crouching Tiger, Hidden Dragon*, a *wuxia* film. The culture of Chinese legendary *xia* has also long fascinated director John Woo in the themes of male individualism and righteous heroism. With a vested interest in the theme of male homosocial bondings, Woo destabilizes the monolithic subjective position of hegemonic masculinity from the subject positions of the Other and problematizes the prescriptive norms of loyalty and belonging. Jackie Chan, a producer, actor, and filmmaker, shuttles between Hong Kong and Hollywood. His martial comedian persona further probes how the geopolitics of capital, people, performances, and cinema continue to shape his works.

Yet, being transnational does not necessarily mean being cosmopolitical. The Wachowski brothers' *Matrix* trilogy seeks to sustain the ideology of hegemonic masculinity and Hollywood's dominance by assimilating special effects–enhanced martial arts choreography and the creation of the Matrix myth. While the dominant global film industry, like Hollywood, shows increasing awareness of Hong Kong martial arts cinema in its creative consciousness, the cosmopolitical film artists shuttle between the different film markets and industries and produce Chinese-language films that embrace contemporary new media technology (as inspired by *The Matrix*) and create works that have established new standards of martial arts/action filmmaking in the Asian film industry. In comparison, Ang Lee's cosmopolitical consciousness, as demonstrated in *Crouching Tiger, Hidden Dragon*, has been reflected in styles, forms, narratives, language, and genre traditions (including ideologies of ideal femininity/masculinity and Chineseness), both in the *wuxia* and Hollywood cross-cultural discursive scales.

Although there has been a wealth of recent publications on Hong Kong cinema and the interconnections between Hong Kong/Chinese and Hollywood film cultures, the scholarship only scratches the surface of a particularly rich topic of inquiry. By definition, research on Hong Kong/Chinese and Hollywood cinemas draws on theories and methodologies informed by film studies, performance studies, Asian and Asian American studies, history, gender, ethnicity, and cultural studies. This book tackles the current state and the historical underpinnings of Hollywood and Hong Kong/Chinese film culture through the genre of common concern: martial arts cinema. The interflows between Hollywood and the Chinese-language film industries are not unilateral but rather multiple. Expanding beyond the border of national cinema studies requires fresh perspectives on how the interflows of people, images, and capital demand scholarship to consider the various cross-cultural links and geopolitical knowledge across the Chinese diaspora in Hollywood, thus invoking issues of gender, class, race, ethnicity, local/translocal political, and cultural affiliations. As I have argued, the transnational trajectories of these film artists address and navigate multiple fields of power, struggle, and inequality through the artists' experiences of the historical processes of colonialism, postcolonialism, nationalism, imperialism, displacement, migration, and exile. Transnational capitalism circulates the cultural production and consumption of cinema. Global flows of capital, images, and ideas through cinema allow the possibilities to transgress boundaries of the nation-state, undermining the yearning for fixation and vitiating the presumably stable categories that the heteronormativity of the nation overdetermines in examining identities and subjectivities.

This book not only focuses on the relationship between Hong Kong/ Chinese martial arts cinema and Hollywood, revealing how the geopolitical influence of the martial arts film genre offers an alternative to the transnational success of Hollywood. More important, this book concentrates on the key and commercially successful figures in the transcontinental martial arts cinema, namely Ang Lee, John Woo, and Jackie Chan, and looks at the way the film artists' works highlight contemporary contradictions involving nation, race, ethnicity, culture, and class. It demonstrates how these film artists' cosmopolitical perspectives reflect the complex and often contradictory interactions of local and global forces, at home and around the world, and their differing effects in contesting boundaries of history, identity, gender, sexuality, and ethnicity. It shows how in this interaction between East and West, and as a result of the necessity of commercial success and survival in the global film world, the subjects' displacements by hegemonic forces and powers result in cosmopolitical perspectives. The film artists I have focused on in this book make use of the martial arts or martial arts–inspired action cinema to provide alternative visions to both mainstream Chinese and Hollywood ideologies in the discourses of gender, race, and sexuality.

Film talents like Ang Lee, John Woo, and Jackie Chan work in Hollywood, producing films that are highly visible and popular. Each intervention into martial arts cinema is different, as is the cosmopolitical consciousness that each demonstrates. Ang Lee's *Crouching Tiger, Hidden Dragon* targets the split of public/private spheres in the *wuxia* genre. Thus, Lee also modifies the concept of *xia*, who generally embodies heroism and justice, and instead portrays both male and female *xia* who have to deal with the repression of their desire by mainstream Confucian and patriarchal society. In *Crouching Tiger, Hidden Dragon*, Lee strategizes the cultural/sociopolitical awareness of emotional repression as the site of contestation. *Crouching Tiger, Hidden Dragon* shows Lee's success in both arts and commercial cinema, and he turns his critical reflection toward Chineseness, Asianness, and femininity as repressed domains and markers on a transnational scale. Ang Lee uses *xia* characters in the *wuxia* film genre to transgress the hegemonic binary split between public and private, masculine and feminine. He feminizes the male *xia* characters by imbuing them with emotion and empowers the female *xia* characters with martial skills to compete with their male counterparts. By invoking strong female fighters and effeminate male warriors, Lee questions the gender construction within the larger framework of Taoism and transnational feminism. The female and male *xia* in the film defy traditional gender representations in which public and private, masculine and feminine get played out through emotion, technology, choreography, and language. Lee's cosmopolitical awareness reveals his geopolitical stances in the global film market, as he navigates between art and commercial cinemas.

As one of the most famous and respected directors from Hong Kong, John Woo has long been a cult favorite in the United States. Known for his choreographed action sequences featuring balletic shoot-outs, Woo's films often engage with themes of loyalty and honor and the place of the loner hero in a world full of corruption and violence. Woo has proved he can make films transnationally without sacrificing the themes and styles that win him international acclaim, as did *The Red Cliff* and its sequel. Woo's cosmopolitical endeavors lead to rethinking the boundaries of history, identity, and a system of polity that governs our sense of belonging, as we have to reconsider the patriarchal structure of homosocial relations that celebrates unilateral and prescriptive norms, such as fatherhood, family, and citizenry, as constitutive of loyalty and belonging. Thus, Woo contests such thematics and representations of homosociality, homogeneity, and the hegemony of subjects in patriarchal masculinity and mainstream Hollywood. He continues to question and investigate the themes of face and honor that exist in every meeting and social encounter in the Chinese context and identity politics in the American context.

As an action film director, he traverses various borders and becomes an active social subject with multiple geopolitical consciousnesses.

Jackie Chan has consistently and dramatically grown in popularity in international media markets since the 1980s, initially in Asia and then in the United States and Europe, thus indicating his broad appeal across national and cultural lines. Chan's comical fighting style in his films undermines the idealized masculine persona of Bruce Lee and other martial film heroes. His performance and fighting style embody the flexibility to put himself momentarily in a vulnerable position in order to trick his opponent and also to distance himself (and audiences) from the rigid norms of heroic masculinity governed by fatherhood and patriarchy (as exemplified by Bruce Lee, Wong Fei-hung, James Bond, Clint Eastwood, and others). Chan's comic displacement of hegemonic masculinity in both Chinese and Hollywood contexts locates the possibilities for men to challenge their constitution as men by multiple ideological practices including sexuality, race, and patriarchy. While Hollywood appropriates the folk customs and traditions of Hong Kong/Chinese martial arts, the Hong Kong film industry reappropriates Jackie Chan's Hollywood success and marketability into its media to enhance a new phase in Hong Kong cinema's transnational trajectory. He continues to make films in Hong Kong and the Mainland. Not only do Chan's works engage in various discourses and contexts of East/West ideologies, but also, more important, as a star, filmmaker, choreographer, and producer, he embodies the cosmopolitical consciousness and awareness of the ways that enable him to work as a major filmmaker/producer/performer in today's global Hollywood.

As directors and very often producers of their own films, filmmakers like Ang Lee, John Woo, and Jackie Chan actively participate in the creative, production, and investment processes and plannings of their works. Their cosmopolitical perspectives stem from the multiply marginalized sociopolitical contexts from which their filmmaking trajectories have diversely criss-crossed. The transnational encounters between East and West result in the crossover of ideologies and local/translocal politics of gender and ethnicity. The interflows of people, media technologies, and capital produce geopolitical consciousnesses as a result of the history of marginalization; the destabilization of the metanarratives of colonialism, Eurocentrism, and Sinocentrism; and the struggles against forms of inequalities in class, ethnic, or gender differences. Such consciousnesses emerge as the result of the necessity for survival in response to the history of displacement by multiple hegemonic forces in the workings of the territorial/national and global terrains and as a form of political resistance both locally and translocally. Different histories of struggles and resistance cannot be defined in the hegemonic, imperialist, or universalist history of the West but rather depend on translocal alliances, encounters, affiliations, and contestations that enable new critical paradigms to imagine race, gender, and power differently. The cosmopolitical in this sense remains compelling because of the engaging and conflicting issues it raises, including the limits of identity and the contradictory spaces of belonging/locality/roots that are based on national entities.

The intersections of multiple differences such as gender, sexuality, class, and ethnicity further problematize the coherent narrative of the nation. There are multiple modernities in the particularity and historicity of communities both locally and translocally. Cosmopolitical perspective requires multiple sites, active tensions/powers, and the recognition of the possibility of inhabiting more than one positionality at a time. This recognition affords the crossing and mutation of multiple sites. Such a geopolitical engagement, however, requires—not simply names— a juncture, a site of articulation, and also addresses how identities and political and economic differences mutually inform and transform each other. In other words, the cosmopolitical consciously addresses the dynamic tensions between categories of power and resistance, hegemony and counter-hegemony.

The egalitarian dimensions of cosmopolitical consciousness sometimes cannot avoid colluding with hegemonic power structures. These film artists' works cannot escape the cultural context of capitalist deterritorialization and reterritorialization in the transnational flows of capital, people, and images. Yet, as I have argued in this book, the collusion also has been accompanied by collisions with mainstream ideologies. For better or worse, the cosmopolitical consciousness is a form of political awareness and agency that is not definable simply in opposition to the hegemonic imperialist forces of the West but instead depends upon multiple engagements and displacements that enable agents to forge new critical paradigms that reimagine race, nation, gender, and power. Lee's *wuxia* epic, Woo's martial arts–inspired action films, and Chan's transnational humor translate across cultural boundaries and appeal successfully to international audiences. Their works displace the hegemonic visions and narratives in Hollywood films and undermine paradigms of Chinese masculinity/femininity in Chinese-language films. During these filmmakers' transnational film careers between Hollywood, Hong Kong, Mainland China, Taiwan, and the rest of the world, they deploy the cosmopolitical perspectives as a form of tactical resistance that allows them to act across diverse power structures. Their works reveal their multiple identifications with and participation in various geopolitical contexts.

As exemplified by the works of Ang Lee, John Woo, and Jackie Chan, the cosmopolitical defies the limits of identity based upon national entities and related issues of belonging and responsibility and raises questions of how to balance the conflicting loyalties of always being a political minority, whether on a regional or transnational basis. Thus, we cannot simply dismiss the cosmopolitical as collusion or idealize it as collision but instead must see it as a complex arena in which agents employ tactical and strategic methods to achieve aims that are themselves complicated by self- and group-motivated interests.

As I have tried to demonstrate in this book, these filmmakers and film talents modify and question hegemonic concepts of social action and interrelated subject positions of gender, ethnicity, and power in the global system. This book critically engages with the politics of gender, ethnicity, the representations of the body, and the critical consciousness that moves beyond the fixed norms of identity in such ways that the geopolitical divisions of Hong Kong, Taiwan, Mainland China, Asia, and America, East and West, can no longer justify or examine the politics of consciousness, knowledge, and power shuttling between and beyond borders and boundaries, struggling to contest competing ideologies. In this light, it is necessary to think comparatively about the diverse routes in which distinctive historical subjects politicize identities across national, ethnic, and gender discourses.

Cosmopolitical thinking destabilizes the inclusion/exclusion binary that extends the nation's reach. It has enabled a structure of identity that continuously calls into question qualities and criteria that try to fix the status of subjectivity contingent upon race, gender, and sexuality. In this book, I have demonstrated how the filmmakers of the Chinese diaspora in Hollywood represent several major trends in film practices that find working power within the Hollywood and Chinese-language film industries. Their works consciously and continuously define and re-define identity politics in Hollywood and the Chinese diaspora. Through examining the transnational trajectories of the filmmakers/film talents who work across cultural and sociopolitical boundaries, this book has led me to reconsider film studies cosmopolitically, particularly genre, auteur, performance theory, and identity politics in gender and ethnicity beyond the notion of the nation, that is, in the new geopolitical era of transnational matrices.

NOTES
BIBLIOGRAPHY
INDEX

NOTES

1. Martial Arts Cinema, the Chinese Diaspora, and Hollywood

1. Poshek Fu and his colleagues edit the volume *Shaw Brothers' Film Empire* and track Shaw Brothers' influences, including the migration from Shanghai (as Tianyi), its significance in Hong Kong from 1930s onward, its growth in Singapore during the 1930s and 1940s, and its expansion in Southeast Asia.

2. Orientalism, proposed by Edward Said, means the network of discourses about the "Orient" constructed in Western civilization. The Orient in Western conceptions is imagined and understood as different from the collective imagination of the civilized West (2). Said's understanding of Orientalism has been extended by postcolonial scholars, such as Homi Bhabha, in ways that rupture Orientalism to create a "third space," which is the mobile zone of interaction and in-between-ness ("Third Space").

3. Sima Qian fulfilled the request of his father Sima Tan (180–110 B.C.) to complete the project that Tan began in gathering materials for a history of China from earliest times to the reign of Han Wudi (140–88 B.C.), a period of three thousand years. Sima Qian is credited solely with the authorship of the work *Records of the Grand Historian of China*.

4. Gina Marchetti's *Romance and the "Yellow Peril": Race, Sex, and Discursive Strategies in Hollywood Fiction* examines the early depictions of Asians in American cinema that often portrayed Asian men as "asexual eunuch figures" (2). Characters such as Fu Manchu and Charlie Chan, played by Caucasian actors, exaggerated the foreign qualities or strangeness of Asians or Asian Americans in order to deemphasize their inherent sexuality and attractiveness. Most Asian male stars in American cinema do not have any physical relations with their female counterparts in films. The Asian females are seen as the docile, submissive, and mysterious Lotus Blossom or China Doll or as the inherent hypersexual and evil Dragon Lady.

5. *Da* (martial arts skill and acrobatics) was one of the four performance skills of Chinese opera, along with *chang* (singing), *nian* (dialogue), and *zuo*

(acting) (Jin, Zhang, and Liu 3–4). Chinese opera is a synthesis of music, dance, art, and acrobatics.

6. *Sheng* is the male role in Chinese opera; *dan* is the general term for the female role. *Jing* refers to the roles with painted faces. They are usually warriors, heroes, statesmen, or sometimes demons. *Chou* basically means "clowns." As *wu* means "martial," *wusheng* therefore refers to actors who excel in riding and archery as well as in martial arts. *Wudan* is the military role for a woman who, like the *wusheng*, is also skilled in martial arts and does a lot of stage-fighting. *Wujing* is a painted-face character with martial arts skills, and *wu-chou* means clown characters that perform stage fighting (Xu 177–94).

2. Ang Lee's *Crouching Tiger, Hidden Dragon*: Gender, Ethnicity, and Transnationalism

1. *Wen* masculinity is associated with the gentleman-scholar or *junzi* promoted by Confucius. *Wu* masculinity is usually associated with the martial masculinity symbolized by the Han Dynasty military leader Guan Yu that emphasizes the homosocial bonds between men, particularly in the outlaw space of the *jianghu* (rivers and lakes) (Louie 10–11).

2. The *yin* and *yang* doctrine in Chinese philosophy is based on the belief that everything in the universe is interrelated and has an opposing, yet inseparable, counterpart. The counterparts are referred to as *yin* and *yang*; they are constantly changing and explain all activity in the universe. This concept of constant change became an approach to understanding the laws of nature. There is no conclusive evidence on when and how the *yin* and *yang* philosophy was first introduced to Chinese culture. This concept was explained in detail during the Zhou Dynasty (1122–249 B.C.), when *Book of Changes* (aka *Zhouyi*) was compiled. *Zhouyi* is a collection of sixty-four six-line figures called hexagrams. See Cheng, "Chinese Metaphysics." *Zhouyi* uses the *yin* and *yang* concept to explain the rules of the universe and to analyze everything in it, ranging from astrology, geology, and meteorology to human relations. In the context of the biography, Ang Lee's usage points to the interstitial areas and the "third space" in the opposing counterparts of *yin* and *yang* between different female subjectivities.

3. Lotus Blossom refers to the submissive stereotype of Asian women that exists in American movies. Lucy Liu's images as Ling in the TV drama series *Ally McBeal* and Alex in the film *Charlie's Angels* (and its sequel) (2000–2003) are representative figures of the Dragon Lady stereotype. Ling's wrath and eroticism in the TV series, for example, reiterate the stereotype of the Orientalist seductress. Both the Lotus Blossom and the Dragon Lady stereotypes work only to uphold the white male heterosexual paradigm with Asian women as exotic, volatile, and seductive sexual objects.

4. Mandarin is the standardized and official language of China. Each region (including different provinces in the Mainland, Hong Kong, Taiwan, and the

other Chinese diasporic communities, such as Yeoh's home country of Malaysia, for example) speaks its own local version of it, usually reflecting influence from the native dialects of the area. Cantonese is the major dialect spoken in Hong Kong. For many years, Chinese dialects like southern Fujianese and Hakka as well as the aborigine languages were widely used throughout Taiwan. The Mandarin spoken by Hongkongese and Taiwanese generally also sounds different from the Mandarin in mainland China.

5. Melissa J. Brown argues that ethnicity (such as Chineseness) cannot adequately address the complexity of identity formation in Taiwan. See Brown, *Is Taiwan Chinese?*

6. In "The Ontology of the Photographic Image," Bazin argues that photography is the discovery that freed plastic arts from its obsession with likeness by satisfying, once and for all in its essence, the obsession with realism in Western painting. The cinematic image shares the being of the photographic model in which reality is transferred to it (166–70).

3. Facing Off East and West in the Cinema of John Woo

1. "Heroic bloodshed" is a term used to describe a subgenre of Hong Kong action film (see Baker and Russell). Rick Baker explains the genre as an example of "Hong Kong action film that features a lot of gunplay and gangsters, rather than kung-fu." He continues, "Sometimes the films do feature martial arts, but it's usually a lot more violent than in the kung-fu movies. Lots of blood. Lots of action. Quite often the hero is either maimed or killed by the final reel" (qtd. in Logan 126). The phrase "heroic bloodshed" is used to distinguish between Hong Kong gangster films and the traditional kung fu and *wuxia* films as guns replaced swords and bullets fly across the screen. Bey Logan contributes a chapter on Woo, titled "Heroic Bloodshed," in his book *Hong Kong Action Cinema*. The phrase later became the title of Martin Fitzgerald's book *Hong Kong's Heroic Bloodshed*, which includes an exclusive chapter on Woo's films.

2. LuMing Robert Mao reviews Penelope Brown and Stephen Levinson's face-saving model of politeness in light of Erving Goffman's original discussion of face and traces the origin of the concept of face in the Chinese context. Mao argues that Brown and Levinson's claim to provide a universally valid model is inadequate because the dynamics of the Chinese notion of face offers an alternative model to their analysis.

3. Turmoil rocked the territory in 1967. Mao Zedong started the Cultural Revolution in China in 1966, which led to a rise of "revolutionary sentiment" among the leftists in Hong Kong. In the early months of 1967, there were a series of labor disputes in Hong Kong. During the disturbances, which occurred between May and October 1967, large posters denouncing British imperialism were put up at the gate of the Hong Kong Government House. Bombs were also planted all over the city, creating a wave of terror. Though the leftists claimed to be anti-British under the banner of nationalism, the majority of their victims

were Chinese. Ho Fung Hung notes that the 1967 riots became the "traumatic kernel" in the formation of Hong Kong's local identity and of its sense as an "imagined community" (99). See Hung, "Discourse on 1967."

4. *Romance of the Three Kingdoms* portrays Liu Bei as a righteous leader who built his kingdom on the basis of Confucian values. The novel emphasizes that Liu Bei was related distantly to the ruling family of the Han Dynasty, thus favoring the argument for the legitimacy of Liu's reign among the Three Kingdoms.

4. Jackie Chan and the Politics of Comic Displacement

1. After creative differences with Jackie Chan, director Lau Kar-Leung left the production. Chan and his team took over as the director and action choreographer for *Drunken Master II*. Lau Kar-Leung was still credited as director for the film.

2. When Jackie Chan first came to Hollywood in the 1980s, directors tried hard to make him speak American English. Chan notes that since he was not raised in the United States, it is natural that he speaks English with an accent. Audiences and the studios also accept "Jackie Chan's style of English" (personal interview).

3. This rendering of the name is, however, different from what appears in the Chinese subtitles of *Shanghai Noon*.

BIBLIOGRAPHY

Abbas, Ackbar. "Cosmopolitan De-scriptions: Shanghai and Hong Kong." *Public Culture* 12.4 (2000): 769–86.

———. *Hong Kong: Culture and the Politics of Disappearance.* Minneapolis: U of Minnesota P, 1997.

Anderson, Aaron. "Violent Dances in Martial Arts Films." *Jump Cut* 44 (2001): 63 paragraphs. 3 June 2003 <http://www.ejumpcut.org/archive/jc44.2001/aarona/aaron1.html>.

Archibugi, Daniele. "Cosmopolitical Democracy." *Debating Cosmopolitics.* Ed. Daniele Archibugi. New York: Verso, 2003. 1–15.

———. "From the United Nations to Cosmopolitan Democracy." Archibugi and Held 121–62.

Archibugi, Daniele, and David Held, eds. *Cosmopolitan Democracy: An Agenda for a New World Order.* Cambridge, UK: Polity, 1995.

Austen, Jane. *Sense and Sensibility.* 1811. Oxford: Oxford UP, 1990.

Baker, Rick, and Toby Russell. "Heroic Bloodshed." Tilston 209–44.

Bakhtin, M. M. *The Dialogic Imagination.* Trans. Caryl Emerson and Michael Holquist. Austin: U of Texas P, 1981.

Bal, Mieke. Introduction. *Acts of Memory: Cultural Recall in the Present.* Ed. Mieke Bal, Jonathan Crewe, and Leo Spitzer. Hanover, NH: UP of New England, 1999. vii–xvii.

Baudrillard, Jean. *Selected Writings.* Ed. Mark Poster. Cambridge, UK: Polity, 1988.

Bazin, Andre. "The Evolution of the Language of Cinema." Braudy and Cohen 41–53.

———. "The Ontology of the Photographic Image." Braudy and Cohen 166–70.

Benjamin, Walter. *Illuminations.* Trans. Harry Zohn. New York: Schocken, 1968.

Berry, Chris. "Taiwanese Melodrama Returns with a Twist in *The Wedding Banquet.*" *Cinemaya* 21 (1993): 52–54.

Berry, Michael, ed. *Speaking in Images: Interviews with Contemporary Chinese Filmmakers.* New York: Columbia UP, 2005.

Bhabha, Homi. *The Location of Culture*. New York: Routledge, 1994.

———. "The Third Space: Interview with Homi Bhabha." *Identity: Community, Culture, Difference*. Ed. Jonathan Rutherford. London: Lawrence and Wishart, 1990. 207–21.

Bliss, Michael. *Between the Bullets: The Spiritual Cinema of John Woo*. Lanham, MD: Scarecrow, 2002.

Bordwell, David. "Aesthetics in Action: *Kungfu*, Gunplay, and Cinematic Expressivity." Yau 73–93.

———. "Hong Kong Martial Arts Cinema." A. Lee et al. 14–21.

———. *Planet Hong Kong: Popular Cinema and the Art of Entertainment*. Cambridge, MA: Harvard UP, 2000.

———. "Richness through Imperfection: King Hu and the Glimpse." Fu and Desser 113–36.

Braudy, Leo, and Marshall Cohen, eds. *Film Theory and Criticism: Introductory Readings*. New York: Oxford UP, 2004.

Bren, Frank, and Law Kar. *Hong Kong Cinema: A Cross-Cultural View*. Lanham, MD: Scarecrow, 2004.

Brown, Melissa J. *Is Taiwan Chinese? The Impact of Culture, Power, and Migration on Changing Identities*. Berkeley: U of California P, 2004.

Butler, Judith. *Bodies That Matter: On the Discursive Limits of "Sex."* New York: Routledge, 1990.

Buxiaosheng. *Jiang Hu Qi Xia Zhuan* [*Legend of the Strange Hero*]. Shanghai: World Book, 1926–30.

Chan, Evans. "Zhang Yimou's *Hero*: The Temptations of Facisim." Marchetti, Tan, and Feng 263–77.

Chan, Jackie. Personal interview. 28 Dec. 2005.

Chan, Kenneth. "The Global Return of the *Wu Xia Pian* (Chinese Sword-Fighting Movie): Ang Lee's *Crouching Tiger, Hidden Dragon*." *Cinema Journal* 43.4 (2004): 3–17.

Chan, Mei-ling. "Shao Shi Xiong Di Zai Xin Jia Po: Er Shi Nian Dai Zhi Qi Shi Nian Dai" ["Shaw Brothers in Singapore during 1920–70s"]. Fu, Liao, Cheuk, and Rong 46–75.

Chapman, James. *Licence to Thrill: A Cultural History of the James Bond Films*. New York: Columbia UP, 2001.

Cheah, Pheng. "The Cosmopolitical—Today." Cheah and Robbins 20–43.

Cheah, Pheng, and Bruce Robbins, eds. *Cosmopolitics: Thinking and Feeling beyond the Nation*. Minneapolis: U of Minnesota P, 1998.

Chen, Pauline. "*Crouching Tiger, Hidden Dragon*." *Cineaste* 24.4 (2001): 71–72, 91.

Chen, Scarlet. "High Flier: Interview with Ang Lee." Garcia 155–58.

Chen Shou. *San Guo Zhi* [*Records of the Three Kingdoms*]. Ed. Songzhi Pei and Naiqian Chen. Beijing: Xin Hua, 1982.

Chen, Xing, Lei Ye, and Yangyin Zhang. "Refusing in Chinese." Kasper 119–63.

Cheng, Chung Ying. "Chinese Metaphysics as Non-metaphysics: Confucian and Daoist Insights into the Nature of Reality." *Understanding the Chinese Mind: The Philosophical Roots.* Ed. Robert E. Allinson. Hong Kong and New York: Oxford UP, 1989. 167–208.

Cheshire, Ellen. *Ang Lee.* Harpenden: Pocket Essentials, 2001.

Cheuk, Pak Tong. "Shao Shi Xiong Di Yu Quan Qiu Hua Yu Dian Shi Wang Guo" ["Shaw Brothers and Global Chinese Television Empire"]. Fu, Liao, Cheuk, and Rong 171–240.

Chiang, Hsiao-hung. "The Unbearable Lightness of Globalization: On the Transnational Flight of *Wuxia* Film." *Cinema Taiwan: Politics, Popularity and State of the Arts.* Ed. Darrell William Davis and Ru-Shou Robert Chen. New York: Routledge, 2007. 95–107.

Chiao, Hsiung-ping. "Bruce Lee: His Influence on the Evolution of the Kung Fu Genre." *Journal of Popular Film and Television* 9.1 (1981): 30–42.

Chiu, Tzu-hsiu (Beryl). "Public Secrets: Geopolitical Aesthetics in Zhang Yimou's *Hero.*" *E-ASPAC: An Electronic Journal in Asian Studies on the Pacific Coast* (2004/2005): 46 paragraphs. 3 Jan. 2009 <http://mcel.pacificu.edu/easpac/2005/tzuchiu.php3>.

Chow, Rey. *Ethics after Idealism: Theory, Culture, Ethnicity, Reading.* Bloomington: Indiana UP, 1998.

———. "Introduction: On Chineseness as a Theoretical Problem." *Modern Chinese Literary and Cultural Studies in the Age of Theory: Reimagining a Field.* Ed. Rey Chow. Durham: Duke UP, 2000. 1–25.

———. *Primitive Passions: Visuality, Sexuality, Ethnography, and Contemporary Chinese Cinema.* New York: Columbia UP, 1995.

Chung, Pei-Chi. "Asian Filmmakers Moving into Hollywood: Genre Regulation and Auteur Aesthetics." *Asian Cinema* 11.1 (2000): 33–50.

Clifford, James. "Mixed Feelings." Cheah and Robbins 362–70.

Dancer, Greg. "Film Style and Performance: Comedy and Kung Fu from Hong Kong." *Asian Cinema* 10.1 (1998): 42–50.

Deleuze, Gilles, and Félix Guattari. "Year Zero: Faciality." *A Thousand Plateaus: Capitalism and Schizophrenia.* Trans. Brian Massumi. Minneapolis: U of Minnesota P, 1987. 167–91.

Derrida, Jacques. *Of Spirit: Heidegger and the Question.* Trans. Geoffrey Bennington and Rachel Bowlby. Chicago: U of Chicago P, 1989.

Desser, David. "The Kung Fu Craze: Hong Kong Cinema's First American Reception." Fu and Desser 19–43.

Du, Jinwen Steinberg. "Performance of Face-Threatening Acts in Chinese: Complaining, Giving Bad News, and Disagreeing." Kasper 165–206.

Du Bois, W. E. B. *The Souls of Black Folk.* 1903. New York: Fawcett, 1961.

Feng, Peter X. "False Consciousness and Double Consciousness: Race, Virtual Reality, and the Assimilation of Hong Kong Action Cinema in *The Matrix.*" Marchetti, Tan, and Feng 9–21.

Fitzgerald, Martin. *Hong Kong's Heroic Bloodshed*. Harpenden: Pocket Essentials, 2000.

Fore, Steve. "Golden Harvest Films and the Hong Kong Movie Industry in the Realm of Globalization." *Velvet Light Trap* 34 (1994): 40–58.

———. "Life Imitates Entertainment: Home and Dislocation in the Films of Jackie Chan." Yau 115–41.

Fu, Poshek. *Between Shanghai and Hong Kong: The Politics of Chinese Cinemas*. Stanford: Stanford UP, 2003.

Fu, Poshek, and David Desser, eds. *The Cinema of Hong Kong: History, Arts, Identity*. Cambridge: Cambridge UP, 2000.

Fu, Poshek, Jinfeng Liao, Cheuk Pak-Tong, and Rong Shi-Sheng, eds. *Shao Shi Ying Shi Di Guo: Wen Hua Zhong De Xiang Xiang* [*Shaw Brothers' Film Empire: The Cultural Imaginary*]. Taipei: Mai Tian, 2003.

———. "Zou Xiang Quan Qiu: Shao Shi Dian Ying Shi Chu Tan" ["Becoming Global: A Historical Survey of Shaw Brothers Films"]. Fu, Liao, Cheuk, and Rong 115–27.

Fuchs, Cynthia J. "The Buddy Politic." *Screening the Male: Exploring Masculinities in Hollywood Cinema*. Ed. Steven Cohan and Ina Rae Hark. New York: Routledge, 1993. 194–211.

Gallagher, Mark. "Rumble in the USA: Jackie Chan in Translation." *Film Stars: Hollywood and Beyond*. Ed. Andrew Willis. Manchester: Manchester UP, 2004. 113–39.

Garcia, Roger, ed. *Out of the Shadows: Asians in American Cinema*. Milan: Edizioni Olivares, 2001.

Gates, Philippa. "The Man's Film: Woo and the Pleasures of Male Melodrama." *Journal of Popular Culture* 35.1 (2001): 59–79.

Gilroy, Paul. *The Black Atlantic: Modernity and Double Consciousness*. London: Verso, 1993.

Glaessner, Verina. "Hard Target." *Sight and Sound* Nov. 1993: 42.

———. *Kung Fu: Cinema of Vengeance*. London: Lorimer, 1974.

Hall, Kenneth E. *John Woo: The Films*. Jefferson, NC: McFarland, 1999.

Hamamoto, Darrell Y., and Sandra Liu, eds. *Countervisions: Asian American Film Criticism*. Philadelphia: Temple UP, 2000.

Han Fei Tzu [Han Feizi]. "The Five Vermin." *Han Fei Tzu: Basic Writings*. Trans. Burton Watson. New York: Columbia UP, 1964. 96–117.

Hanke, Robert. "John Woo's Cinema of Hyperkinetic Violence: From *A Better Tomorrow* to *Face/Off*." *Film Criticism* 24.1 (1999): 39–59.

Hannerz, Ulf. "Cosmopolitans and Locals in World Culture." *Global Culture: Nationalism, Globalization, and Modernity*. Ed. Mike Featherstone. London: Sage, 1990. 237–51.

———. *Transnational Connections: Culture, People, Places*. New York: Routledge, 1996.

Havis, Richard James. "A Better Today: Hong Kong's John Woo Finally Does His Way in Hollywood." *Cinemaya* 39/40 (1998): 29–40.

Heard, Christopher. *Ten Thousand Bullets: The Cinematic Journey of John Woo*. Los Angeles: Lone Eagle, 2000.

Held, David. "Democracy and the New International Order." Archibugi and Held 96–120.

Hu, Hsien Chin. "The Chinese Concept of 'Face.'" *American Anthropologist* 46.1 (1944): 45–64.

Huang, Hai Kun. "A Critique on the Characters in *Red Cliff*" ["Chi Bi Ren Wu De Ji Zhong Ping Jia"] *INK Literary Monthly* 4.8 (2008): 58–74.

Hung, Ho Fung. "Discourse on 1967." *Whose City: Civic Culture and Political Discourse in Post-war Hong Kong*. Ed. Wing-sang Lo. Hong Kong: Oxford UP, 1997. 89–112.

Hunt, Leon. *Kung Fu Cult Masters: From Bruce Lee to "Crouching Tiger."* London: Wallflower, 2003.

Hwang, Kwang-kuo. "Face and Favor: The Chinese Power Game." *American Journal of Sociology* 92.4 (1987): 944–74.

Irigaray, Luce. *This Sex Which Is Not One*. Trans. Catherine Porter and Carolyn Burke. Ithaca: Cornell UP, 1985.

Jayamanne, Laleen. "Let's Miscegenate: Jackie Chan and His African American Connection." Morris, Li, and Chan 151–62.

Jeffords, Susan. *Hard Bodies: Hollywood Masculinity in the Reagan Era*. New Brunswick, NJ: Rutgers UP, 1994.

———. *The Remasculinization of America: Gender and the Vietnam War*. Bloomington: Indiana UP, 1989.

Jiang, Rong Fang, gen. ed. *Zhongguo Da Bai Ke Quan Shu* [*The Grand Chinese Encyclopedia*]. Vol. 12. Beijing and Shanghai: Zhongguo Da Bai Ke Quan Shu, 1983.

Jin, Yao Zhang, Jie Zhang, and Dong Feng Liu. *Zhong Guo Jing Ju Shi Tu Lu* [*The Pictorial Digest of Chinese Peking Opera History*]. Hebei: Hebei Jiao Yu, 1994.

Joseph, May. "Kung Fu Cinema and Frugality." *Nomadic Identities: The Performance of Citizenship*. Minneapolis: U of Minnesota P, 1999. 49–68.

Kaminsky, Stuart. "Kung Fu Film as Ghetto Myth." *Movies as Artifacts: Cultural Criticism of Popular Film*. Ed. Michael T. Marsden and John G. Nachbar. Chicago: Nelson-Hall, 1982. 137–45.

Kasper, Gabriele, ed. *Pragmatics of Chinese as Native and Target Language*. Honolulu: U of Hawaii P, 1995.

Kauffmann, Stanley. "Flying, East and West." *New Republic* 25 Dec. 2000: 22.

King, Geoff. *Film Comedy*. New York: Wallflower, 2002.

Kingston, Maxine Hong. *The Woman Warrior: Memoirs of a Girlhood among Ghosts*. New York: Vintage, 1989.

Koven, Mikel J. "My Brother, My Lover, My Self: Traditional Masculinity in the Hong Kong Action Cinema of John Woo." *Canadian Folklore* 19.1 (1997): 55–68.

Kramer, Peter. "'Clean, Dependable, Slapstick': Comic Violence and the Emergence of Classical Hollywood Cinema." *Violence and American Cinema*. Ed. David Slocum. New York: Routledge, 2001. 103–16.

Kristeva, Julia. *The Powers of Horror: An Essay on Abjection*. Trans. Leon S. Roudiez. New York: Columbia UP, 1982.

Laozi [Lao-Tzu]. *Dao De Jing [Tao Teh Ching]*. Trans. John C. H. Wu. Boston: Shambhala, 1989.

Lau, Jenny, ed. *Multiple Modernities: Cinema and Popular Media in Transcultural East Asia*. Philadelphia: Temple UP, 2003.

Law Kar. "Bullet in the Head." Urban Council, *Fifty* 201.

———. "Hero on Fire: A Comparative Study of John Woo's 'Hero Series' and Ringo Lam's 'On Fire' Series." Urban Council, *Fifty* 67–73.

Lee, Ang. "Preface." A. Lee et al. 7.

Lee, Ang, et al. *Crouching Tiger, Hidden Dragon: A Portrait of the Ang Lee Film*. New York: Newmarket, 2000.

Lee, Bruce. *Chinese Gung Fu: The Philosophical Art of Self Defense*. Burbank: Ohara, 1988.

Leong, Mo-ling, and Tsui Cheong Ming, eds. "Programme Notes of *A Better Tomorrow*." *New Hong Kong Films 86/87*. Hong Kong: Urban Council, 1987. 34–36.

Leung, Grace L. K., and Joseph M. Chan. "The Hong Kong Cinema and Its Overseas Market: A Historical Review, 1950–1995." Urban Council, *Fifty* 143–51.

Li, Cheuk-to. "Through Thick and Thin: The Ever-Changing Tsui Hark and the Hong Kong Cinema." *The Swordsman and His Jiang Hu: Tsui Hark and Hong Kong Film*. Ed. Sam Ho and Ho Wai-leng. Hong Kong: Hong Kong Film Archive, 2002. 12–23.

Lii, Ding-Tzann. "A Colonized Empire: Reflections on the Expansion of Hong Kong Films in the Asian Markets." *Trajectories: Inter-Asia Cultural Studies*. Ed. Kuan-Hsing Chen. New York: Routledge, 1998. 122–41.

Lin Nien-Tung. "The Martial Arts Hero." Urban Council, *Hong Kong Swordplay* 11–16.

Liu, James J. Y. *The Chinese Knight-Errant*. Chicago: U of Chicago P, 1967.

Lo, Kwai-Cheung. *Chinese Face/Off: The Transnational Popular Culture of Hong Kong*. Urbana: U of Illinois P, 2005.

———. "Double Negation: Hong Kong Cultural Identity in Hollywood's Transnational Representations." *Cultural Studies* 15.3–4 (2001): 464–85.

———. "Muscles and Subjectivity: A Short History of the Masculine Body in Hong Kong Popular Culture." *Camera Obscura* 39 (1996): 105–25.

Logan, Bey. *Hong Kong Action Cinema*. New York: Overlook, 1995.

Louie, Kam. *Theorising Chinese Masculinity: Society and Gender in China*. Cambridge: Cambridge UP, 2002.

Lowe, Lisa. *Immigrant Acts: On Asian American Cultural Politics*. Durham: Duke UP, 1996.

Lu, Feiyi. *Taiwan Dian Ying: Zheng Zhi, Jing Ji, Mei Xue, 1949–1994 [Taiwanese Cinema: Politics, Economics and Aesthetics, 1949–1994]*. Taipei: Yuan Liu, 1998.

Lu, Sheldon Hsiao-peng. "Historical Introduction: Chinese Cinemas (1896–1996) and Transnational Film Studies." *Transnational Chinese Cinemas: Identity, Nationhood, Gender*. Ed. Sheldon Hsiao-peng Lu. Honolulu: U of Hawaii P, 1997. 1–31.

Luo Guan Zhong. *San Guo Yan Yi [Romance of the Three Kingdoms]*. 2 vols. Beijing: Beijing UP, 1986.

Lyman, Rick. "Crouching Memory, Hidden Heart: Watching Movies with Ang Lee." *New York Times* 9 Mar. 2001: E1+.

Manovich, Lev. *The Language of New Media*. Cambridge: MIT P, 2001.

Mao, LuMing Robert. "Beyond Politeness Theory: 'Face' Revisited and Renewed." *Journal of Pragmatics* 21 (1994): 451–86.

Marchetti, Gina. "America's Asia: Hollywood's Construction, Deconstruction, and Reconstruction of the 'Orient.'" Garcia 37–57.

———. "Jackie Chan and the Black Connection." *Keyframes: Popular Cinema and Cultural Studies*. Ed. Matthew Tinkcom and Amy Villarejo. London: Routledge, 2001. 137–58.

———. *Romance and the "Yellow Peril": Race, Sex, and Discursive Strategies in Hollywood Fiction*. Berkeley: U of California P, 1993.

Marchetti, Gina, Tan See-Kam, and Peter X. Feng, eds. *Chinese Connections: Critical Perspectives on Film, Identity, and Diaspora*. Philadelphia: Temple UP, 2009.

Martin, Fran. "The China Simulacrum: Genre, Feminism, and Pan-Chinese Cultural Politics in *Crouching Tiger, Hidden Dragon*." *Island on the Edge: Taiwan New Cinema and After*. Ed. Chris Berry and Feiyi Lu. Hong Kong: Hong Kong UP. 2005. 149–59.

Moody, Rick. *The Ice Storm*. Boston: Little, Brown, 1994.

Morris, Meaghan. "Introduction: Hong Kong Connections." Morris, Li, and Chan 1–18.

Morris, Meaghan, Siu Leung Li, and Stephen Chan Ching-kiu, eds. *Hong Kong Connections: Transnational Imagination in Action Cinema*. Hong Kong: Hong Kong UP; Durham: Duke UP, 2005.

Ng Ho. "*Jing Hu* Revisited: Towards a Reconstruction of the Martial Arts World." Urban Council, *Hong Kong Swordplay* 73–86.

Nochimson, Martha P. *Dying to Belong: Gangster Movies in Hollywood and Hong Kong*. Malden, MA: Blackwell, 2007.

O'Hehir, Andrew. "John Woo on *Red Cliff* and the Rise of Chinawood." *Salon*. 18 Nov. 2009. 19 Nov. 2009 <http://www.salon.com/entertainment/movies/beyond_the_multiplex/feature/2009/11/18/john_woo>.

Ong, Aihwa. "Flexible Citizenship among Chinese Cosmopolitans." Cheah and Robbins 134–62.

———. *Flexible Citizenship: The Cultural Logics of Transnationality*. Durham: Duke UP, 1999.

Palumbo-Liu, David. *Asian/American: Historical Crossings of a Radical Frontier*. Stanford: Stanford UP, 1999.

Pollock, Sheldon, Homi K. Bhabha, Carol A. Breckenridge, and Dipesh Chakrabarty. "Cosmopolitanisms." *Public Culture* 12.3 (2000): 577–89.

Prashad, Vijay. "Bruce Lee and the Anti-imperialism of Kung Fu: A Polycultural Adventure." *positions: east asia cultures critique* 11.1 (2003): 51–90.

"Preparing for Battle." *China Daily*. 24 June 2008. 20 July 2008. <http://www.chinadaily.com.cn/showbiz/2008–06/24/content_6790733.htm>.

Pu Song-Ling. *Liao Zhai Zhi Yi* [*Strange Stories from a Chinese Studio*]. Changchun: Jilin Wen Shi, 1995.

Qiu Zhi-Yong. "Tai Wan Dian Ying Yu Di San Shi Jie Dian Ying Lun Shu" ["Taiwanese Cinema and Third World Film Criticism"]. *Dan Dai* [*Contemporary*] 189 (2003): 44–56.

Rao, Shuguang. *Zhongguo Xiju Dianying Shi* [*The History of Chinese Comedy Film*]. Beijing: China Film, 2005.

Reynaud, Bérénice. "John Woo's Art Action Movie." *Sight and Sound* (May 1993): 22–25.

Riley, Jo. *Chinese Theater and the Actor in Performance*. Cambridge: Cambridge UP, 1997.

Rose, Marla Matzer. "Lee Inks 2-Year Consultant Deal with Col for Asia." *Hollywood Reporter* 24 July 2001: 4, 80.

Said, Edward. *Orientalism*. London: Routledge and Kegan Paul, 1978.

Sandell, Jillian. "A Better Tomorrow? American Masochism and Hong Kong Action Films." *Bright Lights* 13 (1994): 23 paragraphs. 25 Mar. 2003 <http://www.brightlightsfilm.com/31/hk_better1.html>.

———. "Reinventing Masculinity: The Spectacle of Male Intimacy in the Films of John Woo." *Film Quarterly* 49.4 (Summer 1996): 23–34.

Sang, Tze-Lan D. "The Transgender Body in Wang Dulu's *Crouching Tiger, Hidden Dragon*." *Embodied Modernities: Corporeality, Representation, and Chinese Cultures*. Ed. Fran Martin and Larissa Heinrich. Honolulu: U of Hawaii P, 2006. 98–112.

Schamus, James. Introduction. *Two Films by Ang Lee*. By Ang Lee, Hu-ling Wang, Neil Peng, and James Schamus. Woodstock: Overlook, 1994. ix–xiii.

Shah, Sonia. "Slaying the Dragon Lady: Towards an Asian American Feminism." *Dragon Ladies: Asian American Feminists Breathe Fire*. Ed. Sonia Shah. Boston: South End, 1997. xii–xxi.

Shek Kei. "A Brief Historical Tour of the Hong Kong Martial Arts Film." *Bright Lights* 13 (1994): 29 paragraphs. 2 May 2003 <http://www.brightlightsfilm.com/31/hk_brief1.html>.

———. "The Development of 'Martial Arts' in Hong Kong Cinema." Urban Council, *Hong Kong Martial Arts* 27–38.

———. *Shi Qi Ying Hua Ji* [*Shek Kei's Film Review Collection*]. Vol. 4. Hong Kong: Ci Wen Hua Tang, 1999.

Silverman, Kaja. *The Acoustic Mirror.* Bloomington: Indiana UP, 1988.

Sima Qian. *Records of the Grand Historian of China* [aka *Shiji*]. 2 vols. Trans. Burton Watson. New York: Columbia UP, 1961.

Smelik, Anneke. "Gay and Lesbian Criticism." *The Oxford Guide to Film Studies.* Ed. John Hill and Pamela Church Gibson. Oxford: Oxford UP, 1998. 135–47.

Stringer, Julian. "Cultural Identity and Diaspora in Contemporary Hong Kong's Cinema." Hamamoto and Liu 298–312.

———. "'Your Tender Smiles Give Me Strength': Paradigms of Masculinity in John Woo's *A Better Tomorrow* and *The Killer.*" *Screen* 38.1 (1997): 25–41.

Sunzi [Sun-Tzu]. *Art of War.* Trans. Ralph D. Sawyer. Boulder: Westview, 1994.

Szeto, Kin-Yan. "The Politics of Historiography in Stephen Chow's *Kung Fu Hustle.*" *Jump Cut* 49 (2007). 45 paragraphs. 3 Jan. 2009 <http://www.ejump-cut.org/archive/jc49.2007/Szeto/index.html>.

Tasker, Yvonne. "Fist of Fury: Discourse of Race and Masculinity in the Martial Arts Cinema." *Race and the Subject of Masculinities.* Ed. Harry Stecopoulos and Michael Uebel. Durham: Duke UP, 1997. 321–42.

———. *Spectacular Bodies: Gender, Genre and the Action Cinema.* London: Routledge, 1993.

Teo, Stephen. *Hong Kong Cinema: The Extra Dimension.* London: BFI, 1997.

———. *King Hu's A Touch of Zen.* Hong Kong: Hong Kong UP, 2007.

———. "Love and Swords: The Dialectics of Martial Arts Romance—A Review of *Crouching Tiger, Hidden Dragon.*" *Senses of Cinema* 11 (2000/2001): 13 paragraphs. 23 Mar. 2003 <http://www.sensesofcinema.com/contents/00/11/crouching.html>.

———. "Tsui Hark: National Style and Polemic." Yau 143–57.

———. "'We Kicked Jackie Chan's Ass!' An Interview with James Schamus." *Senses of Cinema* 13 (2001): 70 pars. 20 June 2003 <http://www.sensesofcin-ema.com/contents/01/13/schamus.html>.

Tilston, Lisa, ed. *The Essential Guide to Hong Kong Movies.* London: Eastern Heroes, 1994.

Turan, Kenneth. "Wire Work." Ang Lee et al. 52.

Urban Council. *Fifty Years of Electric Shadows.* Hong Kong: Urban Council, 1997.

———. *A Study of the Hong Kong Martial Arts Film.* Hong Kong: Urban Council, 1980.

———. *A Study of the Hong Kong Swordplay Film.* Hong Kong: Urban Council, 1981.

Urry, John. *Consuming Places.* New York: Routledge, 1995.

———. *Sociology beyond Societies: Mobilities for the Twenty-First Century.* New York: Routledge, 2000.

Wang, Dulu. *Wo Hu Cang Long* [*Crouching Tiger, Hidden Dragon*]. Ed. Hong-sheng Ye. 2 vols. Taipei: Lian Jing, 1985.

Wang, Gangwu. "Chineseness: The Dilemmas of Place and Practice." *Cosmopolitan Capitalists: Hong Kong and the Chinese Diaspora at the End of the Twentieth Century*. Ed. Gary G. Hamilton. Seattle: U of Washington P, 1999. 118–34.

Wang, Georgette, and Emilie Yueh-yu Yeh. "Globalization and Hybridization in Cultural Products: The Cases of *Mulan* and *Crouching Tiger, Hidden Dragon*." *International Journal of Cultural Studies* 8.2 (2005): 175–93.

Weinraub, Bernard. "A Director's Ballet with Bullets." *New York Times* 22 Feb. 1996: B1+. Woo, John. "Cinema: The Next Mission." *AsiaWeek* 23 June 2000: 36.
——. Preface. Tilston 9–10.

Woodrell, Daniel. *Woe to Live on*. New York: Holt, 1987.

Xu, Mu Yun. *Zhongguo Xi Ju Shi* [*History of Chinese Theater*]. Shanghai: Shanghai Gu Ji, 2001.

Yau, Esther C. M., ed. *At Full Speed: Hong Kong Cinema in a Borderless World*. Minneapolis: U of Minnesota P, 2001.

Ye Hongsheng. *Ye Hongsheng Lun Jian* [*Ye Hongsheng Discusses the Sword*]. Taipei: Lian Jing, 1994.

Yip, June. "Taiwanese New Cinema." *The Oxford History of World Cinema*. Ed. Geoffrey Nowell-Smith. New York: Oxford UP, 1996. 711–13.

Yu, De Hui. "Zhong Guo Ren Xin Di Di Gu Shi" ["The Story inside the Chinese's Hearts"]. *Zhong Guo Ren Di Ren Qing Yu Mian Zi* [*The Chinese Human Relationship and Face*]. Ed. Taiwan Teacher Zhang's Press Editorial Board. Beijing: Zhong Guo You Yi, 1990. 1–12.

Zhang Che. "Creating the Martial Arts Film and the Hong Kong Cinema Style." *The Making of Martial Arts Films—As Told by Filmmakers and Stars*. Hong Kong: Provisional Urban Council, 1999. 16–24.

Zhang, Jingbei. *Shi Nian Yi Jiao Dian Ying Meng* [*Ten Years and a Dream of Film*]. Taipei: Shi Bao Wen Hua, 2002.

Zhuangzi [Chuang Tzu]. "Discussion on Making All Things Equal." *The Complete Works of Chuang Tzu*. Trans. Burton Watson. New York: Columbia UP, 1968. 36–49. *Zhouyi* [*The Book of Changes*]. Trans. Richard Rutt. Richmond, Surrey: Curzon, 2002.

INDEX

Index

Chuang Tzu (Zhuangzi), 67

Clifford, James, 6–7

colonialism, 2–3, 6–8, 20, 27, 56, 79, 82,113–14, 136, 142–43, 146, 148

Come Drink with Me, 22–23, 40, 42–43, 55

comedy,19, 28–29,74, 114–17,134, 137–41,143

Confucianism, 42, 47–48, 64, 66, 75

cosmopolitanism, 4–6, 68, 73

cosmopolitical consciousness, 1, 3, 6–8, 31–32, 34, 36, 60, 61, 66, 69, 71, 73, 77, 88, 105, 111–12, 114, 131, 142, 145, 148, 149

Crouching Tiger, Hidden Dragon (film), 1, 7, 9, 11–12, 18–19, 25, 33–70, 74, 145, 147

Crouching Tiger, Hidden Dragon (novel), 22

Cruise, Tom, 91, 97

da, 29, 153n5

Dao De Jing, 64, 67

Dark Angel, 49

deep focus, 58

Derrida, Jacques, 142

Desser, David, 25–26

diaspora, 2–3, 6, 11–12, 16–17, 20, 45–48, 69, 84, 94 111, 114, 131, 134, 136, 144, 146, 150

double consciousness, 8, 60–61

Dragon: The Bruce Lee Story, 126

Dragon Inn, 23, 55

dragon lady, 43, 48, 64, 68, 153–54

Drunken Master, 116–19, 125, 127, 141

Drunken Master II, 118–20, 156n1

Du Bois, W. E. B., 8

Enter the Dragon, 27, 125

ethnocentrism, 127, 130

Face/Off, 1, 9, 72, 77, 89, 91–94, 96, 108, 110

faciality, 95–97

Fa Mu Lan, 46, 49, 69

femininity, 3–4, 8–9, 36, 38, 41,46–48, 64, 68–69, 105, 108, 145, 147, 149

feminism, 33–34, 63,147

Feng, Peter X., 11, 61–62

Feng Wen. See *Storm Riders, The*

First Strike, 124, 132–34, 136

Forbidden Kingdom, The, 140–41

Fore, Steve, 73, 120

Fu, Poshek, 13, 153n1

Gallagher, Mark, 116

gangster films, 24, 73, 75–79, 86, 92, 96, 107, 155n1

gaze, 34, 56, 60, 132

gender, 3, 8–9, 11–12, 32, 34, 36, 38–39, 42, 44–48, 50–51, 64–65, 68, 73, 81, 90, 96, 99–101, 104, 110, 121, 132, 134, 142, 145, 146–50

geopolitics, 3, 9, 11–12, 45, 68, 112, 142–43, 145

ghetto myth, 28, 31, 129

Gilroy, Paul, 8

globalization, 2, 8, 56, 62–63, 79, 114

Golden Harvest, 26, 114, 134–35

Golden Swallow, The, 23, 42–43, 55

Gong Li, 3, 7

Guan Yu, 106, 154n1

guanxi, 83, 95

Han Fei Tzu. *See* Han Feizi

Han Feizi, 21

Hannerz, Ulf, 4

Hard Boiled, 85–87, 89, 91, 97

Hard Target, 77, 89, 91

hegemony, 11, 32, 50–51, 76, 83,87, 94, 96, 99, 101, 111, 128., 147, 149

Held, David, 4

Hero, 3, 36

heteroglossia, 44, 53, 67, 69

Hollywood, 1–4, 7, 9–20, 24–25, 27, 31–36, 43, 46–51, 53–54, 58, 61–63, 69, 71–73, 76–77, 80, 89–94, 96–97, 103–4, 107–12, 114, 116, 125–27, 129–32, 134, 137–38, 140–42, 144–50, 156n2

homosociality, 72, 79–83, 85, 87, 89, 99–100, 107, 108, 111, 147

Hong Kong, 1–3, 5, 7, 9–22, 24–35, 37, 41–43, 45–46, 51, 55–58, 60, 62–63, 71–93, 97–98, 102, 107–8, 111–14, 116, 118–30, 132–37, 140–50, 153n1, 154n4, 155n1, 155n3; handover (to China) in 1997, 82, 84, 86; Joint Declaration in 1984, 24, 118; New Wave, 24

House of Flying Daggers, 36

Hu, King, 19, 22–24, 26, 30, 37, 40, 42–43, 45, 51, 55, 57, 72

Index

Awarded the PhD in performance studies from Northwestern University, **Kin-Yan Szeto** is associate professor of theater and dance at Appalachian State University. Her research bridges the areas of film, performance, and visual studies. Szeto received her BA in English from the Chinese University of Hong Kong and holds two master's degrees, one in theater and drama studies from the University of London and another in screenwriting and criticism from the Beijing Film Academy. Her articles have appeared in *Modern Chinese Literature and Culture, Visual Anthropology, Dance Chronicle*, and *Jump Cut: A Review of Contemporary Media.*